D1257701

Ghana's
Concert
Party
Theatre

Ghana's Concert Party Theatre

Catherine M. Cole

Indiana University Press BLOOMINGTON AND INDIANAPOLIS

This book is a publication of
Indiana University Press
601 North Morton Street
Bloomington, IN 47404-3797 USA

http://iupress.indiana.edu

Telephone orders   800-842-6796
Fax orders   812-855-7931
Orders by e-mail   iuporder@indiana.edu

© 2001 by Catherine M. Cole

All rights reserved

Portions of this book have been published in earlier versions:

Chapter 2 appeared as "Reading Blackface in West Africa: Won-ders Taken for Signs," *Critical Inquiry* 23, no. 1 (1996): 183–215.

Chapter 6 appeared as "'This is actually a good interpretation of modern civilisation': Popular Theatre and the Social Imaginary in Ghana, 1946–66," *Africa* 67, no. 3 (1997): 363–388.

No part of this book may be reproduced or utilized in any form or by any means, electronic or mechanical, including photocopying and recording, or by any information storage and retrieval system, without permission in writing from the publisher. The Association of American University Presses' Resolution on Permissions consti-tutes the only exception to this prohibition.

The paper used in this publication meets the minimum requirements of American National Standard for Information Sciences—Perma-nence of Paper for Printed Library Materials, ANSI Z39.48-1984.

MANUFACTURED IN THE UNITED STATES OF AMERICA

Library of Congress Cataloging-in-Publication Data

Cole, Catherine M.
    Ghana's concert party theatre / Catherine M. Cole.
        p.   cm.
    Includes bibliographical references and index.
    ISBN 0-253-33845-X (cl : alk. paper) — ISBN 0-253-21436-X (pa : alk. paper)
    1. Performing arts—Ghana—History—20th century. 2. Travel-ing theater—Ghana—History—20th century. 3. Music-halls (Vari-ety theaters, cabarets, etc.)—Ghana—History—20th century.   I. Title.

PN2990.4 .C65 2001
792.7'09667'0904—dc21

                                                            00-044962

1 2 3 4 5   06 05 04 03 02 01

*For Terry Cole, who left this world just as
this book and my son Aaron were entering it.*

And to Kwame, for being there throughout.

Contents

Acknowledgments

Without the generosity of Ghanaians artists who shared their knowledge about the history, practices, and cultural significance of the concert party, this project would not have been possible. Several performance groups were particularly instrumental to my research, including the Adehyeman Concert Party, the Jaguar Jokers, Kakaiku's Concert Party, the Kumapim Royals, and the members of the Ghana Concert Parties Union who performed at the National Theatre. The *ananysesεm* group at Kwansakrom also kindly allowed a storytelling session to be videotaped.

For granting formal interviews, I particularly want to thank Idrisu Abdullahi, Victoria Adoi, Robert Jamieson Amartey, Joseph Benjamin Amoah, Akwasi Ampofo-Adjei, Bob S. Ansah, Sandy Arkhurst, Emmanuel Baidoe, Y. B. Bampoe, David Kwame Blankson, Nathaniel Ekɔw Browne, Francis Edward Cudjoe, Lawrence Cudjoe, Romeo Ampofo Dadah, Beatrice and Kojo Dadson, Joe Eiyson, Atto Essien, George Benjamin Grant, K. Acquaah Hammond, Kwame Mbia Hammond, Samuel Kwame Koomson, Essi Kom, James Kwaku Narkwa, Koo Nimo, Issac Kweku Ntama, Kwabena Onyina, Grace Adom Oppong, Moses K. Oppong Jr., Moses K. Oppong II, Kwaw Prempeh, Margaret Quainoo, Bob Vans, Augustus S. Williams, and A. B. O. Zynenwartel.

The University of Ghana's Institute for African Studies, Language Centre, and School of Performing Arts provided research affiliation and access to libraries, archives, and staff and faculty members. Among the many language experts who taught me Akan and helped with transcriptions and translations, I especially want to thank Lydia Addi, Kwasi Aduonum, Charlotte Akyeampong, O. N. Adu-Gyamfi, Gilbert Ansre, Y. B. Bampoe, K. Acquaah Hammond, K. Keelson, and Moses Narh. During my research trip to Ghana, I depended on several individuals and organizations for advice, emotional support, hospitality, and assistance, among them Kofi E. Agovi, Kwaku and Kafui Alomele, Dr. Gilbert Ansre's family, John Collins, Betty Mayne, Osei Ntiamoa, Adom and Moses Oppong, Robert Henry Suapim's family, and the staff at the United States Information Service, particularly Sarpei Nunoo.

This project received generous financial support from the American Association of University Women, the Harvard Theatre Collection, Northwestern University's Interdisciplinary Ph.D. program in Theatre and Drama, and the University of California Regents. I am indebted to Northwestern University's Program of African Studies for providing financial support for African language study and a pre-dissertation research trip to Ghana. A Fulbright grant supporting a companion project, a video documentary of the Ghanaian concert party on which I collaborated with Kwame Braun, also greatly helped my research.

I especially want to thank my dissertation director, Margaret Thompson Drewal, and committee members Sandra L. Richards and Tracy C. Davis for seeing this project through from inception to its fruition as a doctoral thesis. For their careful and sensitive readings of proposals, chapters, and revisions, I also wish to thank Kofi E. Agovi, Emmanuel Akyeampong, Karin Barber, Kwame Braun, Timothy Burke, Jane Guyer, Jonathan Haynes, Amanda Kemp, T. C. McCaskie, Stephan Miescher, Ikem Okoye, Tejumola Olaniyan, and William B. Worthen. Karin Barber and Amanda Kemp deserve special thanks for their appraisal of the entire manuscript as it neared publication. I am grateful to Janet Rabinowich, Dee Mortensen, and Kate Babbitt for their interest in this book and careful editing during its journey through Indiana University Press.

Without the encouragement of my Cole and Braun family members throughout the long process of researching and writing this book, I might well have lost heart. The final revisions of the manuscript coincided with particularly challenging personal circumstances: the birth of my son, the physical decline and death of my father, and my own battle with a life-threatening illness. That this book manuscript could be completed so close on the heels of these major life events is a tribute to my family's unwavering support. To my husband, Kwame Braun, who collaborated with me on research in Ghana, videotaped interviews, photographed archival images, read multiple drafts of this manuscript, cared for me in my illness, and never lost his cool, I say, *"Esie ne kagya nni aseda."*

Note on Orthography

The Akan language of Ghana has several dialects, two of which feature prominently in the concert party's history: Fante and Asante Twi. The most authoritative Akan dictionary is J. G. Christaller's *Dictionary of the Asante and Fante Language,* first published in 1881 and later revised in 1933. Orthography and spelling of Akan have changed in recent years, as the language is still in the process of standardization. Thus, for advice on Akan spelling, I have relied on the translators with whom I worked at the University of Ghana Language Center.

This book follows the author-date citation system according to the principles set forth in the 14th edition of *The Chicago Manual of Style.* In general, references are cited according to the author's last name and the date of publication, which the reader can then locate in the list of "Works Cited." Interview and newspaper sources required slight modifications of this system. Interviews are cited by giving the name of the individual or group interviewed, followed by a number such as "#95.41." The number preceding the decimal point indicates the year the interview was conducted (in this case 1995). The subsequent number refers to a catalogue number within my collection of field material. Colonial Ghanaian newspapers rarely listed authors' bylines, so I reference most newspaper articles by giving the name of the newspaper, followed by the year the article appeared (for instance, *"Gold Coast Leader* 1903"). In cases when there are multiple articles cited from a particular newspaper in the same year, a letter is appended after the date (for instance, *"Gold Coast Spectator* 1934c").

Ghana's Concert Party Theatre

1

Introduction

The Ghanaian concert party is a form of traveling popular theatre that is a tradition of twentieth-century West Africa. Beginning in the 1920s, African actors trekked the length and breadth of the British colony then known as the Gold Coast, performing comic variety shows that combined an eclectic array of cultural influences. Performers appropriated material from American movies, Latin gramophone records, African American spirituals, Ghanaian *asafo,* and "highlife" songs.[1] They wore minstrel makeup inspired by Al Jolson and played a trickster similar to the famous Ananse character of Ghanaian storytelling.

From colonialism through independence to present-day Ghana, concert parties have undergone constant transformation, readily incorporating new audiences, venues, formats, and styles. While shows were initially predominantly in English, they gradually shifted to Ghanaian languages. Audiences from 1900 to 1930 were generally coastal Africans with some degree of formal Western-style education. But after 1930, concert parties became increasingly accessible to inland working classes and rural populations, with affordable prices and convenient local venues such as open-air cinema halls and large family compounds. The format gradually shifted from an hour-long show of European songs and vaudeville sketches to a protracted event, beginning with an African pop music concert from 8 P.M. to 1 A.M., followed by a full-length comic melodrama punctuated at emotional moments with well-known highlife tunes, the whole performance concluding at dawn. The blackface and vaudeville elements that were once so prevalent ceased to dominate after 1950 as larger casts replaced small trios, elaborate stories supplanted short scenarios about domestic infidelity, and a greater range of characters extended plays beyond three stock roles. Concert party innovators of the late 1950s and early 1960s—such as Kakaiku, E. K. Nyame, the Jaguar Jokers, Bob Cole, and F. Micah—developed the genre into the format as it is known and produced today by commercially successful groups such as the Kumapim Royals and the City Boys. Theatre forms similar to the concert party can be found throughout Africa (see Kerr 1995). West African popular theatre, in particular, has been the subject of a growing body of scholarly literature.[2] In the past two decades, researchers have made great strides in representing and analyzing a theatre form that is highly ephemeral.[3] They have also persuasively demonstrated the *popularity* of traveling theatre among its large and diverse West African audiences. Biodun Jeyifo says that Yorùbá traveling theatre is "produced by and for an aggregate public drawn from all classes and strata of society" (1984, 3). According to him, Nigerian theatre audiences cut "across the nascent division of the people into groups and classes differentiated on the basis of wealth, privilege, and power" (4). While not refuting the heterogeneity of Yorùbá popular theatre, Karin Barber and Báy Ògúndíj assert that Yorùbá theatre is primarily by and for the "underprivileged majority" (1994, 10), the "worse paid, less educated majority who are furthest removed from power" (Barber 1986, 5). Alain Ricard describes Togolese popular theatre in similar terms as the domain of "school leavers, apprentices and the unemployed" (1974, 178). Likewise, it is Ghana's "rank and file," its ordinary citizens, who are the producers and consumers of its popular traveling theatre, according to Kwamena Bame (1985, 63).

Thus, West African traveling theater is considered "popular" for several reasons: Its sociological roots are not in elite and/or privileged minority sub-cultures, but rather in the intermediate and agricultural sectors and the working class. While these audiences statistically constitute a majority population, they nevertheless have limited access to political and economic power. Traveling theatre shows are popular in the sense that they are tremendously well-liked and well-attended. Popular theatre has had a profound impact on other performing arts and cultural forms. For instance, John Collins argues that the Ghanaian concert party has been the "single most important influence and avenue for contemporary Ghanaian performing artists" (1994a, 2). In Nigeria, Onookome Okome and Jonathan Haynes trace the remarkable impact Yorùbá popular theatre has had on emergent cinema (1995, 153–178). Traveling theatre's content and form, its subject and mode of rendering, draw upon what Biodun Jeyifo identifies as a "vast repository of expressive material" available in the everyday popular culture of West Africa (1984, 4). This repository includes slang expressions, political slogans, published histories, traditional folklore, Western vaudeville, and musical riffs from the African diaspora.

What has not yet been fully accounted for in the scholarship on West African popular theatre is historical change, both within particular traveling theatre traditions and in the theatre's relationship to transformations in society at large and to the audiences it serves. How has popular traveling theatre in different West African cultures changed over time? When and why have there been shifts in form, content, the sociology of the audience, size of troupes, use of music, and the relationship between spectators and performers? How do we explain such changes, and what do these transformations tell us about the social history of West Africa? While previous scholarship on West African popular theatre has begun to address these historical questions, it has usually done so through historical preambles to research that is otherwise contemporary in focus (Barber and Ògúndíj 1994; Barber, Collins, and Ricard 1997; Jeyifo 1984). This book is the first study of West African popular theater to be wholly historical, with an empirically detailed portrait of the changing social, political, aesthetic, and economic circumstances of Ghana's concert theatre during the colonial and early postcolonial era.

This book traces the shifting styles, form, and content of Ghanaian concert parties in relation to larger social and cultural conditions from the early twentieth century through the mid-1960s. Because previous scholarship on the concert party covers so thoroughly the period from 1970 to the present (Collins 1994a; Gilbert 2000), this book concludes with the 1960s.[4] The years between 1930 and 1960 most interest me, for it was during this era that concert parties made a dramatic transition from serving as British imperial propaganda honoring "Empire Day" to promoting Ghanaian cultural nationalism and the political career of Ghana's first prime minister and president, Kwame Nkrumah.

Throughout its history, the concert party has dramatized the aspirations, experiences, and frustrations of a large constituency of Ghanaians with limited formal education. Out of the tumult that colonialism and modernization unleashed, actors fashioned comedies. As social roles, class stratification, and regional divisions rapidly shifted throughout the colonial period and the early years of independence, concert party practitioners demonstrated a remarkable ability to adapt to changing circumstances, new technologies, and volatile political climates. An itinerant performance form that responded quickly to subtle changes in the social fabric of colonial Ghana, the concert party provides a unique perspective on the complex experience of British domination, the quest for national identity, and the processes of cultural appropriation and social change.

This project is simultaneously a cultural history of a performance form and a social history of the people who created and consumed it. Like Christopher Waterman's *Jùjú: A Social History and Ethnography of an African Popular Music* (1990) and David Coplan's *In the Time of Cannibals: The Word Music of South Africa's Basotho Migrants* (1994), this study asks historically and ethnographically grounded questions about what a particular performance genre has meant to its participants. Why have people spent effort and money on making concert parties? What have audiences gotten out of these shows? Karin Barber believes these questions are crucial to the study of all popular arts in Africa (1987). In line with new directions in research on African performance as outlined by Margaret Thompson Drewal (1991), this book is part of a shifting focus in scholarship from structure to process, from the normative to the particular and historically situated, and from the collective to the agency of the named individuals in the continuous flow of social interactions. "Shift" is the operative word in Drewal's formulation, for in focusing on process, agency, and the particular, I nevertheless place concert parties within the context of larger structural transformations such as the development of industrialization, migrant labor, wage labor, cash crops, and urbanization.

Inherently interdisciplinary in nature, my research has been variously classified as "social history," "performance studies," "cultural studies," "drama scholarship," and "anthropology." My home discipline of theatre traditionally divides itself into the areas of theory, literary criticism, history, and performance, often treating these categories as though they are discretely constituted. In this book, I insist on the necessity of combining theory, literary analysis, historical research, and performance ethnography, for I find the most compelling insights are gained through interdisciplinary methodologies. For instance, the techniques of literary analysis can illuminate otherwise unseen dimensions of non-literary texts such as newspaper articles, and theory is implicit in the embodied, ephemeral techniques of live performance. I have tried to avoid the hermeticism of formalist literary analysis, the positivism of conventional theatre history, and the lack of empirical research that has marked theoretically oriented work in recent years. As I looked for models of historically grounded, theoretically informed interdisciplinary theatre scholarship, I was most inspired by such recent works as Joseph Roach's *Cities of the Dead: Circum-Atlantic Performance* (1996) and Diana Taylor's *Disappearing Acts: Spectacles of Gender and Nationalism in Argentina's "Dirty War"* (1997). Taylor characterizes her work as an attempt to "look at" history through a performance model, an ambition this present work shares (1997, xi).

I first became interested in the Ghanaian concert party when I learned that under colonial rule concert actors wore blackface makeup, a theatrical convention derived from nineteenth-century American minstrelsy. Knowing the racially charged significance of blackface in North America, I wondered if colonial Ghanaians were expressing through blackface ideas about race and racism. Were these actors consciously subverting racist colonial stereotypes or subconsciously absorbing them? Or did this makeup signify something entirely unrelated to American referents?

I went to Ghana from July to August of 1993 on a pilot trip to ask such questions and to explore whether the concert party was a viable topic for a book-length study. During that trip, I attended the state-sponsored funeral of the famous concert party actor Lord Bob Cole, who passed away just before my arrival. This funeral was my entrée into the community of concert party actors and their families. I initiated relationships that later became central to my research with veteran artists such as Y. B. Bampoe and K. Acquaah Hammond of the Jaguar Jokers, the son and daughter of the late, great Kakaiku, and Bob Ansah of the Gold Coast Two Bobs.

At Lord Bob Cole's funeral I also gained insight into the ambiguous status of the concert party. Located in a cultural no-man's-land, concerts lacked the prestige of Anglophone scripted drama, the "authenticity" of so-called traditional culture, and the financial success of popular music. The Ghana Concert Parties Union had their own stage at the funeral, but it was a poor one with inadequate lighting and bad electronic circuitry that caught fire midway through the wake. The audience area had no seats until spectators themselves sought out benches and chairs. Obscuring the concert party stage was the more centrally located and well-constructed platform belonging to the powerful and lucrative Musicians Union of Ghana (MUSIGA). The MUSIGA stage was the symbolic center of the funeral, in front of which celebrities, state dignitaries, and grieving family members gathered to shake hands, give donations, and perform the elaborate social rituals of Akan funerals.

While the musicians' stage was the center of official activity, the concert party stage appealed to the general masses who turned out for the funeral and for four evenings of abundant, free entertainment. Though the concert party venue was poorly equipped and had no seats, spectators thronged the stage. They stood, sat on the ground, or brought benches of their own. They cheered for the "Bob" solo comedians, wept during a dramatized widow's lament, and sang along with familiar highlife songs that saturated nearly every scene. A crippled man in the audience danced in his wheelchair during one number, and the generally impoverished spectators donated so much money to the performers (a West African tradition of expressing appreciation) that a huge collection basket had to be brought onstage. In the all-star, all-night lineup of concert party acts, most shows were in the Akan language, for the audience was largely Akan-speaking. But when actors performed shows in Ewe and Ga, new voices could be heard in the audience laughing at, rebuking, and commenting on the characters and action.

The popularity of the concert party stage suggested that despite this genre's marginal position in the hierarchy of Ghana's official culture, it had a strong appeal to average working-class Ghanaians: the lorry drivers, market traders, mechanics, seamstresses, cobblers, chop bar proprietors, and farmers who are the lifeblood of Ghana's economy.[5] Hungry for the stories, characters, themes, and *language* of their everyday lives to be represented, these spectators appeared to find in concert parties something not regularly offered through other entertainments such as videos, films, television shows, and scripted dramas.

The insights I gained from Bob Cole's funeral had little to do with my initial research questions about the ideological significance of blackface. Neither performers nor spectators considered blackface painting to be of any particular importance. But if the concert party's connections to minstrelsy were not crucial, what was? How could I explore and elucidate what was clearly such a vibrant and ephemeral performance form?

This book explores how concert parties served as forums for the creation, dissemination, and contestation of identities among Ghanaians in the colonial and early postcolonial eras. What do the concert party's stock characters, thematic concerns, performance styles, and narrative strategies—especially as these changed over time—tell us about the formulation of colonial and postcolonial identities in this African country? A central argument of this book is that concert parties helped colonial Ghanaians re-invent modernity with a critical difference. While embracing and indeed exploiting key features of Western modernization and "progress" such as formal education, industrialization, and wage labor, concert artists interrogated modernity's ideological foundations and the compulsive way in which it was being adopted by Africans. As much as current gender theory has helped untangle the web of assumptions that link sex, gender, and sexuality, the concert party performatively unraveled the insidious link between modernization, civilization, and racism. Concert stages showed how one could modernize without *becoming* "civilized" (i.e., British, white, anti-African). By highlighting the ways in which the "modern" was expressed through behaviors sedimented in the body, concert parties shifted popular understanding about modernization from the essentialized to the performative, from ontology to practice. In concerts, modernization became a "doing" rather than a "being" and therefore a practice open to re-interpretation and re-invention.

The definition of modernity that I use in this book is one advanced in the 1910s by the Ghanaian intellectual Kobina Sekyi. Sekyi rejected the contrast that European conceptions of modernity implied: its implicit comparison with an opposite or antecedent condition variously labeled "primitive" or "traditional." Sekyi was keenly aware of the denigrated role in which such formulations of modernity cast Africa. And he witnessed around him in colonial Ghana African compatriots who, in a rush to "modernize," embraced values, practices, and technology from the West only at the expense and rejection of their African heritage. Sekyi redefined modernity with an African difference. He advocated a self-determined version of modernization as a process of conscious, well-considered choices of inclusion and exclusion. This critical consciousness and re-invention of modernity that Sekyi proposed anticipated the role that concert parties came to serve for colonial Ghanaian audiences in subsequent decades (Langley 1970; Sekyi 1917, 1974).

Postcolonial Interventions

Silence, or at least a problematic and uneasy relationship with language, is a recurring issue of central importance in postcolonial theory. Gayatri Spivak has argued that the "subaltern," the subordinate figure in the allegory of colonial power, is by very definition hopelessly trapped in a narrative of domination. In an essay that has become a touchstone of postcolonial theory, Spivak asks, "Can the subaltern speak?" She concludes there is no place from which the subaltern can "know and speak itself" ([1987] 1988, 285). Bill Ashcroft, Gareth Griffiths, and Helen Tiffin, editors of the volume *The Post-Colonial Studies Reader,* suggest the problem of expression is perhaps one of perception and not an overwhelming "reality" of postcolonial cultures:

> The "silencing" of the post-colonial voice to which much recent theory alludes
> is in many cases a metaphoric rather than a literal one. Critical accounts em-

phasising the "silencing" effect of the metropolitan forms and institutional practices upon pre-colonial culture, and the resulting forces of "hybridisation" which work on the continuing practice of those cultures, make an important point. But they neglect the fact that for many people in post-colonial societies the pre-colonial languages and cultures, although themselves subject to change and development, continue to provide an effective framework for their daily lives. Failure to acknowledge this might be one of the ways in which post-colonial discourse could, unwittingly, become "a colonizer in its turn." (1995, 4)

While I find this categorization of cultures into "pre-colonial," "post-colonial" and "hybrid" problematic, I nevertheless think Ashcroft, Griffiths, and Tiffin raise an issue crucial to the intellectual project of postcolonial theory: Do its assumptions and conclusions adequately represent the experiences of the majority of people in the postcolonial world?

A cursory examination of the evidence from which most postcolonial literary theory draws its conclusions is enough to raise serious doubts. From the work of Homi K. Bhabha, Ngũgĩ wa Thiong'o, and Helen Tiffin to that of Abdul R. Jan-Mohamed and Edward Said, postcolonial theory is dominated by literary analysis of European-language written texts. Very little attention is given to non-textual expressions in so-called indigenous languages of the formerly colonized world. In light of the low literacy rates in many postcolonial nations, one must question whether works of literature are generally representative of the cultures out of which they arise. Is expression for the majority of postcolonial subjects as politically compromised and ideologically overdetermined an act for average citizens as it is for writers of Europhone fiction? To answer this question one would have to examine a wide variety of discourses, including texts in languages that have historically deeper roots than those inherited from colonialism. Non-written media such as theatre, dance, music, street gossip, and radio would assume an importance they have never received in postcolonial literary theory. Such a project would not only recklessly presume that so-called subalterns *can* speak, but that what they are saying is worth listening to, analyzing, and theorizing.

The editors of the *Post-Colonial Studies Reader* enact what has become an all too familiar pattern. Even as they profess to "recognize" the value of work on indigenous languages, the very act of recognition is simultaneously an act of omission. The preface simply states that research on indigenous language, while very "important," is not included in the *Reader*'s 500 pages, nor, one notices, is it even footnoted to help the interested reader look elsewhere. Make no mistake: The silencing of non-Europhone postcolonial discourse is not a mere metaphor, but a chronic fact of postcolonial literary theory. Despite Ngũgĩ wa Thiong'o's impassioned pleas for validating indigenous languages, "decolonizing the mind" and "moving the centre" (1986; 1993), postcolonial theory remains firmly rooted in the imperial metropoles, nourished on material objects such as novels and written dramatic scripts that can be easily transported to and consumed by English- and French-speaking critics who are generally located far from the boisterous hubbub of daily life in Africa.

The Ghanaian concert party offers a perspective on the postcolonial condition not often seen by people located outside the African continent. Created by Ghanaians of modest means and avidly consumed by people of diverse classes, this performance genre represents the way some performing artists in one West African nation have creatively responded to the tumultuous changes wrought by colonialism, industrialization, modernity, independence, postmodernity, and the current neocolonial age. Concert party practitioners do not identify themselves as "subalterns" or "postcolonial subjects." However, throughout this genre's history, most performers have come from the working and intermediate classes. They are individuals with limited formal education who have lived in a country that experienced various degrees of formal British control from 1844 to 1957.

Since the concert party's inception a century ago, it has enjoyed tremendous popularity. Shows attract heterogeneous audiences, from rural agriculturalists to urban wage-earners and even the budding middle class. During thirteen months of field research between 1993 and 1995, every Ghanaian I asked reported that they had seen a concert party at some point in their lives. However, very few of the people with whom I worked had ever read a novel, in English or in Twi, by an African or a Western writer.

Contrary to what postcolonial theory might lead one to believe, concert party artists are not paralyzed by silence or the hegemony of colonial language. Their plays are notable for their loquaciousness and unruly amalgamation of disparate languages. While predominantly performed in the Akan dialects of Twi and Fante, concert parties include English, Hausa, Ga, Yorùbá, Pidgin English, Nzema, Zabrama, and Liberian Kru expressions. Such multilingualism is generally not a problem for Ghanaian audiences, since performances are no more polyglot than any open-air market in the country. But foreigners who do not speak any Ghanaian languages are typically mystified by these shows, which are confidently aimed at local rather than international audiences. Understanding the significance and appeal of the concert party requires at least cursory knowledge of Akan as well as familiarity with the salient issues, characters, and conflicts of Ghanaian life.

Ghana's encounter with Western culture has been an important stylistic and thematic aspect of concert party plays, but the confluence of the "West" and "Africa," the encounter of "self" and "other," the co-mingling of the "modern" and the "traditional" has not been depicted in concert shows as an irreconcilable conflict between two worlds. In concert performances, one sees a multi-ethnic society critically interrogating and robustly consuming disparate cultural influences of which "Western" elements are just one aspect of the form's "radical heterogeneity" (Prakash 1994, 1482). If one were to read concert parties in English translation without any knowledge of Ghanaian languages or cultures, it would be possible to construct a dichotomous interpretation that posited so-called traditional African culture against foreign imports. Yet such a reading is far more difficult to maintain if one views concert parties from within the multicultural and multilingual context of their creation and reception.

A product of the colonial encounter, the concert party has depended as much on Western proscenium staging as it has on British-designed roads and mining towns. However, English and American imports are just part of the diverse palette with which concert parties have depicted life in colonial and postcolonial Ghana. When one forces concert parties to fit into constricting interpretative categories such as "the subaltern" and "the postcolonial condition," cultural nuance and diversity are inevitably suppressed. But any "silencing" of the concert party's discourse, I would argue, is due to the observer's acuity of perception. Concert parties provide evidence that a vast population living in a culture formerly colonized by England are indeed *speaking*. What they are saying is conveyed in African languages and through a non-written theatre form aimed at local rather than international audiences. Even if the postcolonial critic cannot "hear" concert practitioners speaking, Ghanaian audiences surely can. The challenge such popular discourses present to what Anthony Appiah identifies as the "relatively small, Western-style, Western-trained group of writers and thinkers" who write postcolonial theory is whether we are prepared and skilled to understand what is being said (1992, 149).

Knowing and Doing

When I began this research in 1992, I knew little more about Africa than the average North American, which is to say very little besides the usual superficial impressions about famine, war, and wildlife. So why am I now qualified to write this book? My graduate training in African studies at Northwestern University was particularly instrumental in preparing me for this research. Northwestern's Institute for Advanced Study and Research in the African Humanities greatly accelerated my learning curve, for it provided a virtual year-round conference in African studies with a full program of activities by visiting scholars, fellows, and artists. Knowledge of Ghanaian history and culture, familiarity with colonialism in Africa, and acquaintance with the theoretical debates that have driven African studies in recent years is generally considered within the Western academy to be appropriate qualification for undertaking a project such as this one. However, once I arrived in Ghana—first in 1993 for a brief pilot trip and then in 1994 for a year of research—I faced other tests, ones which valued forms of knowledge rarely evaluated in graduate school.

In Akan philosophy, wisdom, or *nyansa,* is an activity and not merely an expression indicating intellectual capacity or accomplishment. Within Akan conceptual schemes, knowing and doing are inseparable (Gyekye [1987] 1995, 61–67). By doing, one knows; and when one has genuine knowledge, it leads to action. During my field research there were many occasions when I experienced this principle. At the invitation of the Jaguar Jokers Concert Party, I performed at the National Theatre in a concert play called *Onipa Nyi Aye,* or *People Are Ungrateful* in March of 1995. In March of that same year, both my husband Kwame Braun and I performed in another Jaguar Jokers play entitled *The Wedding Day*. Both of these shows were later broadcast on television by the Ghana Broadcasting Corporation. Acting in such a highly visible venue was an entirely unanticipated development in my dissertation research. My academic training had led me to value performance ethnography and to privilege participation as a means of producing knowledge (Conquergood 1991 and 1992; Drewal 1991, 33–35). However, through these concert performances I became a nationally recognized television personality, a far more conspicuous participatory role than I had ever imagined for myself. After these shows were broadcast, hospital workers in the northern town of Worawora, Asante market women in Kumasi, and pedestrians in the western city of Tarkwa easily recognized and identified me with my theatrical role. Children who followed me on the street began calling out my most memorable line from the play, *"Opia ɔnyare! ɔnyare koraa!"* ("Opia is not sick! He's not sick at all!"). While such attention was at times exhausting, I appreciated that their chant was at least more personalized than the all-purpose *"oburoni kɔkɔ makye"* (literally "red white person, good morning") with which children usually greet white foreigners.

Performing with the Jaguar Jokers benefited my research in several ways. First, it gave me insight into the concert party creation and rehearsal process and the dynamics of troupe organization. I saw how Y. B. Bampoe, the leader, transmitted new ideas to the company, and how K. Acquaah Hammond refined and directed these ideas during rehearsal. The experience also deepened my relationship with Hammond and Bampoe. The time we spent together preparing for the show created trust and provided a relaxed and informal context in which to ask questions about concert party history and consult with them on particular diplomatic or interpretive dilemmas I faced in my research. Finally, my performance created public interest in this project. Wherever I traveled, people immediately associated me with the concert party. This facilitated new relationships with practitioners and also prompted spectators to share spontaneously their opinions and recollections.

But perhaps the most profound outcome of my performing with the Jaguar Jokers was the general perception among Ghanaians of various ranks—from concert actors and university professors to lorry drivers and market women—that because I had performed in a concert party, I was now qualified to *write* about them. Within an Akan frame of reference, "objective," distanced observation —no matter how well informed with secondary literature, how thoroughly immersed in archival documents—does not constitute "knowledge" in its fullest sense (Gyegye [1987] 1995, 62–63). Aside from appearing at the National Theatre, the most important active expression of my budding knowledge about Akan culture was through language. I studied the Twi dialect of the Akan language for four years, both in Chicago and Accra. Like many African languages, Akan is proverbial and highly idiomatic. Deep knowledge of the language comes from a lifetime of experience for which four years of intensive language study is no substitute. At my best, I have spoken Twi like a fairly articulate teenager: I was often able to understand every single word in a sentence yet not understand the deeper meaning of a sentence which drew upon proverbs or idioms. A common expression of praise for someone undertaking a difficult task is, *"Wo bɔmoden,"* or "You try." I did indeed try, and Ghanaians generously rewarded and praised my language efforts, however faltering.

In Akan philosophy, one not only gains knowledge about something by doing, but one must also express that knowledge through action. As Kwame Gyekye explains, "The wise person in the Akan conception is one who can 'analyze' (*mpaepaemu, mpensempensemu*) the problems of people and society with a view to suggesting answers" ([1987] 1995, 65). So what problems does this present work tackle and what answers does it suggest? One of my objectives is to identify and analyze Akan-based theories of creativity that undergird concert party practices. In seeking to uncover embedded theories that are germane to this art form, this book intersects with recent debates in African studies about the appropriateness of European and North American research agendas and theories which are routinely imposed on African subjects with little regard for existing indigenous paradigms.[6] In Chapters 4 and 5 in particular, I analyze and theorize the proverb *"ohia ma adwennwen"* as it expresses Akan understandings about the relationships between power, creativity, improvisation, and performance.

A related agenda of this book is to interrogate the implicit Eurocentrism in contemporary critical theory. For instance, Chapter 5 examines concert party female impersonation in relation to North American drag and gender performativity theory. By its very lack of cultural specificity, drag theory tends to assume universal applicability. Yet when tested on African ground, this theory appears provincial and culturally biased. Upon hearing earlier versions of my work on concert party transvestism, some scholars argued that drag theory is so overwhelmingly associated with North American queer theory that it is not possible or even appropriate for an Africanist to inhabit this discourse. I vehemently disagree. Africa has much to contribute to the production of knowledge outside the African continent, and I believe that only by placing Africa front and center will its contributions move beyond the peripheral, token "multicultural" position to which it has been relegated by the Western academy. It is for this reason that an overarching concern of this book is African perspectives on modernity, for the "modern" is a phenomena of the twentieth century that the West usually conceives of in culturally exclusive terms.

Concert party veterans, scholars based in Africa, and theorists, cultural critics, and theatre historians residing in Europe and North America voice competing perceptions about what exactly makes the concert party interesting. Underlying the disjunctions between these various perspectives is an extremely problematic issue: the politics of the production of knowledge in and about Africa. With so many competing interests, whose research agenda will be served? In a provocative study of the imposition of Western gender discourses on Africa, sociologist Oyèrónké Oyêwúmí charges that "in African studies, historically and currently, the creation, constitution, and production of knowledge have remained the privilege of the West" (1997, x). Within African studies, one sees a widespread tendency to impose Western conceptual categories, theories, and research agendas in ways that predetermine research outcomes. As Oyêwúmí rightly points out, "We should recognize that theories are not mechanical tools; they affect (some will say determine) how we think, who we think about, what we think, and who thinks with us" (24).

While the poststructuralist critique of anthropology has led to much hand-wringing about the politics of Western-educated scholars objectifying Africa, it has not led to a radical reformation of the epistemologies and theories that researchers bring "to the field" in Africa. Recent Africanist scholarship is still overwhelmingly dominated by agendas derived from outside the continent. The relationship between social structures and individual agency is a driving question of the Western-derived discipline of anthropology. Yet how many Africans whose lives are marshaled as evidence in this discourse see process versus structure as the most burning question to be asked about their lives? How often are the subjects of Africanist research included as worthy partners of debate and key figures in establishing the framing arguments of new scholarship? As Paulla Ebron has argued, even when Western-trained scholars are highly self-conscious about the notions of "Africa" they generate, it rarely occurs to them "to ask Africans to join them in their ruminations on the problem of how to generalize about Africa" (1996, 21). And what if African subjects' own interpretations of their lives contradict the explications woven by authors of books on Africa? On the few occasions when the opinions of the "subjects" of Africanist research are included in scholarly texts, their words are rarely incorporated *on an equal footing* with those of published authors.

Inclusion can take many forms, and the *means* by which the subjects of African research are incorporated into the knowledge production process is critical. For example, performers' perspectives are foregrounded right from the beginning of Veit Erlmann's study *Nightsong: Performance, Power, and Practice in South Africa* (1996a) on *isicathamiya* choir performances in South Africa. The book begins with an introduction by Joseph Shabalala, a leading innovator of the *isicathamiya* genre. Erlmann's second chapter reproduces a discussion that took place among the Kings Boys choir after they watched a video Erlmann shot of one of their shows. *Nightsong* appears, on initial perusal, to include and highlight the perspectives of *isicathamiya* performers themselves. Yet upon closer examination it becomes clear that the voices of practitioners are bracketed off, treated differently from sections of the book that quote ethnomusicologists and other published scholars. For instance, in the Kings Boy's discussion of Erlmann's video in Chapter 2, the performers complain that they did not know in advance that their show would be videotaped. They object that they did not have an opportunity to choose which songs they were going to record, nor were they able to rehearse in advance for this new media and adjust their performance for maximum visual impact. The Kings Boys apparently had little agency over Erlmann's documentation and distribution of their creative material. Since the performance

Erlmann recorded was in effect a "first draft" of this choir's work and the performers themselves were so dissatisfied with the results, one wonders why Erlmann chose to focus on this event in his book and also publicly distribute this
videorecording along with the book (1996b). Erlmann himself offers no explanation. Imagine the controversy an academic author would provoke if she quoted
and reproduced liberally from first drafts of essays written by fellow academic
authors. Clearly the creative and intellectual property of *isicathamiya* performers
and that of academic scholars are included in the book *Nightsong* under very
different terms.

One of the contentions of this present book is that the politics of knowledge
production are enacted in the everyday details of research and academic writing.
While African studies has made great strides in deconstructing its colonialist
heritage, our field has yet to address the ways in which the mundane aspects of
research performatively re-enact outmoded epistemologies. I do not wish to construct an either/or dichotomy, as if the epistemological traditions of Africa, Europe, and North America could somehow be disentangled after six centuries of
intensive intermixture. Yet I do want to suggest African studies needs to bring a
great deal of new energy and creativity to the challenge of decentering Western
discourses, and that methodological issues should command as much attention as
philosophical ones, for the two realms are inextricably linked.

Structure and Approach

Rather than presenting one main argument about the Ghanaian concert party, this
work makes several different arguments about the concert party's changing significance over a seventy-year time span. Chapter 2, "Reading Blackface in West
Africa: Wonders Taken for Signs," addresses the question that first sparked my
interest. I explore the significance of concert party blackface. This section not
only analyzes what this appropriation of American and British theatre conventions represented, but also critiques the ahistorical and acultural assumptions in
much postcolonial literary theory. Drawing upon current work on the African
diaspora and the black Atlantic, I argue for the necessity of a transnational paradigm when interpreting concert party blackface.

That this study begins with the question of concert party blackface reveals
the political economy of its creation and consumption. This book is part and parcel of a North American tradition by which scholars advance their careers through
publication. The primary distribution of the book is likely to be in Europe and
North America, since scholarly books are too expensive for widespread distribution in Africa. Blackface is the feature of concert parties that first ignited my
interest. It is also the aspect of my work that most interests my North American
compatriots upon whom I am dependent for a living. By beginning with a chapter
that caters to the preoccupations of this audience, I have fallen into a common
trap, one that has ensnared other scholars—such as V. Y. Mudimbe (1988), Mar-

garet Thompson Drewal (1991), and Oyèrónké Oyêwúmí (1997)—who have criticized the hegemony of European epistemologies in African studies. In devoting so much energy and attention to dismantling the prejudices of Western discourse, deconstructive analysis can ironically end up reinforcing the West's centrality. While I have fallen into this common trap, I have a strategy for escape: The reader should consider this first chapter a space-clearing gesture, one in which North American preoccupations are addressed so that they can be laid aside, making room in subsequent chapters for questions that Ghanaian concert practitioners advance as being more germane to their performance tradition.

Subsequent chapters are organized chronologically, covering the years from 1895 to 1965. I divide this history into three eras. The first period, between 1895 and 1927, can be thought of as the era of the "concert," since performances during this time had not yet adopted the name "concert party." Turn-of-the-century "concert" entertainments were based on European models of performance, particularly vaudeville and music hall. However, the years from 1927 to 1945 saw a much more thorough incorporation of African languages, idioms, and references into this genre. This second period, which I identify as the "trio era," also saw the development of a distinctive three-character format with highly formulaic sketches about domestic situations. The third period of concert party history extends from 1946 to 1965. I call this the "troupe" era, since concert parties at this time grew from simple three-character scenarios to extended plays incorporating anywhere between fifteen and twenty-seven characters. Such periodization can make distinctions between eras appear far more pronounced than they actually were in the historical past. Each era of the concert inevitably bleeds into the one that follows. For instance, while larger troupes became popular in the 1950s and 1960s, many retained the name "trio," calling themselves names like the "Akan Trio" or "Bob Cole's Ghana Trio." Even if such groups performed complex tales involving many characters, they would incorporate older elements, such as the classic trio-style "opening chorus." Thus the periodization I present here is based upon general principles rather than unequivocal rules of historical change.

Chapter 3, "The Rowdy Lot Created the Usual Disturbance," spans the period from the late nineteenth century, when amateur concerts first appeared in the city of Cape Coast, through the 1920s, when concerts became a thriving semiprofessional activity in the cities of Accra and Sekondi. I examine the relationship between this novel performance form and its newly emergent "publics," the incipient classes of coastal society. This chapter explores Kobina Sekyi's ideas about modernization and civilization in an African context as expressed in his play *The Blinkards*. It also addresses the performative way in which Western culture was disseminated, adopted, and adapted by coastal populations.

Chapters 4 and 5 focus on the concert party's most formative years, the period when school boys Bob Johnson, E. K. Dadson, and others from the Western Region used their wits and ingenuity to make concerts accessible to new social classes and geographical regions. By incorporating indigenous languages, blending imported characters with homegrown tricksters, and taking their shows on the road, these youngmen made concert parties a genuinely popular theatre form. Chapter 4 covers the pragmatics of performance, from the sociology of actors and troupes and the history of theatrical conventions to the details of concert party plots, venues, audiences, touring routes, and life on the road among itinerant performers. Chapter 5 considers the poetics of concert party invention, particularly as they arise from Akan notions of creativity and improvisation. This chapter concludes with an analysis of female impersonation and the political efficacy inherent in *how* concert party characters were constructed and enacted.

Chapter 6 examines the changes the concert party underwent during the period just before and after Ghana's independence in 1957. In the aftermath of World War II, African self-rule in the Gold Coast appeared to many inevitable. Yet the struggle to define the first independent nation of modern Africa took years. As Africans envisioned the new Ghana and its relationship with Pan-Africanism and the African diaspora, concert parties imaginatively blossomed forth with a huge range of characters, more elaborate plots, supernatural creatures, and a diversity of themes more closely tied to the lives of ordinary people. This chapter looks at the period between 1946 and 1965 when concert parties expressed everexpanding ideas of community, as Ghanaians shifted from local and regional to ethnic, national, and Pan-African affiliations.

Chapter 6 analyzes in particular concert plays of the early 1960s that were audiotaped and preserved by the University of Ghana. I worked with linguist K. Keelson to transcribe and translate these plays, producing five complete scripts: *Beautiful Nonsense* and *Man Must Work Before He Eats* by the Fanti Trio, *Don't Covet Your Neighbor's Possessions* and *Life Is Like a Mirror* by E. K. Nyame's Akan Trio, and *The Family Honors the Dead* by the Ahanta Trio. While these plays contain enough material to sustain a book-length study of their own, Chapter 6 focuses primarily on two plays. Because my readers do not have access to these unpublished texts, close analysis of any one play requires a fair amount of contextualization in terms of plot, characters, action, conflict and theme. I analyze in detail the two plays that seemed the most representative of dominant trends of this period.[7]

Access to the past is always mediated through the present, particularly when using oral and ethnographic sources. For instance, few actors who performed during the 1930s are still alive. So in order to find out how this generation of actors went about creating their shows, I interviewed those who studied under them. This research method results in apparent anachronisms within particular chapters. For instance, Y. B. Bampoe and Kakaiku are central figures in Chapters 4 and 5 (which cover the period 1927 to 1945), even though they did not begin their professional careers until the 1950s. However, Bampoe is a key eyewitness to the 1930s and early 1940s because during that time he worked in an informal apprenticeship system whereby young boys assisted touring troupes. By studying under his concert party predecessors, Bampoe learned how to compose stories, entice the audience with jokes, and perform musical numbers according to established theatrical conventions. When Bampoe subsequently became a professional actor and created his own stock character "Opia" in the 1950s and 1960s, his creative process of invention was based upon what he had observed among the "pioneers" of the concert party form. Kakaiku's signature song "Ohia Ma Adwenwen" likewise informed my interpretation of the 1930s and 40s, even though this song had not yet been composed. Kakaiku's tune illustrates a fundamental principle of Ananse storytelling (*anansesɛm*) and Akan proverbial wisdom, and thus serves as documentation of oral traditions that predate Kakaiku's career.

Readers of this book may wish to consult its companion videotape, *Stage-shakers! Ghana's Concert Party Theatre,* created by my collaborator and husband Nathan Kwame Braun, with whom I shared my research in Ghana. Comprised of performance footage, interviews, and images of a concert party troupe on "trek," the video is intended as a teaching resource to be used in tandem with this book. *Stage-shakers!* brings the concert party to life with images in motion and music, without which it is impossible to appreciate concert theatre in all its dynamism. An accompanying instructors' guide provides suggestions for integrating text and video into the curriculum.

Dynamic and vibrant, the concert party—in all the forms it has taken over the course of its hundred-year history—expresses a culture in the throes of intense social change. Through its topsy-turvy style, passionate engagement with audiences, polyglot dialogue, and raucous, irreverent humor, concert performances reflected and help constitute Ghana's colonial and postcolonial realities. The history of this form attests to African agency in the midst of economic exploitation and artists' ingenuity even in the face of oppressive limitations. The concert party also testifies to the mysterious power of comedy to turn reality on its head, providing all of us with a fresh perspective.

2

Reading Blackface in West Africa

WONDERS TAKEN FOR SIGNS

I first encountered the Ghanaian concert party in the Northwestern University library in 1992. It was there I found Efua Sutherland's small booklet *The Original Bob,* a biography of the famous concert party actor Bob Johnson (1970). On the cover was a picture of Johnson in top hat and tails, wearing a plaid tie, his beaming smile broadly painted in white, his hands extended outward at his sides: a perfect evocation of Al Jolson exclaiming "Mammy" (figs. 1 and 2). This picture of Johnson, so suggestive of the controversial and racially charged American minstrel genre, raised questions about how blackface traveled all the way to West Africa. Why did Africans wear blackface? Did this makeup, clearly influenced by American and British minstrelsy, signify ideas about race circulating during British colonial rule?

Perhaps colonial Ghanaian performers were offering what Homi K. Bhabha calls a "revaluation of the assumption of colonial identity through the repetition of discriminatory identity effects" (Bhabha 1986, 173). Blackface performance practices might have been subversive strategies through which Africans disrupted racist colonial domination by turning "the gaze of the discriminated back upon the eye of power" (173). Yet as someone who strongly believes that postcolonial theory is desperately in need of historical specificity, I question just how such an interpretation of concert party's subversiveness could be supported with historical evidence. Would it require intentionality on the part of the performers? Or would audience reception be more important? Subversiveness may not be consciously articulated at all, for concert parties are comedies, and humor, as Freud has shown us, registers in regions of the human psyche often beyond the reach of rationality, inaccessible to the historian searching for evidence firm enough to move an argument beyond speculation and surmise.

While questions of audience reception in theatre history are notoriously problematic, they are especially so in Africa. Spectators of colonial concert parties had extremely limited access to writing and preservation, thus diaries or memoirs recording their recollections are not to be found in the archives. Oral history, the mainstay of African social history since Vansina's foundational treatise (1985), is of limited use: Spectators' memories of ephemeral theatricals enacted over sixty years ago are sketchy at best, when even extant. Performers' recollections are far more vivid and accessible through oral interviews, and their testimony supplemented with contemporaneous performance reviews in colonial African newspapers as well as my experiences in Ghana of the 1990s constitute the evidentiary basis for this chapter's exploration.

My concern to find evidence substantiating how a performance convention such as blackface was interpreted in the historical past arises from what I see as a problematic gap between academic disciplines in the study of colonial and postcolonial cultures. Postcolonial literary theory has converged on occasion with debates in colonial and postcolonial historiography, most notably in Gayatri Spivak's critiques of the Subaltern Studies Group ([1987] 1988). However, there has been a tendency for the fields of literary study, history, and political science to explore issues of subaltern agency and colonial power independently, since a common ground between disciplines is difficult to maintain when accusations of history's empiricism are countered by rejections of literary theory's ahistorical flattening of the experiences of colonized people (Ahmad 1996; Cooper 1994; McClintock 1992; MacKenzie 1994; Slemon 1994). Postcolonial literary theory makes generic claims about "the postcolonial condition," a state of being that freely transgresses historical and cultural boundaries (Ashcroft, Griffiths, and Tiffin 1995). This leads, as Aijaz Ahmad points out, to some rather peculiar assertions, as when one postcolonial primer suggests, in reference to the *fatwa* on Salman Rushdie's *Satanic Verses,* that the Indian government is Islamic and Irani clerics are postcolonial (1996, 277).

While poststructural theory, upon which much postcolonial theory is based, has undermined facile claims to empirical truth, it has authorized, ironically, truth-claiming interpretations of entire cultures and epochs. Consider the work of Eric Lott, a literature scholar whose award-winning book *Love and Theft: Blackface Minstrelsy and the American Working Class* (1993) explores the historical significance of American minstrelsy. Lott offers at one point an extensive analysis of a single illustration from a 1901 edition of *Huckleberry Finn.* As is typical of his overall methodology, Lott treats one image as sufficient basis upon which to interpret the thoughts and feelings—the "structure of feeling"—minstrelsy cross-dressing inspired in nineteenth-century working-class spectators (1993, 166). By what logic can one illustration from a novel published in 1901 tell us so much and so definitively about a form of "lowbrow" theatrical entertainment enjoyed by thousands of Americans during the previous six decades? Why we should consider this one image so emblematic?[1]

I want to locate my work precisely between the disciplines of history and literature: My research questions arise from issues in postcolonial theory, but the methods I deploy are grounded in established modes of historical inquiry. Has the concert party blackface had the subversive elements ascribed to colonial mimicry by postcolonial theory? For evidence I turn not to literary texts in a colonial language, the basis of much postcolonial theory and criticism, but instead I examine oral histories and interviews in both English and Akan languages, American minstrelsy archives, colonial Ghanaian newspapers, and ethnographic material gathered during thirteen months of field research.

As scholars such as Paul Gilroy have demonstrated, empirical methods demanding transparent sources must be suspended when considering performance practices forged, as blackface was, under conditions of exploitation and domination. Yet despite the ultimate failure of empirical models, I argue that a thorough immersion in evidentiary sources is especially crucial where conditions of domination prevail. Postcolonial theory asserts that colonial mimicry and stereotypes were ambivalent. But to speak of mimicry and colonial ambivalence ultimately does not tell us very much. What is much more revealing is to analyze in detail *how* specific valences were created, reproduced, and transformed through particular representations over time. What did blackface come to "mean" as it moved geographically from Boston to Hollywood, from London to Africa, and temporally from the late nineteenth through the twentieth centuries? Looking at the particular valences of ambivalent signs may take us much further into understanding the cultural maelstrom where colonialism and performance converge.

Questioning the Question

Even when the focus of our attention is on the historical past, the exigencies of the present impinge, shaping our perception of what is worthy of attention (Carr 1961, 35). Thus, before asking why colonial Ghanaians wore blackface, we must ask why and for whom such a question is interesting. Blackface, or the concert party's appropriation of theatrical conventions from minstrelsy, is what most fascinates many North Americans when they learn about the concert party. Throughout the 1990s as I have talked about, lectured, and written on this art form, images of the darkened faces and whitened lips donned by colonial concert party actors have generated the most sustained interest among my North American audiences. Yet among Ghanaians I interviewed, concert party blackface is of no particular importance. Some, such as Sandy Arkhurst at the University of Ghana's School of Performing Arts, say that focusing on Western aspects of concert party genealogy re-enacts a colonialist obsession: Non-Africans all too often see in African practices only what is familiar and relevant to the West, thereby failing to perceive what is pertinent to local populations (#95.58). Kwabena N. Bame, author of *Come to Laugh,* finds that among "outsiders learning for the first time of Ghanaian concert parties, there is a particular fascination in attempting comparison with the more familiar historical dramatic tradition of their own countries" (1981, 6).

Having often witnessed such blinding self-absorption, Ghanaian scholars listened to my initial research questions about the ideological significance of concert party blackface with polite tolerance, their smiles and lack of engagement masking, I eventually realized, exasperation. Highlighting the Western derivations of the concert party also raised questions about the genre's cultural authenticity. Arguments about the foreign inspiration of concert parties engendered counter-assertions about its indigenous roots in storytelling traditions known as *anansesɛm*.[2]

While scholars are caught in a gridlocked debate about the concert party's hybridity or authenticity, concert party practitioners themselves are much less concerned about the origins of their art form. Senior actors I interviewed, while acknowledging multiple influences, did not categorize their ideas as "Western" or "African." In response to questions about where performance ideas came from, actors gave short, disinterested answers. They were far more galvanized when talking about how well actors could execute those same ideas. Bob S. Ansah of the 1940s troupe the Gold Coast Two Bobs prides himself on his chameleon-like ability to transform his identity. He told me how he alone, in a single performance, could enact multiple stock characters:

> I could act as the gentleman, and then lady impersonator, and then boy actor—at the same time, when the show is going on, by changing. While we are doing the dialogue, hardly before you could know I am the one appearing as lady impersonator, I am also appearing as a gentleman, and also as a boy actor. Because of the attire and the language and the voice I use, you will never detect that I am the one who acts as the lady impersonator. (#93.10)

In the sixty formal and many informal interviews I conducted, concert practitioners chose narratives highlighting personal agency and individual talent. They boasted about how a Fante actor could portray a Muslim northerner by praying to Allah in perfect Hausa; how E. K. Dadson, son of an Axim merchant, convincingly impersonated King George VI on his coronation day in 1936; or how Mr. E. C. Baidoo could mince in European-style shoes and women's attire, uttering the refined English of an educated "lady." Practitioners did not locate meaning in the content of performances—the semiotics of face painting or the lyrics of a song. Nor did they consider the genealogy of particular performance conventions such as blackface especially meaningful. Rather they identified the *doing* of performance as the aspect which should be the focus of study, for *how* a gesture is enacted often conveys far more meaning than what the ostensible content of the gesture may signify.

Concert practitioners generally do not find blackface the most compelling or illuminating aspect of their work. However, they were willing to engage in debates about the history and relevance of this feature of their art form. Their perspectives and opinions thus feature prominently here. While it would be naive to interpret actors' intentions as the incontrovertible source of "true" meaning, ignoring their perspectives altogether would willfully exclude African artists from scholarly discourse on their work. The issues of agency and performative competence that performers themselves articulated as being more germane to the history and practice of their art form are taken up in later sections of this book, especially in Chapters 4 and 5.

Genealogies of Performance

Throughout the twentieth century, an endless parade of stock characters trod the boards of concert party stages: the Fante "gentleman," the anglicized African "lady," the domestic worker from Liberia, the Muslim malam, the urban good-time girl, the traditional Ghanaian "cloth" woman, and the city-slicker young man. These stereotypical characters, forged under British colonial rule, codified and delimited particular behaviors into generic tropes. Though broadly drawn and ideologically overdetermined, these tropes had valences that far exceeded firm empirical grasp. Homi Bhabha argues that it is precisely the ambivalence of the colonial stereotype which must command our attention, for ambivalence ensures the stereotype's "repeatability in changing historical and discursive conjunctures; informs its strategies of individuation and marginalization; reproduces that effect of probabilistic truth and predictability which, for the stereotypes, must always be in excess of what can be empirically proved or logically construed" (1994, 66).

The performance genealogy of the concert party extends to many traditions and conforms to no clear legitimate or illegitimate lines of descent. As is generally true of performance practices in the diasporic frame that Paul Gilroy calls the "black Atlantic" (1993), concert parties partake in a process of displaced propagation in which historic practices adapt to changing conditions and new locales (Roach 1996, 28). The process of transmission follows no clear path or predictable pattern. Old meanings are cast off and new ones adopted with little ceremony or reverence for origins. Even when lines of descent can be clearly traced, origins only tell fragments of a much larger story. Positivist theatre historians have sometimes responded to my work by asserting that Ghanaian concert parties are merely derivative of North American minstrelsy, British seaside entertainments, or European commedia dell'arte. Yet concert parties developed in the "behavioral vortex" of the circum-Atlantic, a place where, as Joseph Roach has demonstrated, absolute interpretations are quickly thwarted. Locating unequivocal meaning at the busy intersection of Atlantic cultures is a fruitless exercise. Rather than constructing forthright arguments tracing origin, the challenge such performances pose for scholarship lies in identifying the many routes available to practitioners and spectators and uncovering the reasons why people followed particular trajectories.[3]

The use of blackface in colonial Africa is of particular interest in light of the historical development and ideological significance of "blacking up" in Western theatre. To historicize blackface is to experience what anthropologist Michael Taussig calls "mimetic vertigo," a dizzying whirlwind of identity and alterity in which actors along different racial and cultural divides adopted the superficial identity effects of various "Others" (1993, 237). George Rehin dates the mask of blackness in Western theatre as far back as 1377 in England, when Richard II hosted a performance in which actors impersonated African princes (1975, 686). In an article entitled "Harlequin Jim Crow," Rehin speculates that the black mask worn by the commedia dell'arte Harlequin may have carried racial valences in popular imagination and reception (1975, 692). The mid-nineteenth century saw the birth of the wildly popular American minstrel genre in which whites "delineated" so-called Ethiopians, apparently using as source material their observations of the behavior and culture of Southern plantation slaves.[4] After the Civil War, African Americans also entered the minstrel field, for the only way they could be accepted on the American stage was by blackening their faces (Toll 1974, 195–233). When European immigrants flooded New York at the turn of the century, blackface offered Irish, Italians, and Jews a means of becoming "American," for burnt cork erased their ethnic differences from—and highlighted their racial affinities with—hegemonic culture (Roediger 1991, 95–163; Rogin 1996).

In the 1920s and 1930s, Al Jolson transposed minstrel theatrical conventions from New York vaudeville houses, where the form was nearly defunct, to Hollywood celluloid. Films such as *Mammy,* which re-created in 1930 a classic nineteenth-century minstrel show, were distributed throughout the world and played in colonial outposts such as the British Gold Coast in West Africa. There, Jolson's movies generated tremendous enthusiasm among Africans, who were quick to copy the fashions, dance steps, and performance conventions they observed. In December of 1934, a traveling Ghanaian comedian named Mr. Smart-Abbey staged a variety performance called a "concert party" in the Government Gardens of Cape Coast Castle (fig. 3). In a deeply ironic twist of history, this building had served in previous centuries as a storehouse for slaves awaiting export to the New World. Mr. Smart-Abbey's variety show began with a "real hot tune" called the Charleston, which "took the house by storm," followed by musical solos and a comic sketch of romantic "spooning." Then, according to newspaper accounts,

> the atmosphere all of a sudden changed when it came to the item of the "Reminiscence of the 'Singing Fool'." We were all enjoying the fun of the Singing Waiter in the theatre, and expecting more from him when apparently news came that the famous Singing Waiter has lost his only son, "Sonny Boy Junior." (*Gold Coast Spectator* 1934i)

Overcome with grief, the waiter felt unable to perform, but the theatre manager prevailed upon him with threats of breach of contract. The waiter eventually capitulated. "He came out sorrowfully and sang in the most pathetic strains the famous song the son loved, 'Sonny Boy.' Then he collapsed."

The singing waiter's doleful, pathetic display was in fact entirely staged. The whole scenario of the dying child, the fight with the theatre owner, and the ballad "Sonny Boy" was a fabrication adapted from the 1928 Al Jolson film *The Singing Fool.* Thus an African actor, performing in a former slave castle, imitated an American Jew, imitating a white nineteenth-century minstrel actor, who imitated

American slaves, who came from Africa in the first place. Enacted on what Michael Taussig calls the "colonial stage of historic surreality," this performance makes it "far from easy to say who is the imitator and who is the imitated, which is the copy and which is the original" (Taussig 1993, 78–79).

Concert parties demonstrate how deeply, if problematically, implicated are the performance traditions of Europe, America, and Africa. From the inception of the African slave trade in the fifteenth century through European colonialism in the twentieth century, performance styles traveled—like raw materials, commodities, traders, and slaves—through vast maritime networks linking nations, colonies, and empires. The slave trade brought African storytelling, music, and dance traditions to the New World. White American actors observed plantation culture, copied what they perceived, and refashioned this material to suit the tastes and prejudices of white audiences. Minstrelsy became, in the words of Michael Rogin, the "first and most popular form of mass-culture in nineteenth-century United States," a position later usurped by Hollywood (1996, 5). Minstrelsy also anticipated Hollywood's role as an exporter of North American culture: In the nineteenth century, minstrelsy traveled throughout the world, most notably to England and throughout the British empire. Blackface was performed in Cuba, Jamaica, Nigeria, the Gold Coast (Ghana), South Africa, India, China, Indonesia, and Australia.[5] In many of these places, minstrelsy not only took root, it flourished, finding fertile soil in the ideology of white supremacy that shaped relations between white and nonwhite populations.

For North Americans, blackface is a highly charged signifier, intimately tied to an unresolved history of racial exploitation, segregation, and derisive stereotyping of people of African descent. Whites created minstrelsy to represent blacks, and the images they presented were overwhelmingly degrading. Blacks were portrayed as either dandies or buffoons, with a transition between these two extremes woven into the very dramaturgy of the shows.[6] Typically the first half of a performance depicted the so-called northern Negro and his ineffectual attempts to assimilate into polite society. Meanwhile the second part showed southern slaves in their presumed natural state frolicking blissfully on the old plantation. The evening was structured around a transition from civilized to savage, from performers in formal evening dress singing refined and sentimental ballads to men in crude farm clothes dancing plantation breakdowns (fig. 4). The first half of a show, visually represented on the top half of many minstrel playbills, featured modes of performance centered on the head—singing, facial expressions, and verbal antics—whereas the rest of the body predominated in the latter half: high stepping, clog dancing, boxing matches, military drills, and men wearing women's dresses. Performances began in a highly ordered semi-circle with stock characters named Tambo and Bones at either end and the Interlocutor in the middle. Yet as the evening progressed, the action built to a crescendo of disorder, sometimes climaxing in an explosion that sent performers crashing through drums, violins and chairs sailing perilously through the air, arms and legs flailing about in puffs of smoke (fig. 5).

What made the American minstrel show so racist was that blackness and

African American culture became the unequivocal signifiers for ignorance, disorder, and the grotesque. Shows were dramaturgically structured to create a dichotomy between high and low, between black and white. As Ralph Ellison (1964, 45–59), Eric Lott (1993), Marlon T. Riggs (1986, 1991), David Roediger (1991), Robert Toll (1974), and many other scholars have demonstrated, blackface in America was and continues to be expressive of divisive relations among races, classes, and ethnicities.

When blackface and other elements of minstrelsy traveled to the Gold Coast, these theatrical conventions were once again used in a setting where whites dominated blacks based upon racist notions of white superiority. What did blackface signify for colonial Ghanaian audiences? To answer this question requires further consideration of the scope and nature of the relationship between concert parties and various minstrel-derived performance conventions. The documentable performance connections between these genres are numerous. Aside from Mr. Smart-Abbey's direct appropriation of "Sonny Boy" in Cape Coast Castle, many older actors say they copied Al Jolson's minstrel greasepaint (Amartey and Williams #95.51; Ansah #93.10; Hammond #93.6). A photograph of the Ghanaian troupe the Dix Covian Jokers taken in the mid-1940s gives visual evidence of stylistic appropriation of makeup and costume: The bow ties, plain suits, and controlled makeup closely match Jolson's cinematic appearance (figs. 6 and 7). Both concert parties and minstrelsy were exclusively male genres, with men in drag playing female roles. In minstrelsy, the "wench" and "prima donna" roles were specialty acts at which certain performers excelled, most notably Francis Leon, "the Only Leon" (fig. 8). Likewise Ghana had its stars of lady impersonation such Kwaw Prempeh the "Danger Woman" of Kakaiku's Band, Joseph Emmanuel Baidoe of the Akan Trio (fig. 9), and the impressive troupe of drag queens assembled by the Jaguar Jokers (fig. 10).

Ghanaian concert parties have a direct connection with—indeed they are widely acknowledged to be derived from—amateur British theatricals promoted in colonial schools. On special occasions, such as end of school term and British Empire Day, African school boys were encouraged to stage "concerts" (Narkwa #94.21; Sutherland 1970, 6; Vans #95.30). Imagine, as a colonial African subject, attending a performance celebrating Empire Day in the Gold Coast in 1930. The show, staged in the auditorium of the Bishop's School of Accra, begins when three African schoolmasters in blackface "acquit themselves creditably in the rendering of . . . humorous 'Plantation Songs.'" Among the eighteen items on the evening's bill are African schoolchildren dancing the Scotch reel and the sailors' hornpipe, followed by renditions of "Negro Spirituals" and sea shanties "sung with expression and feeling" (*Gold Coast Times* 1930). The evening concludes with African schoolmaster Ayittey starring in a comic dialogue in which he plays a troublesome servant who nearly sets his master and himself on fire. The huge African audience that gathered for this performance is reported to have reeled "with bursts of laughter from beginning to the end of the dialogue." Thus on a day intended to celebrate "the desirability of thinking Imperially and for doing [one's] best for the Empire as a whole" (*Gold Coast Times* 1932b), black Africans wore minstrel makeup, sang African American spirituals, did "humourous" American plantation songs, danced the Scotch reel, and laughed uproariously at the antics of a disruptive servant.

Although concerts began in colonial schools, Ghanaian school boys soon discovered their popular appeal and exported these variety entertainments to more accessible venues. Bob Johnson, a pioneer of the concert party, and his friends in the Versatile Eight used holiday breaks to earn money by staging concerts for the general public. They took the shows on the road, touring coastal towns and villages. Johnson recalls, "At weekends, we would travel from Sekondi to as far west as Axim—for small concerts around the villages. . . . Soon our pockets began to swell up with coppers—and that was a lot of dough for young school boys like ourselves" (*Sunday Mirror* 1960c). The Versatile Eight appealed to non-English-speaking audiences by incorporating Ghanaian languages and music. Actor, director, and historian Bob Vans recounts:

> During those days, some school boys were practicing, but unconsciously. They didn't know they were starting something. Those school boys, Mr. Horton, Bob Johnson, and Tackey were attending Methodist School in Sekondi. . . . It came to a point that they were able to perform satisfactorily and so they started going to villages. They will go to a village, and then they will perform. They will go here, and perform. And then they toured, very nicely. (#95.30)

By adapting Empire Day school concerts to suit the general public and by taking these performances to the villages, these school boys created, though probably "unconsciously" (as Vans contends), the prototype of the professional traveling theatre that came to be known as the concert party.[7]

Like American minstrelsy, concert parties were itinerant shows that brought alien lifestyles to remote areas: Minstrelsy staged southern Black plantation life for Americans living in the north, while concert parties represented elite coastal life to farmers living in the Gold Coast hinterland. Both genres began their spectacles with a brass band parade through town, drawing spectators to the evening's performance. Concert parties and minstrelsy shared presentational styles, operating within an aesthetic that careened wildly from sentimental pathos to ridiculous buffoonery. Shows in both genres were improvised, not scripted, combining music, dance, and story within a formulaic three-part structure that allowed ample opportunity for variations.[8]

However, there were important differences between concert parties and minstrelsy. First, the dichotomy that minstrel shows created between white and black, between order and chaos, and the genre's derisive stereotyping of African culture seems to have been largely unknown on concert party stages. Second, concert parties and minstrelsy developed within very different constellations of power. Whereas American minstrel shows were performed by and for people who had considerably *more* power than the characters they represented onstage, Ghanaian concert parties were created and consumed by people who generally had *less* power than the elite "ladies" and "gentlemen" they depicted.[9] Finally, Africans, who statistically far outnumbered Europeans in the colonial Gold Coast, chose to adopt blackface, whereas African Americans, a minority population, had burnt cork stereotypes imposed upon them by a materially and numerically dominant white culture (Toll 1974; Riggs 1986, 1991).

During the course of my field research in Ghana, I asked many people where blackface, or "tranting" as they call it, came from and what it meant.[10] I never met anyone, either among performers or spectators, who explicitly said blackface carried any notable ideological weight in terms of race. When I asked the leaders of the Jaguar Jokers why they painted their faces, they said, "Because it is attractive. In fact, it creates laughter too. When you wear the trant, it creates laughter" (Bampoe and Hammond #93.11). Kwame Mbia Hammond said actors do it "just to crack jokes to the audience. If you don't make up your face and disguise yourself to the audience, you don't get laughs" (#93.6). Blackface is part of a whole aesthetic of artifice in which actors use self-consciously presentational conventions to foreground the artifice of performance. Conventions such as female impersonation, non-naturalistic staging, cartoonish characterizations, and a broad acting style create comic distance between the actors and their characters.

When I visited Ghana in 1993, the Concert Parties Union was preparing a proposal to perform at Ghana's 1994 Pan-African Historical Theatre Festival (Panafest). This semiannual event attracts participants from throughout the African diaspora, for it commemorates the devastation of the African slave trade and reunites African peoples whom slavery dispersed throughout the world. The Ghana Concert Parties Union members discussed their participation in Panafest not as an occasion to reflect on diasporic issues, but as an opportunity to advance the Union's reputation (GCPU 1993). Knowing that many Americans would come to Panafest, they decided to feature the American-derived aspects of their art form by doing an old-style show in which blackface featured prominently. The show was to be performed on a stage constructed within the Cape Coast Castle, the symbolic center of Panafest and site of the historic "Gate of No Return" through which Africans embarked on the Middle Passage. Union members seemed entirely innocent about how offensive blackface comedy performed in a former slave castle was likely to be for African Americans, especially those motivated to make a pilgrimage all the way to the Motherland. Fortunately, this particular Panafest show never materialized, perhaps due to sluggish bureaucracy or a diplomatically astute festival organizer's intervention.[11]

When I returned to Ghana in 1994, I asked performers more questions about blackface, but my inquiries led to blind alleys. Everyone said blacking up was done just to make people laugh—it meant nothing. Tranting was but one of the many techniques concert party actors use to transform themselves "for show." So I decided to give actors more information about why I was interested in this particular feature of their shows. On one occasion I gathered together six older actors for a reunion during which I showed them pictures of nineteenth-century American minstrelsy and early vaudeville. These performers, ranging in age from sixty-three to seventy-seven, were among the first and second generations of concert party practitioners: Bob S. Ansah of the Gold Coast Two Bobs, Jimmie Narkwa of the Dix Covian Jokers and the West End Trio, Joseph Emmanuel Baidoe of the West End Trio and the Axim Trio, and Y. B. Bampoe and K. Acquaah Hammond of the Jaguar Jokers. These actors began their careers in an era when blackface was used in concert parties much more frequently than it is today. They also began acting at a time when African contact with British culture and the ideologies of colonialism were most intense. If blackface carried racial meanings in Ghana, I suspected this generation was most likely to be aware of it.

At the reunion, I showed the concert party elders a photograph taken in 1874 of American vaudeville actors Harrigan and Hart (fig. 11). Everyone immediately exclaimed, "Oh! They are Bob Johnson! Both of them are Bob Johnson!" recalling the pioneer of the Ghanaian concert party whose career began in the late 1920s (CPMR #95.27). Rather than interpreting the photograph as evidence that Bob Johnson's wastrel attire and stage makeup came from American precedents, these actors initially perceived Harrigan and Hart as having copied Bob Johnson. After discussing the date of the photograph further, the actors decided, "What she is showing to us simply means the face painting aspect of shows is not new. It has been there over the years." Everyone readily perceived the continuities between the makeup and costume styles used by Harrigan and Hart in the 1870s and those of Ghanaian troupes in the 1930s and 1940s, such as the Yankey Trio (fig. 12).

I then tried to explain what blackface means in America and why it is now considered to be very offensive. Perhaps reacting to the seriousness with which I conveyed this information, actor K. Acquaah Hammond interpreted what I said to mean, "Today . . . if someone should paint his face while staging a show [in America], one would be shot dead on the stage. He will be shot dead immediately." During our conversation, there were many misunderstandings, which suggested to me these older actors were genuinely unaware of the history and ideological significance of blackface as practiced outside of Ghana.

When I asked the performers if they found blackface offensive, Y. B. Bampoe, leader of the Jaguar Jokers, offered his own interpretation. On previous occasions, Bampoe and I had talked extensively about blackface because he would like to come perform in America someday and wanted to know how his performance needed to be altered to appeal to U.S. audiences. At the reunion, Bampoe absented himself briefly from our discussion and returned wearing minstrel makeup fashioned impromptu from cooking charcoal and blackboard chalk purchased at the local food market. Bampoe addressed his fellow performers, myself, and Kwame Braun, my partner and videographer. He at times spoke in English rather than Fante, knowing that by doing so on camera he was addressing a general American audience:

> (*In Fante*) I want to give some explanation. The fact is some of our brothers elsewhere, we have been made to understand that if they see someone staging a show in Ghana or elsewhere with some paint applied to that actor's face, it means the actor is insulting them. I am referring to those who were sold into

slavery. But that's not the idea. Here in Ghana are many occasions when people apply paint to their bodies. When the Krobos are undergoing Dipo rituals, the body is smeared with some paint. The Nzemas apply some colors to their bodies during the Kundum festival. The Akuapem have a ritual known as *bragor* for young girls who have had their first menstrual period. The young girl and her intimate friends have some colors applied to their bodies. The Abiriws, Guans, perform the same rituals for young girls. . . .

When therefore we apply colors to our bodies, nobody should think that he or she is being made fun of. It is customary. We normally paint our faces. Some people apply paints to their bodies before they attend some functions. We have the colors. We have all the colors: blue, green, red. . . . (*Switching to English*) Some people over the globe have different understandings or different interpretations that we are reminding them that they are slaves: is never true. It is completely out of gear. So nobody should think of that. We should all co-operate. When you see Africans painting their face, you should not be offended. It's for fun's sake. (*Switching to Fante*) It is something we do, and people are happy about it. I would like to go to America in future. I have learned that the blacks in America don't like the idea. They should take it from me that there is no bad intention behind the scenes. If I go to America or Europe and do it, it must be taken in good faith. Our African priests and priestesses practice it a lot, and at some of our festivals many people do it. . . . That's all I have to say.

What Bampoe sees in concert party blackface are connections not to American minstrelsy, but to Ghanaian puberty rites, annual festivals, and ritual practices performed by priests and priestesses of traditional religion. Body painting sets these occasions *and* concert parties apart from everyday life and highlights the liminal status of key performers.[12] When I told Mr. Bampoe not all types of body painting were problematic in America, just black face painting, he said, "Oh, I see. Then it means when I come to America, I should paint my face green."

Bampoe's interpretation of blackface as being part of a tradition of ritual body painting was far from typical. In fact, he was the *only* Ghanaian I interviewed, either among practitioners or spectators, who expressed this particular reading. Bampoe's interpretation was also not categorical, for while he at one point disavowed racial connotations and emphasized reading blackface within a local, ethnically specific semiotic field, he later drew upon a much wider geographical frame, one with a distinct racial element. Bampoe asserted that in concert party blackface,

> there is a reason for using black and white: Dr. Aggrey used the keys of an organ to explain a point. He said that whites can't live happily without the blacks and the blacks also can't live happily without the whites. Furthermore, much of the raw materials they use are imported from Africa. After they've been used, they come back to us. We are, therefore, one people. If someone applies black and white to his face, it shows unity.

Bampoe alludes here to a piano metaphor associated with Dr. James Emman

Kwegyir Aggrey, known throughout much of the world simply as "Aggrey of Africa" (Smith [1929] 1932). Born in the Gold Coast in 1875, Aggrey came to the United States, earned degrees at Livingstone College and Columbia University, and then returned to Africa in the 1920s as part of the Phelps-Stokes Education Commission to Africa. This initiative was aimed at formulating new educational policies for Africa, ones which would synthesize African and European cultures. Aggrey was instrumental in the founding of Achimota School in the Gold Coast, a school that remains today a flagship campus in Ghana. A piano keyboard was the central image of Aggrey's philosophy of education. He likened cooperation between black and white races to the harmony achieved through black and white keys on a piano keyboard, and he advocated for a school curriculum that would achieve such harmonic synthesis.

Thus, in our conversations about blackface, Mr. Bampoe first argued that nothing about this theatrical convention is considered racially derogatory in Ghana because body painting is more readily associated with African rituals than performance traditions propagated across the Atlantic. But he simultaneously asserted that the colors used in concert party blackface *do* indeed have racial connotations. Just as black and white together on a keyboard symbolize unity, so a blackened face with whitened lips signifies racial harmony. Adding a further layer of complexity to Bampoe's exegesis of concert party blackface, one must consider his desire to tour professionally in North America and to make his performances accessible and palatable to audiences across the sea. His relationship with me and interview on video provided what he saw as an opportunity to make professional contacts for his desired tour abroad.

Diaspora Longings and Mediated Perceptions

I began this chapter by asking why Africans in colonial Ghana wore blackface. Did this makeup signify ideas about race circulating during British colonial rule? In addressing this question I have thus far traced the trajectory of blackface as it moved from U.S. minstrel and vaudeville stages in the late nineteenth and early twentieth centuries to Hollywood movies that were viewed and consumed in colonial Africa in the 1930s and 1940s, and with Negro spirituals and American plantation songs performed in British schools on special occasions such as Empire Day. I have analyzed some of the similarities and differences between blackface as practiced in North America and the Gold Coast, both formal conventions and the sociology of actors, characters, and audiences. I have incorporated opinions of senior Ghanaian actors in the concert profession, those who performed in the 1930s and 1940s, a time when blackface in the Al Jolson makeup style was most prevalent on concert party stages.

Other than Y. B. Bampoe, who connected the black and white colors of blackface to Dr. Aggrey's piano metaphor of racial harmony, no Ghanaians whom I interviewed explicitly identified race as a component of concert blackface. However, ethnographic and archival evidence suggested the possibility of racial connotations, however latent. When I told concert party elders that "tranting" in America was done primarily by white men, everyone laughed. No one could explain why this struck them as funny, it just *was*. When I tried to probe the sources of such laughter, I had difficulty framing questions about race that were meaningful to Ghanaians. I believe this was due to a lack of vocabulary, however, and not an absence of racial issues in Ghanaian life.

In nearly every aspect of my family's life in Ghana in the mid-1990s, our *whiteness* mattered, for foreigners with light skin are accorded enormous privileges and status. Preferential seating on buses, unquestioned access to university facilities, relatively benign encounters with bureaucracy, and outpourings of hospitality at enstoolments of chiefs and public festivals were automatically extended to my husband and me as *aburofo* (that is, Europeans, foreigners, whites) in a way that was *much* less frequently extended to African American researchers we knew, some of whom experienced downright harassment on account of their status as "those who were sold into slavery." The ideology of white supremacy appeared to me to be pervasive in Ghana, not only in the prevalence of straightened hair and skin bleach, but in everyday casual encounters at taxi ranks, chop bars, and food markets. Countless times during our stay, Ghanaians would marvel at our electronic equipment and ask what was wrong with "the black man" that he could not design such machines. My husband and I found ourselves in the strained position of trying to dissuade people of apparently sincere opinions such as, "You whites are wonderful," "I know I can trust you because you are white," and "The black man is bad and lazy."

My impressions of contemporary racial issues in Ghana are just that—impressions. They are not based on methodical study. Yet as Liz Stanley and Sue Wise contend, the lived experience of research must be recognized, for it is an "invisible yet crucial variable present in any attempt to 'do research'" (1991, 266). I suspect many researchers of European descent working in Africa enjoy privileged access to resources, people, and information on account of their whiteness. Yet I can think of no occasions when the specific dynamics of white skin privilege as experienced during research are acknowledged, much less analyzed, in scholarly publications. As Kofi Agawu argues, the self-reflexive turn in anthropology is usually not extended to many common features of Africanist research. Agawu points out that "one rarely encounters statements like, 'I was only there for two weeks,' 'I lived in a hotel in a city and visited the villages daily,' 'I did not speak a word of the language'" (1992, 257).

My experiences of race in everyday Ghanaian life in the 1990s—the prominence of racial issues and simultaneous absence of an explicit discourse about race—led me to consider archival evidence in new ways. Race arose in parenthetical comments, in laughter, on the periphery of conversations. I returned to the archive wondering if the racial dimensions of concert performances would be similarly located on the margins, in between lines, in the silences of archived texts.

Extant documentation of performances from the 1930s and 1940s is limited to occasional performance reviews in African newspapers. I culled through stacks of Ghanaian newspapers from the 1930s and 1940s, several of which are now housed at the University of Ghana's Institute for African Studies Library. Newspapers such as the *Gold Coast Spectator* and the *Gold Coast Independent* were generally published and consumed by a relatively educated sector of colonial Ghana. While this constituency cannot be considered representative of all concert party spectators during this period, many of whom were illiterate and resided in rural areas, a large segment of the audience at urban venues such as the Palladium in Accra and the Optimism Club in Sekondi were indeed drawn from the "Standard VII" class.

Few performance reviews mentioned blackface and none discussed explicitly its meaning. Yet as I scanned entertainment pages, I began to notice the prevalence of articles and feature stories on black American or "Negro" culture. Colonial Ghanaian newspapers from the 1930s and 1940s express a keen interest in the African diaspora, evident through regular feature articles on leading African American entertainers, editorials on discrimination laws in England, and stories about economic exploitation of blacks in America and the West Indies. Newspapers reveal that the 1930s saw an awakening of racial consciousness in colonial Ghana, at least among the coastal populations these newspapers generally addressed. For the first time in the seventy-year history of the local press, newspapers such as *The Gold Coast Provincial Pioneer, Gold Coast Spectator,* and *Vox Populi* began to carry regularly articles on "The World Situation and the Negro." Journalists reported news from America on the Scottsboro trial, lynch terror, and the activities of Marcus Garvey. Editorials connected racial discrimination in America with the color bar in England and the "brutal treatment of the African" locally (*Gold Coast Spectator* 1932c, 1932d, 1934d).

This nascent diaspora consciousness in the realm of politics arose in the Gold Coast precisely when colonial Ghanaians became interested in studying and emulating American Negro artists. An editorial on the future of Gold Coast culture challenged readers to "look at all the great philosophers, the great educationists there are in Negro America. . . . Paul Robeson, the actor and singer, is believed to be the greatest living Negro. We want our Paul Robesons in acting, singing; in playing the piano [and] violin" (Musing Light 1932b). Throughout the thirties, the *Gold Coast Spectator* covered Robeson's European travels extensively. Newspapers also followed the careers of Louis Armstrong, Coleman Hawkins, Ethel Waters, and Noble Sissle and reported on developments in Harlem theatre.

Just as editorialists were demanding Gold Coast Paul Robesons, local theatre artists began impersonating icons of Negro entertainment on Accra stages. Soon after audiences in the Gold Coast flocked to see the "great coloured actress" Ethel Waters in the film *On with the Show,* an African performer named Miss Aurora Cato created her own vaudeville act in which she impersonated Waters singing

"Am I Blue?" Cato appeared in a variety show hosted by the Ladies Musical League in Accra in 1932. The African reviewer known as "Musing Light" described her performance:

> Just as I took my seat and started to devour the programme, the curtain rose displaying attractive scenery and a bevy of chorus girls in charming costume. Their opening chorus "Dawn is Breaking" was nicely rendered and the reception healthy. Then came the Negro Troupe like lightening wizards and cut some capers which brought the house down with tremendous laughter and applause.

> Next was Miss Aurora Cato's solo "Am I Blue?" the famous song of the film *"On with the Show,"* now showing at the Palladium. She went through the piece beautifully; and, considering the fact that she had no training, I should say her rendition was excellent. (Musing Light 1932a)

Miss Aurora Cato's act was hardly an isolated occurrence. Variety shows such as the one described above were quite common at this time in Accra and Sekondi, the major port cities of the Gold Coast. Performances of Negro jokes and spirituals, as well as imitations of specific American movie stars dominated colonial Ghanaian stages in the 1930s.

What did these performed emulations of Negro entertainers signify? Why did reading about African Americans musicians and actors and seeing them in Hollywood movies prompt Africans in colonial Ghana to perform impersonations on local stages? What was the relationship between performances of diaspora identification on stage and textual representations of the Negro world published in local newspapers? What is, in effect, the connection between performing and writing the African diaspora?

"That the people have become race-conscious there can be no two opinions," wrote an anonymous reader to the *Gold Coast Spectator* on April 28, 1934. A swelling tide of racial sentiments and the circulation of Negro literature in the Gold Coast did not go unnoticed by the government. The Gold Coast legislature passed in 1934 an amendment to the Criminal Code Ordinance that banned the importation and even possession of literature deemed to be subversive. Governor Thomas justified the controversial Sedition Bill by saying that "the people . . . in their present stage of development should be protected from disloyal intrigue and subversive propaganda."[13] Among the literature considered particularly inflammatory were the *Negro Worker,* a Paris-based organ of the International Trade Union Committee of the Negro Workers (ITUC-NW); publications of the International League Against Imperialism; the *Negro World,* founded by Marcus Garvey; all the writings of George Padmore; and Nancy Cunard's edited anthology *Negro.*[14] These publications represented the prime networks through which Gold Coast newspapers obtained news of the larger black world.

When colonial representatives described such literature, they frequently took exception to the communist, "Red," or "Bolshevik" sentiments expressed therein (Shaloff 1972, 242, 246, 255, 262). While the rhetorical construction of this literature as communist helped mobilize support for sedition legislation in both

London and Accra, the banned literature was in fact as much about race and white supremacy as it was about class and capitalist oppression. The *Negro Worker* treated race and class as inextricably linked oppressions. The journal's stated aims included equal pay for equal work irrespective of race, color or sex; an eight-hour workday; freedom to organize trade unions; elimination of racial barriers in trade unions and industry; and the elimination of lynching, which they identified as an example of "capitalist terror" (*Negro Worker* 1933). Nancy Cunard's *Negro* anthology was explicitly about race, with essays on racial injustice, Negro history, music, and poetry, and the political situation of black people throughout the world. The colonial impulse to ban such literature was widespread, extending to such places as Trinidad, the Gambia, South Africa, and Nigeria (*Negro Worker* 1934a, 1935).

"Negro" as a transnational and transcultural identity was subversive precisely because it linked the labor struggles of South Africa with strikes in the West Indies, the plight of farmers in the Gold Coast with Negro soldiers in France, and the exploitation of Negro seaman and stevedores in ports throughout the world (*Negro Worker* 1931). A poem entitled "The Same" by Langston Hughes published in the *Negro Worker* articulates a perception of the transnational consistency of racial exploitation:

> It is the same everywhere for me:
> On the docks at Sierra Leone,
> In the cotton fields of Alabama,
> In the diamond mines of Kimberly,
> On the coffee hills of Haiti,
> The banana lands of Central America,
> The Streets of Harlem
> And the cities of Morocco and Tripoli.
>
> Black:
> Exploited, beaten, and robbed,
> Shot and killed,
> Blood running into
> >> Dollars
> >> Pounds
> >> Francs
> >> Pesetas
> >> Lire
> For the wealth of the exploiters.
> Blood that never comes back to me again. (Hughes 1932)

Such pronouncements of racial and class affiliation prompted British Colonial Secretary Sir Cunliffe Lister to deem the *Negro Worker* a "foul and obnoxious" tract. He asked, "With that kind of seditious stuff coming into the country, with that kind of filth . . . is it to be supposed for a moment that the Government can tolerate it to go on?"[15] Global affiliations among blacks were tolerable and even desirable when based upon the "imagined community" of the British Empire, as the annual colonial ritual of Empire Day made abundantly clear (Padmore 1932). But transnational identifications that highlighted the racist foundations of imperial rule were deemed foul, obnoxious, filthy, and seditious.

The Gold Coast Sedition Act of 1934 censored the importation, possession, and publication of various literatures about the "Negro." However, the colonial government did not ban colonial Ghanaian performances of Negro spirituals, comedies, and popular songs. There is no evidence that such performances were ever subject to censorship, legal proceedings, or even mild government intrusion during this period. What accounts for this discrepancy in the government's reaction to performing versus writing the African diaspora? I believe the mediated nature of perceptions upon which colonial Ghanaian performers based their "Negro" acts explains, at least in part, this apparent contradiction. Gold Coast performers gathered much of the creative material for their theatrical shows from the cinema. Unlike the politically charged and critical visions of black identity and white supremacy presented in publications such as the *Negro Worker,* the *Negro World,* and Nancy Cunard's *Negro* anthology, Hollywood films represented African American culture from an overwhelmingly racist and derogatory perspective. In affiliating with Negro Americans through performed impersonations, Ghanaian actors consumed and reproduced racist stereotypes from abroad. For instance, African actors copied minstrel imagery from Hollywood films under the misguided perception that plantation songs, Sambo plays, and Al Jolson actually *were* representative of Negro culture.[16]

I argued earlier in this chapter that minstrel blackface did not carry in Ghana the same racist connotations it held in Britain and America. However, theatrical impersonations of Negroes in colonial Ghana were part of a growing popular discourse on black identity. While blackface in the Gold Coast was not *racist,* it was on some level *about race* and racial affinity. The adoption of this makeup expressed a burgeoning interest in the black Atlantic. Representations of the larger Negro world were controversial, both among British colonials who banned the importation of "seditious" literature from the black Atlantic and among colonial Ghanaians who debated the appropriateness and authenticity of performed emulations of American Negro culture.

Let me narrate here briefly one particular example. The Ghanaian popular press in the early 1930s contained a running series of articles that debated the pros and cons of singing Negro spirituals. Teachers at Achimota school believed these songs represented one of "the African's great achievements in music." An editorialist at the *Times of West Africa* thought Negro spirituals should be discouraged because they reminded people of the slave trade. Yet an editorialist in the *Gold Coast Spectator* questioned this assessment:

> In an issue of the *Times of West Africa* in the past year, were some statements in Zadig column, meant as a criticism of Achimota, to the effect that Negro Spirituals are not desirable in the country as they tend to remind people of the Slave Trade. Teachers, who had up to that time regarded Negro Spirituals as the African's great achievement in music, were disappointed and had to discuss it in a

refresher course in July, 1931. Then came Professor Ballanta this year to this country to give organ and pianoforte recitals, Negro Spirituals and lectures on African music, in some of which functions the one responsible for Zadig columns was undoubtedly present. *The Times of West Africa* joined the community and other presses in eulogising Professor Ballanta for his recitals, his lectures, and these very Negro Spirituals that were deprecated some months previously as I have already stated. In a citizenship lesson after Professor Ballanta's performances, a keen student wanted to know why the Negro Spirituals that were deprecated some months in the past year as undesirable, and praised this time by the papers. Reader, how would you answer this if you were a Teacher? (*Gold Coast Spectator* 1932g)

Not knowing who Professor Ballanta was and if he was of European descent, it is difficult to interpret the full dynamics of this controversy. But the terms of the debate clearly revolved around whether African American spirituals signified cultural achievement, progress, and black agency or whether these songs represented a more bleak and disempowering image of blackness, one too closely associated with slavery. Behind this extended controversy about how to classify Negro spirituals was an unspoken question: Within the colonial grand narrative of cultural evolution, where were Negro spirituals to be placed? Was this music to be extolled as evidence of Negro "progress"?

Debate about the appropriateness and significance of singing Negro spirituals in the Gold Coast formed the subtext of ad copy promoting Al Jolson's movie *Big Boy.* The advertisement for the film's 1932 debut in Accra read:

BIG BOY—What is he? BIG BOY—who is he? Leave it at that, because Al Jolson himself will tell you all about it. You may also not have heard Negro Spirituals sung properly, but when you hear Al Jolson sing Negro Spirituals as one should be expected to sing them, perhaps you will be disposed to occupy your spare time in learning some negro spirituals. This is a talkie full of coloured men. It will show you exactly how black men suffer in some parts of the world. (*Gold Coast Spectator* 1932f)

While the ad claims *Big Boy* is full of "coloured men," the film had relatively few black actors and none playing central roles—unless, of course, one perceives the black-faced Jolson himself to be a "real Negro." Jolson's so-called proper style of singing spirituals was stilted and operatic. He sang to the accompaniment of an African American chorus which lounged on the front lawn of a southern plantation, the white overlords looking on with paternalistic appreciation.

While the controversy at the Achimota school revolved around the cultural value of spirituals, the Jolson ad copy signaled questions of authenticity. Newspapers reflect preoccupations about whether Al Jolson and African performers in the Gold Coast sang spirituals "properly." Concern with the "real" informed local performances of Negro spirituals as well. For instance, the Musical Dragons, who performed in Accra in February 1932, promoted their show by asking, "Have you heard a Real Negro Spiritual? If not, book your seat for the M.D.E. [Musical Dragons Entertainment] of February 5" (*Gold Coast Spectator* 1932a). A review of the performance found the singing adequate, but inauthentic: "The Dragons Quartet sang remarkably well the Negro Spirituals 'Steal away to Jesus,' 'I've got a robe,' and 'Nobody knows the trouble I've seen;' but we have heard better singing than to say this was 'real;' all the same their ensemble was good." Following the Dragons Quartette in this variety show was the "dapper" Augustus Williams, who performed an imitation of Al Jolson playing the "Singing Fool." Unlike the spiritual singers, this performance of Negro identity was praised for authentically reproducing its model. The reviewer praised Williams's makeup for so accurately replicating Jolson's in the movie *The Singing Fool.*

Public concerns over the authenticity of Negro culture and misunderstandings about Jolson's ethnic and racial identity expressed in the Gold Coast press exemplify precisely the sort of ironic disjunctures and misperceptions that riddle the discourse of the black Atlantic. Colonial Ghanaian performers saw Al Jolson on film and then imitated him on local stages, just as they imitated Ethel Waters in *On with the Show.* Among many colonial Ghanaians represented by these newspapers, Al Jolson's makeup, Sambo plays, plantation sketches, and spirituals accurately represented Negro life. As literate Africans in the Gold Coast living under British rule searched for models of successful black identity within a racist social order, they found Negro American life of particular interest. Yet among British colonial authorities, no doubt familiar with the racist pedigree of blackface in Britain and America, Jolson's films and Sambo plays represented no particular threat.

That so many different and ostensibly incompatible meanings can be found in just one aspect of the Ghanaian concert party—the use of blackface—is entirely in keeping with larger patterns of cultural transmission in the black diaspora. The circulation of performance cultures within the black diaspora, Paul Gilroy has argued, rarely follows any clearly defined or traceable trajectory. "Black performance . . . is a profane practice. It has been propagated by unpredictable means in non-linear patterns. Promiscuity is the key principle of its continuance" (1995, 15–16). Forged under conditions of domination, exploitation, and desire, black Atlantic cultures demand that we re-conceptualize the whole problematic of origins. Scholars must dispense with evolutionary paradigms that impose a teleological model of development. Genealogical paradigms that imply notions of purity and legitimate lines of descent are similarly problematic. And positivist procedures that assume stable, unified meaning are utterly useless in this context. The challenge of African diaspora performance scholarship lies in representing and analyzing the multiple, contradictory perspectives found in the "behavioral vortex" of the circum-Atlantic, to use Joseph Roach's terminology (1996). We must identify the routes that were available to practitioners and spectators and ask why people followed particular trajectories through the busy intersection of cultures.

Popular discourse in this period of Gold Coast history also has two implications for Africanists. First, it highlights the performative nature of identity

construction, for embodied knowledge and behaviors were central to the transmission and formation of new subjectivities in colonial Ghana.[17] Africans imagined themselves as members of an expanded transnational and transcultural black
community. These new geographies of identity arose not just through print culture and mass media—as Benedict Anderson's work would lead us to believe—
but also through an active, performative process of consumption (1991). Colonial
Ghanaians not only watched Hollywood films and read newspapers articles about
the Negro: They *performed* Negro identity and thus imagined new communities
through their bodies.

That Ghanaians under colonial rule so quickly gravitated toward performed
emulations of African Americans is not astonishing, considering the performative manner in which many encountered British culture in educational settings.
Schools were a primary institution for instilling not only the skills of reading and
writing and knowledge about subjects such as history and math, but also the embodied behaviors fundamental to the civilizing mission. Attending school meant
learning to wear Western clothes, speak English well, eat in the European manner
with knife and fork, and conform to the manners of polite British society. During
the annual Empire Day celebrations on May 24, schools mounted variety shows
in which students exhibited their mastery of English singing, speaking, and dancing. At an Empire Day celebration held at the Presbyterian School in Christians-
borg in 1932, students staged a play called "Brittania and her People."

> Brittania, robed in the traditional costume was sitting in all majesty, when her
> men of renown were introduced to her, with a short sketch of their achieve-
> ments. You ought to see Nelson in his nineteenth-century costume, with epau-
> lets and sword complete. It was a truly patriotic play, with which His Excel-
> lency was highly satisfied. (*Gold Coast Spectator* 1932f)

Such performances exhibited for the governor, the teachers and the colonial Ghanaian public that students had mastered the embodied behaviors of Western culture. Among those who attended colonial and mission schools, colonial identity
was well understood as a performative act.

Thus, when concert entertainers in Accra and Sekondi began mounting variety shows in which they impersonated American movie personalities and sang
Negro spirituals, they were responding to representations from abroad using the
same performance skills that colonialism had inculcated. The whole question of
the ways in which colonial ideology was transmitted, resisted, and reformulated
among Africans through embodied, performed behaviors has yet to be explored
adequately by Africanist researchers. Further consideration of the ways in which
performance was central to the process of cultural transformation in colonial Africa might illuminate a great deal that textually oriented research has failed to
investigate.

The popular print and performance culture of colonial Ghana also illustrates
the deficiencies of nationalist paradigms. Gold Coast popular press and theatrical culture of the 1930s and 1940s transcended colonial boundaries and local

particularities. Our theoretical paradigms must account for this heightened interest among colonial Ghanaians in the affairs of black people in Haiti, Trinidad, South Africa, Harlem, Alabama, Kenya, Germany, and London. How else can we explain the popularity in the Gold Coast of films representing American Negroes and the preponderance of theatrical performances imitating "Negro" culture unless we consider the imaginative implications of the black Atlantic? Diaspora consciousness is neither a presentist projection nor an imposition of black nationalist or Pan-African desire: It was a historical fact of Ghana's past, though one that has heretofore escaped scholarly attention.

In *The Black Atlantic,* Paul Gilroy argues that "nationalist paradigms for thinking about cultural history fail when confronted by the intercultural and transnational formation" of the black Atlantic (1993, ix). The nation as a category of analysis—whether defined geographically as the modern nation-state or ideologically as black nationalism—can be a crude and inadequate tool for understanding the historical processes by which individuals and ideas moved across space and time. The intercontinental and transnational journeys of black intellectuals such as J. E. K. Aggrey of the Gold Coast, I. T. A. Wallace-Johnson of Sierra Leone, and Richard Wright and W. E. B. DuBois of America disrupt nationalist narratives. Similarly unsettling are instances of the global circulation of cultural idioms among geographically disparate black populations, such as the consumption of West Indian reggae music in Britain, the importance of Motown music in South Africa, and the ubiquity of Ghanaian kente cloth in the material culture of American-based Afrocentrism. Interpretive frameworks have a profound impact on whether scholars perceive such transcultural phenomena at all. Conceptual models also determine whether such practices are seen as important or marginal, part of a coherent discourse or simply isolated aberrations.

The concert party provides an unusual perspective on the changing social, political, and cultural climate of one formerly colonized country. Blackface is but one issue in the genre's complex and varied history, though as Prof. Bame argues, it happens to be the feature that most *interests* many Western observers (1985, 6). Reading blackface in West Africa is complicated: Documentary evidence in colonial newspapers unsettles categorical dismissals of race as a valid line of inquiry, for race was clearly a preoccupation among some spectators six decades ago. Likewise, testimonies by veteran actors disrupt facile conclusions about the inherently subversive nature of concert party "hybridity," conclusions that contemporary theories of "the postcolonial condition" could easily authorize. A careful look at Ghanaian concert party blackface demonstrates that by placing "wonders" from the postcolonial world in a detailed historical and social context, postcolonial studies can go much further than merely declaring all hybrid cultural phenomena to be subversive signs.

FIGURE 1. Bob Johnson is shown on the cover of this pamphlet in a pose and costume reminiscent of Al Jolson. Courtesy of Efua Sutherland.

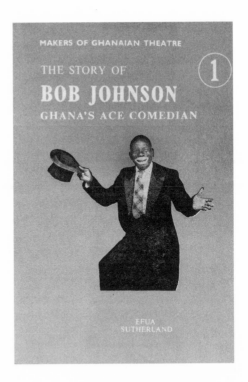

FIGURE 2. Al Jolson in the classic "Mammy" pose. Courtesy of the International Al Jolson Society.

FIGURE 3. In the late nineteenth century, Cape Coast Castle housed a company of West Indian soldiers who had been brought to the Gold Coast to fight in the Ashanti wars of 1874. From Dennis Kemp, *Nine Years at the Gold Coast* (New York: Macmillan, 1898). Courtesy of Macmillan Press.

FIGURE 4. American minstrel advertisements often depicted the dramaturgical structure of minstrel show: the first half represented freed slaves of the north, while the latter portion featured "the Ethiopians of the Southern States." Courtesy of the Harvard Theatre Collection, Houghton Library.

FIGURE 5. American minstrel shows were constructed around a dichotomy between order and chaos, beginning with an ordered semi-circle of performers who enacted a structured series of songs and jokes revolving around the stock characters of Tambo, Bones, and Mr. Interlocutor. Next came "olio" acts of solos and duets. The action gradually built to a crescendo of disorder. Courtesy of the Harvard Theatre Collection, Houghton Library.

FIGURE 6. The Dix Covian Jokers in their prime during World War II. From left to right are Bob Anderson, Atoo Essien, and James Kwaku Narkwa. Courtesy of Atoo Essien.

FIGURE 7. Al Jolson's makeup and costume served as inspiration to many concert party performers. Sketch by Nathan Kwame Braun.

FIGURE 8. Frances Leon, known as the "Only Leon," was one of the most celebrated female impersonators of American minstrelsy. Here he portrays Sarah Bernhardt. Courtesy of the Harvard Theatre Collection, Houghton Library.

THE ONLY LEON,
AS
SARAH BERNHARDT.

FIGURE 9. Joseph Emmanuel Baidoe in this photo from the mid-1950s is dressed in the classic costume of a concert "Lady": hat, glasses, lipstick, earrings, gloves, and a frock. Courtesy of J. E. Baidoe.

FIGURE 10. The 1960s saw an explosion of female types. Pictured here in a pose reminiscent of Diana Ross and the Supremes is the Jaguar Jokers' cadre of female impersonators. From left to right are Kwasi Owusu, Yaw Nyamekye, E. C. Baidoo, Yaw Werenko, Kwao Mamful, and Kwaku Okyere. Courtesy of K. Acquaah Hammond.

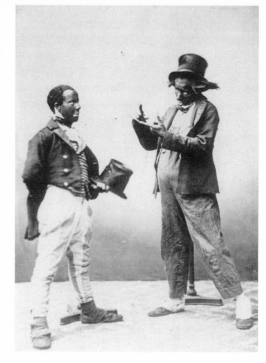

FIGURE 11. In the early 1870s, American actor Edward Harrigan left minstrelsy for the variety stage, teaming up with Tony Hart. Together they did plays about immigrant life in New York. Courtesy of the Harvard Theatre Collection, Houghton Library.

FIGURE 12. When Y. B. Bampoe's cousin returned from World War II with a trunkload of costumes, Bampoe and his friends put these items to good use. K. C. Bampoe, K. M. Hammond, and Y. B. Bampoe (from left to right) used top hats, frocks, and grease paint to impersonate concert party troupes such as the Axim Trio and the West End Trio who regularly toured their home town of Suhum. Courtesy of K. Acquaah Hammond.

FIGURE 13. Woman wearing a kente cloth wrapped in traditional style. Courtesy of Philip Turkson.

FIGURE 14. While some men in the early twentieth century wore their cloth with bare shoulders exposed, others started wearing shirts underneath their wraps to conform with European notions of modesty. Courtesy of Philip Turkson.

FIGURE 15. The comedy team of Williams and Marbel, who performed at the Accra Palladium in the early 1920s. Courtesy of A. S. Williams.

FIGURE 16. The Two Bobs and Their Carolina Girl, c. 1934: from left to right are J. B. Ansah as the Gentleman character, Charles B. Horton as the Lady, and Bob Johnson as the disruptive Houseboy "Bob," whose behavior and large belly resembled the trickster Ananse. Courtesy of C. K. Stevens.

FIGURE 17. An artist's depiction of the Ananse story "How the Spider Got a Bald Head." By permission of Oxford University Press.

Ananse putting the beans in his hat

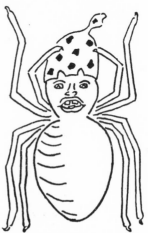

Ananse caught hold of his hat

FIGURE 18. Opia, the stage persona of Y. B. Bampoe, the leader of the Jaguar Jokers. Courtesy of Y. B. Bampoe.

FIGURE 19. This production shot from the Jaguar Jokers' play *Wo Tu Aduru Bone a, Edi Ka Wo Ano* was probably taken in the late 1950s, prior to the development of Y. B. Bampoe's signature stage persona, "Opia." Bampoe, on the left, appears as a typical "Bob" clown with painted face and tattered clothes. He is accompanied by K. Acquaah Hammond, who plays the role of the Gentleman. Courtesy of Jaguar Jokers.

FIGURE 20. The cover illustration of the Ghana Concert Parties Union membership card shows the classic "trio" format. Courtesy of the Ghana Concert Parties Union.

GHANA CONCERT PARTIES UNION
(In Affiliation with the Arts Council of Ghana)

Membership Card

Motto: UNITED WE STAND

FIGURE 21. The Akan Trio during an opening chorus, late 1950s. Joseph Emmanuel Baidoe, playing the Lady, is flanked by Kobina Okai on the left and E. K. Nyame on the right. Courtesy of J. E. Baidoe.

FIGURE 22. Female impersonator E. C. Baidoo "on the platform" with K. Acquaah Hammond in a play by the Jaguar Jokers. Courtesy of K. Acquaah Hammond.

FIGURE 23. Kwaw Prempeh plays a damsel in distress in Kakaiku's play from the 1960s, "*Sasabonsam Fie,* or The House of the Forest Monster." Courtesy of Kwaw Prempeh.

FIGURE 24. The white American performer Charley Backus and other female impersonators, c. 1880s. Courtesy of the Harvard Theatre Collection, Houghton Library.

FIGURE 25. E. K. Nyame on guitar sings with Kobina Okai and another musician. Courtesy of the Institute of African Studies Library, University of Ghana.

Figure 26. Kakaiku (second from left) with his band in Sekondi in 1961. Other musicians are I. K. Amissah on sax, Mr. Lasina on drums, Mr. Wood on trumpet, and C. K. Mann on guitar. Courtesy of I. K. Amissah.

"The Rowdy Lot
Created the Usual Disturbance"

CONCERTS AND EMERGENT PUBLICS, 1895–1927

Akan culture is highly performative and has long been so. Some Akan perform-ance modes such as Ananse storytelling, *adowa* dancing, and *odwira* festivals have deep historical roots, far predating the advent of colonial rule (Amegatcher 1968, 11–30; Lokko 1980; McCaskie 1995, 144–242; Nketia 1965). However, theatre as it is known in Europe and North America is a fairly recent innovation. Playwright Efua Sutherland claims that prior to the European presence in the Gold Coast, Africans "did not stand on a platform to sing songs and say things, and dance to entertain static audiences ranged on chairs before them" (1969, 84–85). Sutherland and J. H. Kwabena Nketia link the adoption of theatrical conven-tions such as raised stages, written texts, and a bicameral separation between performers and spectators to African contact with Europeans who settled on the shores of the Gold Coast (Nketia 1965, 33).

Europeans first brought scripted dramas to precolonial Ghana in the eigh-teenth and nineteenth centuries (Lokko 1980, 314–315). In fortresses at Elmi-na, Cape Coast, and other coastal towns, Europeans formed schools to educate their mulatto children (Foster 1965, 45). Castle schools hosted drama groups that mounted plays. Inhabitants of the castles also put on occasional shows, as when Governor Sir George Maclean supervised the staging of Shakespeare's *The Mer-chant of Venice* in Cape Coast in 1840 (Lokko 1980, 315). As formal education became more accessible to Africans in coastal cities of the late nineteenth cen-tury, so too did school theatricals.

Schools and social clubs mounted loosely structured variety shows known as "concerts," and it is from this tradition that concert parties most likely got their name (Sutherland 1969, 84–85; Bame 1985, 8; Collins 1994a, 3).[1] Early colonial concerts featured English-language comedy sketches and Western songs such as the "Song of the Fairies" and "Kiss the Little One for Me" (*Gold Coast Nation* 1914e).[2] Nothing quite like this had ever been seen in Akan cultural life. Their novelty necessitated the adoption of a new word among Akan speakers. While storytelling, singing, and dancing were referred to with the Akan word *agoro,* school theatricals were called concerts or *concets* among coastal Africans. According to Efua Sutherland, "concert" means

> any performance by actors on a stage, that is, an acrobatic display by a Chinese troupe; straight Shakespearean drama by a British troupe; a performance of modern dance by an American troupe. The words Drama and Theatre are foreign words and incomprehensible to everybody else except a mere sprinkling of people. But CONCERT has become a Ghanaian word which is comprehensible, and for the people who use it, it serves instead of drama and theatre. (1969, 84–85)

Concert is thus a loan-word from English that has gained widespread currency among Akan speakers. In popular parlance, "concert" denotes a theatrical show with an ordered, pre-established program, enacted on a raised platform with a proscenium-style division between actors and audience (Amegatcher 1968, 1, 4; Lokko 1980, 314). Such staging conventions contrast with performances of storytelling, dancing, music, and festivals, which tend to have fluid spatial relationships, multiple centers of focus, and looser temporal structures (Cole 1975; Kedjanyi 1966; Sutherland 1987, 5). Performer Y. B. Bampoe contends that if concert parties were "traditional" Akan culture, "we would have an Akan name for it— not 'concert'" (Bampoe #95.55).

Between 1900 and 1940 journalists in colonial newspapers generally referred to European-style theatrical performances as "concerts," though they also called them "costume concerts," "promenade variety performances," "theatrical entertainments," "vaudeville entertainments," and "nocturnal amusements." The phrase "concert party" does not appear at all in the historical record until 1933, when it was adopted by a short-lived Accra troupe called the "Co-Optimists Concert Party" (*Cost Coast Independent* 1933).[3] Some performers and spectators argue that the phrase "concert party" signifies a major historical shift in the genre that occurred between World War II and independence. Whereas all touring theatrical groups in the Gold Coast in the 1930s and 1940s were three-member troupes known as concert trios, those from the 1950s onward had twenty to thirty members. Because of their large size, these troupes became known as "parties" rather than "trios," and the term "concert party" thus gained widespread currency (de Graft 1976, 15; Nketia 1965, 42; Oppong and Oppong #95.40).

Concert theatricals of the early twentieth century were almost exclusively urban and coastal diversions, produced by and for the incipient social classes who lived and worked in the major cities along the Atlantic shore: Cape Coast, Sekondi, and Accra. Of all inhabitants in the Gold Coast, those living in these coastal cities had the most contact and familiarity with English language, manners, customs, and prejudices. Such familiarity bred, if not contempt, at least a vibrant engagement with European rituals and behaviors, and this engagement was the creative wellspring from which concert entertainers drew performance material.

The history of concerts in colonial Ghana begins in Cape Coast, for it was in this town that these amusements first appeared in the late nineteenth century. Of the major coastal cities, Cape Coast was the most coherent and well established. It was a center of education, the early seat of the British colonial administration, and the long-standing home of the Fante intelligentsia.[4] Cape Coast also had the most thorough contact with Europeans during precolonial times, and performances drew upon and exploited this familiarity with the rituals and behaviors of white people from *aburokyir,* across the seas. As the center of colonial activity moved to other coastal cities, concert performances spread to those locales as well, first to the burgeoning commercial town of Accra in the east and then to Sekondi in the west.

Concert audiences in each of these cities were far from representative of the colonial population at large, most of whom had no access to Western education. Yet concerts in Cape Coast, Accra and Sekondi drew a socially stratified crowd. Spectators ranged from lawyers, district commissioners, clerks, and teachers to semi-skilled laborers, merchants, and small traders. With little historical documentation about these early colonial concerts and few eyewitnesses alive today, it is difficult to know how audiences interpreted performances. But the historical record clearly demonstrates that since their inception, concerts served as forums through which Africans expressed an active and irreverent engagement with Western performance conventions—both theatrical conventions such as proscenium-style staging and variety show program fare and the performative conventions of daily life inculcated through institutions such as school, work, and church.

Concerts put Western behaviors and lifestyles on stage at a time when new constituencies were emerging in Gold Coast society. Africans who performed in and patronized concerts belonged to the incipient classes, their newfound rank and social mobility intimately linked to the introduction of formal education, wage labor, and large-scale cash crops. While some refer to this class using the umbrella term "Westernized elite," this is an inadequate and reductive description. Turn-of-the-century coastal society was densely textured, with overlapping layers of stratification and parallel indices of social value. Africans with access to new occupational opportunities afforded by the cash economy formed a conglomeration of publics and counterpublics—dominant and subordinate social groups with competing agendas and divergent interests—rather than a cohesive unit.[5] Further complicating analysis of interpublic relations in the colonial Gold Coast is the fact that individual Africans were often simultaneously affiliated with several different constituencies. Fante society during this early colonial period had multiple overlapping layers of affiliation based on class, lineage, education, and associations ranging from exclusive European-style "gentlemen's" clubs to precolonial militias known as *asafo* companies.

In the city of Cape Coast, concerts brought together different classes and became, however inadvertently, occasions for the public expression of social tension between various strata of society. Concert performances found their most demonstrative fans among waged workers, people with Standard VII level of education or less.[6] In contrast to these spectators, journalists who reviewed concerts in local newspapers represented the politically dominant interests of the more highly educated and well-established Fante intelligentsia.[7] Newspaper columns from the early twentieth century reveal that interpublic relations between these segments of the Cape Coast populous were neither amicable nor calm. Spectators were reputed to be rowdy and unruly, and their undisciplined habits of spectatorship scandalized journalists. Rather than criticizing the theatrical shows themselves, newspaper reviewers composed diatribes condemning raucous audience behavior.

Focusing on the concert party's early years, this chapter illuminates the relationship between an evolving theatrical form and its diverse audiences from 1895, when amateur concerts first appeared in the city of Cape Coast, through the 1920s, when concerts became a thriving semi-professional activity in the cities of Accra and Sekondi. Previous scholarship on the concert party has dated its origin from the mid-1920s, when a man named Teacher Yalley began performing in the Optimism Club in Sekondi (Bame 1985, 8). However, archives have collected material that reveals that concert performances began in coastal cities of colonial Ghana in the late nineteenth century, some three decades before Yalley's heyday.

It is impossible to examine a concert per se—for there are no extant scripts from this era. Instead, a written play by Kobina Sekyi, the distinguished writer and nationalist leader from Cape Coast, serves as a referent for the local stereotypes and social tensions that concerts satirized. In 1915, Sekyi wrote *The Blinkards,* the first scripted drama from the Gold Coast. This comedy of manners, written in both Fante and English, satirizes the class conflicts that permeated Cape Coast society. Though *The Blinkards* is far too thoroughly scripted and extensively plotted to be classified as a "concert," its vivid depiction of the absurdities of colonial Cape Coast life provides valuable insight into the performative dimensions of colonialism that concerts also lampooned. *The Blinkards* is also a fruitful place to begin an examination of early colonial concerts, for Sekyi identified in this play the need for integrative mechanisms in Akan society, mechanisms that would facilitate an African-centered process of modernization. Sekyi anticipated the integrative role that "concert parties" eventually came to serve in Ghana during the colonial and postcolonial periods.

Modernity with a Critical Difference

Kobina Sekyi's play *The Blinkards* provides an astonishingly prescient analysis of what modernization and civilization meant and could mean for Africa. Sekyi defined "modernization" as a process of critical evaluation and selective appropriation. He contrasted modernization with "civilization," which he defined as the compulsive tendency to adopt anything associated with British and/or white culture and categorically denigrate and reject all aspects of African/Akan culture. Sekyi advocated modernization with a critical, African-centered difference: a deliberate consideration of what was useful and detrimental about ideas and practices adopted from abroad, and a circumspect integration of those ideas with local Fante culture.

The Blinkards was first performed in 1915 at a men's organization known as the Cosmopolitan Club in Cape Coast. Little is known either of the club or the production, but Sekyi's play appears to have been an aberration in the history of Ghanaian theatre. Gold Coast Africans wrote no other major scripted dramas until J. B. Danquah's *The Third Woman* (1943) and F. Kwasi Fiwaoo's *The Fifth Landing Stage* (1943). While *The Blinkards* is distinct from the "concert" genre that was popular in Cape Coast, the play does have clear affinities with concerts. Both were performed by and for people involved in new social networks, such as the Boy Scouts and exclusive ladies' and men's clubs. Both concerts and *The Blinkards* used comedy as a medium for expressing the absurdities and stresses of modern Gold Coast society.

The Blinkards evokes in rich detail the city of Cape Coast in the 1910s and dramatizes the distinctions and conflicts between disparate strata of Fante society. The play revolves around the Anglo-maniacal obsessions of Cape Coast citizens and portrays how individuals with affiliations to commercial, educational, traditional, and peasant sectors negotiated a complex and changing social reality. Among the major characters in this play—all of whom are African—are a merchant, a barrister, a cocoa magnate who wants his daughter to be educated in British customs, a doctor, a Kru servant boy from Liberia, fishermen, esteemed gentlemen of the Cosmopolitan Club, an uneducated elderly woman who comes to the defense of her matrilineage, and an anglicized society lady who is a "leader of fashion." Such characters represented major constituencies of Cape Coast society.

The plot of *The Blinkards* revolves around the daughter of the Tsiba family who have made their fortune in the new export crop of cocoa. Aspiring to acquire the educational status commensurate with their newly achieved socio-economic rank, this nouveau rich family places their daughter under the tutelage of Mrs. Brofusem, whose name literally means "foreign matters." Mrs. Brofusem is to teach the Tsiba girl how to speak and act like a "white woman," in other words, an English lady. The conflict of the play arises when Miss Tsiba becomes so enamored with English culture she decides to follow British rather than Fante customs when she becomes engaged to marry a young man named Mr. Okadu. According to Fante traditions, marriages are arranged by the extended family and are never formalized solely through the negotiations of the prospective bride and groom. Miss Tsiba's and Mr. Okadu's autonomous decision to marry violates Fante conventions, and Miss Tsiba's maternal extended family angrily confronts those responsible for this travesty of Fante tradition. As the plot unfolds, Miss Tsiba's mother dies of shock over her daughter's impending marriage. The Christian wedding of Miss Tsiba and Mr. Okadu nevertheless proceeds as planned, but the reception is interrupted by women from Miss Tsiba's extended matrilineage, who come to repossess the bride. They say they have not sanctioned the marriage and according to Fante matrilineal tradition Miss Tsiba belongs to them, not to her nuclear family or her new husband.

Sekyi's satire is most biting when directed at those who imperfectly and uncritically mimic British culture. Mrs. Brofusem, who is to teach Miss Tsiba to "behave like a white lady," copies everything she observes about English culture, often hilariously misinterpreting her sources. As J. Ayo Langley points out in his introduction to *The Blinkards,* Mrs. Brofusem often mistakes English working-class culture for *"the* English culture" (Sekyi 1974, 12). She believes that it is customary in England to deposit cigar ashes on the carpet to discourage moths, and she greets people by touching her fingertips to theirs. At odds with African customs, she tries to get her husband to kiss her, a habit that many in the play find overwhelmingly repulsive and alarming. When Mrs. Brofusem's husband rejects her smooching, she scolds "My mouth is not smell," using her characteristically ungrammatical English. Mrs. Brofusem is prone to malapropisms and mangled idioms, as when she says she wishes to "kill one bird with two stones" and teases Mr. Onyimdzi for having a white girl "in" (rather than "up") his sleeve (38, 41). Mrs. Brofuseum's incomplete comprehension of what she imitates is the source of much hilarity in the play.

Even more Westernized than Mrs. Brofusem is her husband, who was born and raised in an Anglicized Fante household and is clearly much more fluent in English. Mr. Brofusem is amused by his wife's aping of British culture, but he objects to the compulsive nature of her mimicry. Cursing the day his wife went to England, Mr. Brofusem complains that ever since then,

> I have had nothing but we *must* do this, because it is done in England, we *mustn't* do that, because it is not done by English people and so on *ad nauseam.* (*Throws away newspaper, gets up, and walks up and down.*) The worst of it is that some of us got into these foreign ways through no fault of our own. We were born into a world of imitators, worse luck . . . and blind imitators, at that. . . . They see a thing done in England, or by somebody white; then they say we must do the same thing in Africa. It is that confounded *must* that annoys me. Why *must*? (21–22)

Mr. Brofusem sees his wife's compulsions as symptomatic of a widespread problem in Fante life, one that extends much further back in history than 1915. Mr. Brofusem complains that he himself did not chose his own way of life, for his parents "set out to make me as much like a European as possible, before they sent me to England. They would have bleached my skin, if they could" (22). Because his parents raised him in such an Anglicized manner, Mr. Brofusem now feels "hampered" that he does not know how to wear "native" dress properly, nor can he express himself as eloquently in Fante as he can in English. An unhappy hybrid of two cultures, Mr. Brofusem objects to his lack of agency in constructing his own identity.

At the other end of the spectrum from such overtly Anglicized characters as the Brofusems are characters who are "Fantes among Fantes," such as fisherman, servants, and relatives from the Tsiba matrilineage who have no formal education, speak Fante rather than English, consume *dɔkono* instead of cake, eat with their hands rather than forks and knives, and wear traditional cloth and sandals rather than frocks, slacks, and covered shoes. As depicted in *The Blinkards,* clothing is the ultimate symbol of a person's identity and cultural affiliation. Anybody who does not follow British customs is referred to as *efuratam-nyi,* which literally means one who wears cloth in the traditional style. In Fante, for a man to *fura ntama,* or "wear cloth," means he drapes an 8- to 12-yard piece of fabric over his shoulder, toga style. For women, "wearing cloth" means wrapping one unsewn piece of cloth around the hips as a skirt and another piece around the bust (see figs. 13 and 14).

However, the term *efuratamfu* connoted much more than style of clothing. What one wore represented that person's essential nature, their location within the Enlightenment teleology of cultural "progress." Wearing cloth stigmatized a person as "savage" and "uncivilized." "Without tailors and hatters and shoemakers, gentlemen, we are nothing," says a member of the elite men's organization the Cosmopolitan Club to his compatriots. "Without tailors hatters and shoemakers, we will be savages" (92). Clothes not only made the man, they were the quintessential measure of worth in early twentieth-century Cape Coast society. Even a highly educated person would be considered "savage" if he did not wear Western clothing. For instance, during the garden party scene in *The Blinkards,* the lawyer Mr. Onyimdzi appears wearing cloth rather than European attire, and a group of Anglicized young women find his behavior most confusing. One of the girls chides, "You don't behave yourself. Look at your cloth: it is savage" (57). Her comment sparks a heated discussion among her friends, who also condemn Onyimdzi for dressing in a "savage" manner incompatible with his level of education:

> 4th Girl. Yes. You have English education, yet you wear cloth. Don't you misbehave, then? . . .
> 5th Girl. You are not a lawyer if you do not go England [i.e. behave English].
> 6th Girl. Yes. You do not behave yourself; you come to garden-party in native dress. (58)

When someone as highly educated as lawyer Onyimdzi wears cloth or "native dress," he undermines his rank in the social hierarchy. Despite his English education, prestigious law degree, and successful law practice, Onyimdzi is as uncivilized as a "bushman" if he wears native rather than European dress.

While clothing indicated a person's location on the continuum between "civilized" and "savage," status was also expressed through a host of other embodied behaviors. Civilization was understood as a performance involving speech, gesture, dress, and manners. According to Mrs. Brofusem, even the pitch and timbre of one's voice changes when one has been to England (27). When Miss Tsiba's suitor, Mr. Okadu, sings a patter song during the garden party scene, he details the performative nature of civilization:

A product of the Low School, embroidered on the High,
Upbrought and trained by similar products, here am I.
I speak English to soften my harsher native tongue:
It matters not if often I speak the Fanti wrong.
I'm learning to be British and treat with due contempt
The worship of the fetish, from which I am exempt.
I was baptized as an infant—a Christian hedged around,
With prayer from the moment my being was unbound.
I'm clad in coat and trousers, with boots upon my feet;
And *tamfurafu* and Hausas I seldom deign to greet:
For I despise the native that wears the native dress—
The badge that marks the bushman, who never will progress.
All native ways are silly, repulsive, unrefined.
All customs superstitious, that rule that savage mind.
I like Civilization, and I'd be glad to see
All people that are pagan eschew idolatry. (46–47)

As Okadu's song makes clear, civilization is sedimented in the body, enacted through language, tone of voice, religious rituals, style of dress, and manner of greeting. The motivation for performing this role lies in aspirations for material advancement. The opening line of the song—"a product of the Low School, embroidered by the High"—alludes to the social mobility available to many Cape Coast citizens at this time due to the introduction of large-scale cash crop farming, merchant capitalism, and wage labor. What drives many of the characters in *The Blinkards* is their desire to better their material circumstances. They perceive the road to material advancement to lie in the performance of a "civilized" self.

In the performance of self in everyday life as depicted in *The Blinkards,* "civilized" and "savage" formed a fundamental and mutually exclusive dichotomy. Each of the characters faces the burden of being labeled as one or the other. Yet many characters and incidents depicted in *The Blinkards* do not fit neatly within either category, and it was precisely the gray areas, the places where the so-called civilized and savage mixed, that most interested Kobina Sekyi. Such hybridity is evident in clothing, as when some fishermen in the play gawk at a female *tamfura-nyi* (one who wears cloth) because she combines traditional clothing with petticoats, stockings, shoes, a parasol, and a handbag (109–111). The barrister Mr. Onyimdzi is a similar hybrid. He provides in *The Blinkards* an alternative between the misguided, obsessive Anglophilia of Mrs. Brofusem and the traditionalism of *efuratamfu*. Mr. Onyimdzi is a long-standing member of the African intelligentsia, a "true" bearer of high British culture, largely due to his advanced education abroad. But Onyimdzi rejects the bifurcated way in which Western culture is being adopted in the Gold Coast. He charts instead an idiosyncratic course, defying the expectations and rules those around him try to impose. When he goes to work at his law office, Onyimdzi wears European slacks, an Inns-of-Court gown, and covered shoes. But he changes into "native" garb of draped cloth and sandals as soon as he reaches home. When Mrs. Brofusem comes calling at Mr. Onyimdzi's house with her debutante Miss Tsiba, he serves them cake, wine, and a tin of chocolates, as would be expected of a Western-educated host of his standing. However, Onyimdzi also sets out more traditional Fante snacks such as boiled peanuts with a finger bowl, since it is customary in Akan culture to eat with one's hands and to wash at the table just before eating. While perfectly articulate in English, Onyimdzi often speaks Fante, and he completely flabbergasts Mrs. Brofusem when he artfully delivers a Fante proverb. Proverbs are a rarified and sophisticated dimension of Akan orality and only those who know the language well are generally inclined to use them. Mrs. Brofusem exclaims, "Well, I am surprise! Fancy being able to talk Fanti like that, when you have spend many years in England. How can you remember? Most young men don't able to understand vernacular when they return from England" (41). Onyimdzi explains that while he is one of the Gold Coast's "social hybrids, born into one race and brought up to live like members of another race," he has always tried to keep up his Fante, communing with himself in this African language even while he was in England.

The character Onyimdzi has much in common with the author of *The Blinkards,* Kobina Sekyi. Both were lawyers educated in Britain, and many of the philosophies espoused by Onyimdzi are evident elsewhere in Sekyi's life and writings. Onyimdzi claims that he found himself more Anglicized by his schooling in the Gold Coast than he was as a result of living in England for six months. His education in Britain made him "a Fante man who had studied and thought in England, rather than an anglicized Fanti or a bleached Negro" (58). The latter, by implication, is what Gold Coast education tended to produce. Sekyi himself apparently had a similar experience with his education overseas. K. A. B. Jones-Quartey contends that the more European philosophy Sekyi read at school abroad, "the more African he became" (1967, 74–78).

While *The Blinkards* portrays the Fante educated intelligentsia in a favorable light, Sekyi is nevertheless highly critical of Westernization. This is nowhere more evident than in the play's radical bilingualism.[8] Written in both Fante and English, *The Blinkards* is the only published drama from sub-Saharan Africa that I know of to so thoroughly intermix both a European and an African language. Sekyi's choice of language reflected his abiding concern with the dangers of Anglicization and its detrimental effect on African cultures. In this regard, Sekyi was far ahead of his time. His bilingual African play preceded by seventy years Ngũgĩ wa Thiong'o's now legendary treatise on the politics of language in African literature (1986).

Lawyer Onyimdzi is appropriately named, for his name translates as "one who knows how to live." Onyimdzi is Sekyi's model of a well-balanced, "modernized" African who has not lost his identity in the civilizing mission. Even though he has an advanced Western education, Onyimdzi avoids the compulsive drive to "civilize" (i.e., adopt European customs) in every aspect of his life. At one point in the play some women question him about the peculiar way in which he combines African and Western customs and one woman asks, "You mean to say you are not glad that you are educated?" Onyimdzi responds, "I am sorry I am civilized." While the general assumption at the time was that civilization and education were synonymous, Onyimdzi carefully separates the two. He says that when one is civilized, "your wants increase and your contentment decreases in proportion" (58). Onyimdzi's response to the woman's query is overly self-deprecating, for he is one of the few characters in *The Blinkards* whose wants are moderate and whose contentment is clearly evident. He is comfortable and at ease with his lifestyle, which balances and gracefully integrates Fante and English customs. Onyimdzi embraces aspects of European modernization such as formal education and law courts, but he uses these institutions for self-determined and unconventional ends. For instance, by the end of the play he uses his mastery of English language and law in order to defend the sanctity of the Akan matrilineage and the right of the extended family to negotiate marriage arrangements for young women such as Miss Tsiba. Onyimdzi rejects civilization as a compulsive drive to Westernize but embraces his own definition of modernization as a process of critical evaluation and selective appropriation. Cape Coast citizens of the 1910s as depicted in *The Blinkards* perceived "civilization," "education," "progress," and "modernization" as inherently related. It was this linkage that both the character Onyimdzi and the writer Sekyi sought to combat.

J. Ayo Langley argues that throughout Sekyi's life, he "condemned not modernization whose benefits he praised and highlighted, but the particular character which that process assumed in his own country during the colonial era up to the eve of independence" (1970, 1). Sekyi advocated modernization with a critical difference. He embraced Western education, English law, and the material developments of "progress." But he rejected "civilization," the foundation of which was a dichotomizing paradigm that pitted "tradition" against "modernity," "savage" against "civilized" cultures. The question that drove Sekyi's life, according to Langley, was "how to Westernize without being Westernized." Sekyi promoted a process of inner development and rejected the frantic "catching up" attitude he saw infecting Africans around him. He wrote in 1917, "Let us not induce ourselves to think and believe that the *only* way to 'survive' Europe's aggression is by organising on European (including American) lines. . . . If we are to formulate any really sound and practicable scheme for our future, let us set before us, and try to understand, the ideal of *living* as men, and not seek the compromise of *surviving* as persecuted persons" (Sekyi 1917, 78). In his writings, Sekyi identified the need for effective integrative mechanisms that would help mediate between the Western economic and social systems being introduced in the Gold Coast and the pre-existing cultures and social systems of West Africa (Langley 1970, 46). He envisioned that imaginative and responsible leaders would serve this integrative function in African life. In *The Blinkards,* Mr. Onyimdzi is a perfect model of Sekyi's ideal of an African who harmoniously integrates Western customs into a life that is firmly rooted in Akan customs and also mediates among his compatriots, advising them on the differences between civilization and modernization. Sekyi believed enlightened individuals such as Onyimdzi would help colonial Ghanaians combine the best of African and Western worlds. However, as I will argue throughout this book, rather than enlightened individuals such as Sekyi, concert parties came to serve this mediating function in colonial Ghana.

Concerts and Cape Coast Society

One of the earliest historical references to a concert-type entertainment in the Gold Coast appears in the memoirs of Wesleyan missionary Dennis Kemp (1898, 169–170). Kemp describes a show he saw in Cape Coast in 1895 in which the performers satirized a drunken Englishman:

> Towards the latter part of the year, the patriots of Cape Coast decided to arrange a purely native entertainment. Every syllable of every song was rendered in the vernacular; the dresses of the artists were certainly made after the fashions of the country, though I have no doubt the material itself for the most part came from Manchester.
>
> One item of the programme necessitated the adoption of an English dress—for the actor was supposed to represent an English father. A translation of that pathetic ballad, "Father, come home!" was sung by a little girl. At the end of the first verse, a youth dressed in ragged attire, with a battered silk hat, came reeling on to the platform. I naturally felt very much ashamed at the thought that to obtain an illustration of the evils of the drink traffic the actors found it necessary to personate an Englishman. I felt still more ashamed that the acting of a song which represents the anguish of so many broken hearts in this country should have provoked only mirth in the audience.

Like many outsiders who encounter West African syncretism, Kemp struggles to categorize the elements of this performance as either foreign or indigenous, a project in which he is greatly handicapped by his ignorance of Fante culture and language.[9] The use of "the vernacular" is enough for him to deem this a "purely native entertainment," though the show clearly had more cosmopolitan origins. Kemp describes several elements that eventually were of central importance to the concert party genre and distinguished it from precolonial performing arts. He notes a raised platform, an ordered program, and a comic sketch that mocked and travestied European behaviors. Kemp's description indicates neither who sponsored and attended this event nor what type of music was performed. Kemp says, "Every syllable of every song was rendered in the vernacular." However, this is no guarantee that the music was, as he claims, "purely native." Popular Fante vocal music of the time ranged from *adenkum* songs, a precolonial music genre, to "singing band" music, a syncretic form of Christian hymns that combined Western melodies, "vernacular" lyrics, and African rhythms and instrumentation.[10]

While the absence of accurate description makes interpretation of this performance difficult, contextual background on the importance of alcohol in early colonial history reveals the significance of this parody of a drunken father. In *Drink, Power, and Cultural Change: A Social History of Alcohol in Ghana, c. 1800 to Recent Times,* Emmanuel Akyeampong argues that the late nineteenth century saw a dramatic increase in the trade of imported spirits and the incidence of public drunkenness in the Gold Coast (1996c, 47–69). The expansion of coastal trade and the emergence of wage labor undermined the monopoly on alcohol previously enjoyed by land-holding male elders. Prior to colonial rule, elders tightly controlled the distribution of locally brewed palm wine, an alcohol used for ritual purposes. However, the influx of imported spirits and the burgeoning cash-earning population in urban centers gave rise to a new class of Africans, some of whom displayed their newly acquired wealth and political autonomy through conspicuous consumption of alcohol. This was particularly true of young men who migrated to urban centers such as Cape Coast for education and trade. Their behavior undermined the authority of elders and chiefs. In an effort to control consumption of imported spirits, numerous temperance societies formed in the late nineteenth century. These organizations played a formidable role in colonial politics from the 1860s through the 1930s (Akyeampong 1996c, 70–94; 1996b). Temperance adherents particularly objected to public drunkenness among African young men and European colonial administrators because both groups were notorious for their excessive consumption of spirits.

Alcohol was thus central to the renegotiation of power in the early colonial period. Controversies over alcohol consumption masked deeper social conflicts arising from a shifting of power and wealth. Christianity and missionaries played a role in such conflicts as supporters of temperance. However, if the sketch of the drunken Englishman is any indication of public sentiment, Africans perceived Westerners' role in the alcohol situation in the Gold Coast in a more ironic light. Whatever perceptions and criticisms undergirded this Cape Coast performance Kemp witnessed in 1895, it provides documentary evidence that theatrical concerts, from their inception in the Gold Coast, served as forums for the expression of topical issues and volatile social tensions, particularly through the use of comedy and satire.

Another early reference to a performance called a "concert" in the Gold Coast appeared in a review of "Amagic [*sic*] costume Ball and Concert" printed in the *Gold Coast Leader* in 1903. This event, the first to be advertised explicitly as a "concert," was an elite and racially mixed affair, "patronized by the Ladies and Gentlemen of the town and was well attended by the European residents also" (*Gold Coast Leader* 1903; Akyeampong 1996a). It was held in the Great Hall of Cape Coast Castle, a room that by day served as the courthouse. Ironically, this same room had functioned in previous decades as an auction room for slaves prior to their trans-Atlantic passage. The Great Hall was transformed on this occasion into a "fairy hall" with Chinese lanterns and flowers. The most elite members of Cape Coast society attended the ball, including the district commissioner, lawyers, doctors, judges, and their wives. Party guests "performed" offstage, appearing in costume as characters such as the "Queen of the Night," "Ben Hur," "Truly Sweet Daisy," "Pierrot," and a "Mohammaden aristocrat." Meanwhile, a raised platform erected in the hall was a venue for more formal theatrical performances. The Amagic Band played brass music, Prince John of Asante "sang lustily," and other vocalists sang to a piano accompaniment "of the first order." Magicians in claret-colored turbans entertained the crowd, and the program finally concluded with two employees from the African Association, a trading company, appearing as the "Two Macs" in a "strikingly original and funny" routine.

While turn-of-the-century performances such as the one witnessed by Rev. Kemp in 1895 and the "Amagic Costume Ball" of 1903 were occasional events, by the 1910s concerts had become an institution in Cape Coast. Organizations such as schools, ladies' clubs, the Cape Coast Literary and Social Club, and even the Automobyle [*sic*] Club regularly hosted concerts. Early twentieth-century concerts resembled American vaudeville or British music hall variety shows. They had a program with an pre-established sequence of songs, recitations, dialogues, and sketches. Concerts featured a wide range of music, including sentimental ballads and popular tunes from abroad as well as Fante sacred "singing band" music. In a concert in Cape Coast in 1914, the Boy Scouts performed songs ranging from "God Bless the Prince of Wales" and "Genevieve" to "I'll Sing a Pretty Song" and "Where Did You Get That Hat?" (*Gold Coast Nation* 1914e). Recitations on the program included "Colonial Loyalty," "My Good Right Hand," "Excelsior," "Chickadee," and "Loss of the Royal George." The Fox Patrol enacted a comic scene called "Camp Life," and the Lion Patrol did a "Mock Trial." As was typical of many formal public events in the colonial Gold Coast, the whole program ended with a chorus of "God Save the King." Patronage was a key feature of early concerts, and L. W. S. Long, the district commissioner, chaired this Boy Scouts Association concert of 1914.

While contemporaneous newspaper accounts of early colonial concerts do not provide detailed descriptions of dramatic sketches, titles such as "Mock Trial," "Playing at Parliament," "Camp Life," and "The Battle of the Books" suggest performers creatively engaged with Western rituals of law, order, and education (*Gold Coast Nation* 1914c, 1914e). Other favorite acts of the time were drilling exercises and scenes about drunkards.[11] One sketch at a "Singing Band Fanti Sacred Concert" mocked the Dutch conscription of Gold Coast Africans into military service in Southeast Asia in the nineteenth century (*Gold Coast Nation* 1914d).

That this active engagement with Western culture through performance happened first in coastal cities is no accident. Seaside towns had long served as the "border zone" of contact between Gold Coast Africans and people from *aburokyiri*, overseas, "the white man's country, Europe and America respectively" (Christaller [1881] 1933, 54). Europeans had been frequenting this portion of the Guinea Coast since the late fifteenth century. Once formal British colonial rule began in the 1870s and Europeans settled in coastal towns and founded schools and churches which actively recruited African participants, *aburokyiri* began to have a profound and lasting impact on local culture.

Early colonial concerts were closely connected to Western education. A "Grand Concert" given by the Ladies' Club of Cape Coast in November of 1914 brought together performers from different schools, including the Wesleyan, A.M.E. Zion, Government Boys, Catholic Boys, Mfanstipim, Catholic Girls, Government Girls, and Training Home Girls schools (*Gold Coast Nation* 1914c). Schools and social clubs represented a particular segment of the urban population. People who sent their children to colonial and mission schools or belonged to Good Templars, Oddfellows, and Ladies societies, shared in common certain class aspirations: They sought the social and economic mobility that successful performance of British culture made possible. By speaking English, being able to read and write, attending church, wearing Western dress, and eating with knives and forks, these individuals hoped to gain economic opportunities and social advancement. At school or in a social club, one performed rarified customs of Anglo-African culture. Formal concerts with Western songs, sketches, and lusty renditions of "God Save the King" in the vernacular were merely extensions of the performances of everyday life enacted by members of upwardly mobile Westernized coastal society (*Gold Coast Nation* 1914d).

Literary and social clubs drew their members from the barely literate to the most bookish of Africans. Fluency in English was often the only requirement for admission. That "concerts" were performed at both social clubs and schools is more than a coincidence: In the absence of widespread secondary education, clubs served as centers for continuing adult education. Club members, according to Kwa O. Hagan, "were convinced that by study and personal advancement, they could come by opportunities for a fuller life, socially and economically" (1968, 81).

The adoption of European lifestyles as an alternative status index among Fantes was part and parcel of large-scale transformations in the Gold Coast in the late nineteenth and early twentieth centuries (Kimble 1963, 1–60, 125–167). Stratification, in and of itself, was by no means a new phenomenon. Precolonial Akan culture was itself extremely hierarchical (Arhin 1983; Wilks [1975] 1989). Prior to the nineteenth century, a Fante person's connections to chieftaincy, principal lineages, voluntary associations, and *asafo* military companies determined status (Arhin 1983, 14; Casely Hayford 1991; Casely Hayford and Rathbone 1992; Cole and Ross 1977, 186–199; de Graft Johnson 1932). While most aspects of "traditional" ranking were hereditary, some positions depended on wealth that could be earned (Arhin 1983, 15). Fante entrepreneurship has a long history, dating as far back as the late fifteenth century, when the commercial presence of Europeans spawned a new class of Fante middlemen and brokers. From the fifteenth to the twentieth centuries, Fantes mediated between Europeans on the coast and Africans such as the Asante in the interior while trading slaves, ivory, gold, food staples, guns, and liquor. Fante middlemen prior to the nineteenth century had only modest commercial success, however, for this period produced neither major merchants nor deep changes in the political order (Arhin 1983, 15).

But the advent of industrial capitalism in the nineteenth century sparked an economic revolution in the Gold Coast with profound consequences for the country as a whole, and for Fante society in particular. Through the cultivation and trade of such export crops as palm oil and rubber, a few members of the Fante brokering class became extremely wealthy (Hinderink and Sterkenburg 1975, 30, 34–35). The ascendance of this mercantile class transformed the economy, opening new channels for personal acquisition and ambition. Rank and status could be secured not only through family ties, as was formerly the practice, but also through financial success in the burgeoning cash economy and the acquisition of rarified Western speech, manners, and dress. According to Kwame Arhin, there arose in Fante society in the nineteenth century two parallel systems of social differentiation: one based upon established modes of Akan authority, and one based upon wealth, mobility, and a Western frame of reference (1983, 17; see also Foster 1965, 91–93).

The introduction of formal education in the nineteenth century accelerated new class formations (Foster 1965, 74–111). Western-style schools had existed in the Gold Coast prior to 1800, but these were primarily for the mulatto offspring of European inhabitants based in coastal forts and castles. In 1821, however, the Crown authorities decided to provide a chain of schools, financed through government funds, to educate the general population (Foster 1965, 49). Shortly thereafter, Christian missionaries also opened schools. Attendance at government and mission schools was voluntary, and families with ties to chiefly authority initially were reluctant to enroll their children because Western education, according to popular belief, could make one unfit to assume traditional roles of leadership (Foster 1965, 96). However, among the incipient merchant classes, demand for education was great because education was perceived as the key to upward social mobility. As a result, Gold Coast education, much of which was based in Cape Coast, grew dramatically in the late nineteenth century. Whereas in 1891 there were only 53 government and assisted schools, just ten years later there were 135 schools (Foster 1965, 79). This expansion was largely due to African demand for education, and in many cases African initiative in founding schools, particularly at the secondary level. African desires to obtain formal education, according to historian Philip Foster, reflected a "realistic perception of the differential rewards accorded to individuals within this occupational structure" (1965, 105).

Jobs available to "scholars," as students were called,[12] ranged from work as interpreters and catechists in the missions to clerkships in government and the business sector. Kwame Arhin says graduates who worked in business "could keep memoranda, copy papers and accounts, and supervise labourers in the shipyards, on the building sites and in the mission plantations. They became shop clerks or agents, self-employed businessmen, supervisors of works and artisans" (1983, 17). Clerkships in the government were among the most prized jobs, the benchmark against which other positions were measured. However, few channels for mobility were available to Africans within the colonial administration. According to I. M. Wallerstein, Western education essentially socialized individuals "to anticipate career patterns which they were not permitted to fulfill" (1962, 59).

Collective labels denoting class have limited value in describing Fante culture, for such labels, as Augustus Casely Hayford argues, are unable "to cope with the contradictions that are seemingly evident in most Fante families and individuals" (1991, 52). Because of the continued importance of the extended family structure, Cape Coast citizens were not divided into discrete categories of traditional, educated, mercantile, and peasant classes. Fante society by the turn of the century was densely layered with overlapping hierarchies and nuanced gradations. Not only did this period see the emergence of dual ranking systems, "the typical Akan system, consisting of the hierarchy of rulers and the ruled" but also "an emergent class system based on differences of wealth, strengthened by education and adoption of European life styles" (Arhin 1983, 18); individuals and families also held multiple affiliations. Members of the most highly educated minority, for instance, "were particularly proud if they could trace their affiliations to 'noble lines'" (Foster 1965, 99). There was a simultaneity of status structures linked to chieftaincies, clans, schools, churches, *asafo* companies, social clubs, shrines, and the government. Status *simultaneously* depended upon one's level of education, scale and type of trade, connection to traditional lines of authority, seniority, gender, marital status, whether one had children, how long one's family had been established in coastal society, and whether one had traveled *aburokyir,* overseas.

While Fante society consisted of a complex layering of affiliations and parallel status structures, there were nevertheless clearly articulated divisions and conflicts, as the work of Emmanuel Akyeampong so lucidly and richly details (1996c). One of the more salient divisions in Cape Coast life in the 1910s was between the nascent intermediate classes and the established Fante intelligentsia. Concert performances served as key sites for the public expression of conflict between these two constituencies. Newspaper reviews indicate audiences were disorderly and boisterous. Students and "youngmen" in the audience made loud comments on the action and hooted at bad actors. Critics invariably struck a censorious tone when discussing concert audiences. At a Wesleyan School concert in June of 1914, "scholars" in the audience who created "too much" noise provoked a reviewer to admonish the headmaster and other teachers to see that their "youngmen will not behave so badly again as this casts a bad shade on the rising generation and gives one the occasion to ask 'can this race stand'?" (*Gold Coast Nation* 1914b). At another concert that same year, a newspaper reviewer deplored spectators' "uncivilized" behavior:

> The lighting was very poor and it greatly helped the rowdy lot to create much noise and disturbance. We were pained to notice some educated young men among them who ought to know better. This time we are giving them a timely warning to put a stop to their disgraceful conduct otherwise it will be our bounden duty to give publicity to their names if they persist in repeating their conduct at public gatherings in future. No one grudges an orderly and decent audience enjoying themselves and according plaudits to deserving performers or coldly acknowledging the efforts of an unfortunate performer who either from stage

fright or other incapacity had not merited commendation. But to make it a rule to pass rude remarks about every performer, and to hiss and hoot at a high personage rising to counsel decent behaviour is to reveal a regrettable state of affairs which does little credit to the reputation of this ancient town. (*Gold Coast Nation* 1914d)

Such disruptions occasionally escalated into fistfights, as when a Mr. Weber of the district commissioner's office and one Mr. Sarsah reportedly created a "great uproar" with a public brawl (*Gold Coast Nation* 1914e).

Raucous audience behavior at concerts and the moralistic critiques of journalists reveal deeper social tensions within the educated ranks of Cape Coast society. The active and vocal engagement of audiences with the performance was in keeping with Akan modes of spectatorship at performances such as festivals and Ananse storytelling sessions. But hooting, hissing, and engaging in loud talk and fisticuffs did not conform to the notions of "civilized" spectatorship held by the writers of *The Gold Coast Nation*. This newspaper was an organ of the Aborigines Rights Protection Society, an early nationalist organization comprised of esteemed members of the African intelligentsia, many of whom had advanced degrees from British universities (Jones-Quartey 1968, 42; Kimble 1963, 313, 358–403). In contrast, the boisterous "scholars" and "youngmen" attending concerts were drawn from the intermediate classes, those with limited formal education who aspired to work as commercial clerks, civil servants, or teachers.

The appellations reviewers used to describe these young spectators provide important clues to the social composition of audiences at early colonial concerts. "Scholar" and "youngmen" carried very specific valences. British missionary Dennis Kemp explained in his memoirs that a scholar in the Gold Coast "does not necessarily come within the category of divines and scientists of our own country. The 'scholar' of the Gold Coast may have spent only sufficient time at school to enable him to write a misspelt letter, but he is still known by the title" (1898, 60). African lawyer and nationalist leader John Mensah Sarbah corroborates:

> In the ranks of the educated Africans, one finds all grades of European learning and culture—the man who can only scrawl his name, and cannot without much labour struggle his way through the spelling primer; the petty clerk, who having a fair knowledge of reading, writing, arithmetic, had received some Christian instruction of a superficial kind, thinking himself very high above the masses; he despises the dignity of labour, because he has not been taught a more excellent way; called by everybody a scholar, he has no ambition to acquire more learning. Next to the scholar are the intellectually ambitious men, who by assiduous application have mastered the English language, and attained the proficiency in many subjects of commercial utility. ([1906] 1968, 246)

Sarbah was himself a member of the "intellectually ambitious" ranks, and his disdain for lowly "scholars" is palpable. Sarbah attributes the lack of advanced education among scholars to their lapsed moral character or want of personal ambition. However, Philip Foster's history of education in Ghana demonstrates that formidable institutional and economic barriers, rather than lack of ambition, deterred the majority of students from pursuing education beyond the elementary level (1965, 102, 133–139). The financial burden of school fees, the lack of sufficient secondary schools, and problems of unemployment among educated classes all made secondary education futile for many school leavers.

"Youngmen," or *nkwankwa,* was another highly charged designation in the colonial Gold Coast. This constituency eventually played a decisive role in the rise of modern mass nationalism. Described as "aspirant businessmen," "petite bourgeoisie," "commoners," or "veranda boys," youngmen were defined by occupation and social position rather than age. As the work of Jean Allman (1993) and Emmanuel Akyeampong (1996c, 47–69) illustrates, youngmen were a disruptive force not only at school and social club concerts, but within Gold Coast society as a whole. They were dissatisfied with established authority, whether of chiefly or intellectual bent (Allman 1993, 28–36). The newly acquired Western education of youngmen, their growing economic power, and their widening occupational roles gave them confidence and a sense of autonomy. They flaunted their independence through a display of material wealth, social drinking, and general disregard for authority, particularly in the growing urban centers (Allman 1993, 32; Akyeampong 1996c, 47–69). In Kofi Agovi's opinion, this class was among the most exciting in the Gold Coast at this time, for they

> embodied the nascent spirit of the Ghana to be. This group was both daring, creative and full of initiative. Possessing neither firm roots in English cultural traditions nor a complete allegiance to their native African heritage, the only cultural models available to them for emulation were the cultural activities of the Merchant-Lawyer class and those of the Colonial Administrative officers. In this regard, they were prepared to learn, to emulate and above all, to venture. (1990, 10–11)

But it was precisely youngmen's exuberance, their daring, unruly creativity that most distressed representatives of traditional authority and the Westernized intelligentsia who reviewed concert shows to which youngmen thronged and at which they "misbehaved."

What was it about concerts that so captivated the interests of youngmen? I believe the answer to this question lies in the ability of concerts to provoke laughter. By putting Western appearances and manners on stage, by presenting in a self-consciously performative mode behaviors that were rapidly becoming institutionalized within everyday Fante life, concerts created a space for laughter *at* these behaviors. Concerts appealed to the intermediate sector by dramatizing their own ambiguous social position. Elementary students, clerks, and petty traders were simultaneously included *and* excluded from Anglo-African culture. They had enough education to understand the English language and the peculiarities of Western behavior portrayed on stage, but not enough education to *belong* truly to the westernized elite of Cape Coast society. Lawyers and intellectuals such as John Mensah Sarbah looked down upon semi-educated Africans, accusing them of laziness, lack of ambition, or ignorant delusion. But the intermediate classes, rather than loathe their inadequate embodiment of English manners, laughed in the face of Western pretensions. Comic sketches such as "Mock Trials," "Playing at Parliament," drilling exercises, and impersonations of drunken Englishmen did not offer a lasting purgative for the restlessness of youngmen. However, hooting and guffawing at these shows did provide emotional release in an atmosphere rife with economic inequities and rapidly changing social expectations and indices of value.

Accra and Sekondi

After concerts in schools and social clubs flourished in Cape Coast in the 1910s, semi-professional amusements subsequently developed in other coastal cities, such as Accra and Sekondi. Concert performances in these other cities do not seem to have been as volatile and contentious as those of Cape Coast. At least newspaper reviews give no indication of such controversy, and critics rarely struck the censorious tone one finds in Cape Coast newspapers. What is more notable about the concerts of Accra and Sekondi was their commercial and semi-professional nature. Shows were performed in spaces specifically dedicated to entertainment. These theatrical halls charged a gate fee, with stratified ticket prices based upon where one sat in the house. Like Cape Coast audiences, Accra and Sekondi shows were not patronized solely or even predominantly by the "westernized elite," for the cheapest tickets to concerts were affordable to most citizens. There were, to be sure, lawyers, doctors, and other members of the highest strata of coastal society in attendance. But concerts in Accra and Cape Coast, as well as Sekondi, catered as much to the intermediate classes, as they did to the so-called westernized elite.

When the capital of the colonial Gold Coast moved from Cape Coast to Accra in 1877, Accra's population and commercial activity burgeoned (Hinderink and Sterkenburg 1975, 33). According to census figures, the population doubled between 1911 and 1921, increasing from 18,500 to 38,000. By 1931, the city's inhabitants had grown to 61,500 (Acquah [1958] 1972, 30–31). During this same period, Accra experienced a tremendous expansion of roads, housing, commercial activity, communication, schools, and health care (Acquah [1958] 1972, 27–29). The *Red Book of West Africa* of 1920 lists more than sixty major enterprises in Accra, as compared with seven in Sekondi, twelve in Kumasi, and none in Cape Coast (MacMillan [1920] 1968, 139–228). "No town in West Africa provides more contrasts in material progress, more wide divergences between the old and the new, more demonstrations of the past and the present, than Accra," reported the *Red Book of West Africa* (MacMillan [1920] 1968, 176). It was indeed a city of contradictions: Although Accra was the center of foreign commerce with more imports and exports than any other city in the colony, it had no harbor. And while it had the finest and most up-to-date retail stores and business in all of West Africa, the city was not illuminated either by electricity or gas (MacMillan [1920] 1968, 175).

With Accra's burgeoning and cosmopolitan population came a growing appetite and audience for "modern" entertainments. The first building in Accra devoted solely to amusement was the Merry Villas cinematograph palace, constructed in 1913 with an audience capacity of 1,000 (MacMillan [1920] 1968, 176). Built by W. Bartholomew and Co., a merchant of automobiles and other goods, the Merry Villas showed imported films. In the late 1910s and early 1920s, two other theatres were built in Accra: the Cinema Theatre at Azuma and the Palladium built by Alfred John Kabu Ocansey (Williams 1995).

Alfred Ocansey was a highly successful African merchant who traded cars, trucks, and other goods (MacMillan [1920] 1968, 203). During one of his business trips to London, Ocansey attended a music hall performance at the London Palladium, "the greatest Variety theatre in the world" (Amartey and Williams #95.51; Pilton 1976, 11). He was so captivated by the show and the building that he decided to build a similar music hall in Accra in the early 1920s. Ocansey initially called his entertainment house the "West End Kinema [sic] Palladium," but it soon became known simply as "The Palladium" (Amartey and Williams #95.51). It was an unusual enterprise for the Gold Coast, for unlike private social clubs in Cape Coast and Sekondi, the Palladium was a commercial venture devoted solely to public entertainment and open to the general public. With widely stratified admission fees, a great range of Accra citizens could attend. Attracting both African and European patrons, the Palladium "was a thing which had never happened in Accra," says Augustus Williams, an actor who frequently appeared on its stage (Amartey and Williams #95.51).

In addition to showing films from abroad, entertainment houses such as the Palladium, Merry Villas, and Azuma Cinema Theatre held variety entertainments, magical acts, social evenings, and dances. In 1921, Mr. Kitson Mills, the principal of the Accra Royal School, organized a fund-raising "variety entertainment" at the Cinema Theatre under the patronage of Acting Governor Justice Nettleton (*Gold Coast Independent* 1921). A newspaper advertisement for the Merry Villas in 1924 read:

Always in the Centre
Merry Villas Cinema and
General Entertainments
Social Evening and Dance To-day
2nd August
Commencing at 8 P.M. precisely
Music by the famous WURLITZER BAND ORGAN
Admission: Gentlemen 2/-
Ladies free.
(*Gold Coast Independent* 1924c)

That same weekend in 1924, the Palladium featured the comedian Augustus Williams and his party in "Our Parochial Gathering," along with Professor Cheotoo, the Great Wizard of the North, who exhibited "his surprising deceptions in Arabian magic" (*Gold Coast Independent* 1924b).

Only a year after Ocansey opened his entertainment hall, critics reported that the Palladium was "rapidly coming into its own":

> We are rather agreeably surprised at the progress that has been made by our local comedians Mr. Williams and his party, who are just now performing on the Palladium stage. It would be invidious to differentiate, but we think that given a little more opportunity to study details, Williams will soon be fully fledged into a first rate comedian. (*Gold Coast Independent* 1924a)

With three different venues and a rapidly expanding audience, concert-style entertainments became one of the most popular leisure activities in Accra in the 1920s.

The entertainer mentioned in the above review, Augustus Alexander Shotang Williams, is an important figure in the history of the concert party. He was one of the first actors in the Gold Coast to earn a substantial portion of his living through concert entertainment. Williams completed his education at the Government Boys School, and then worked briefly as a lawyer's clerk. In the evenings, Williams attended the pictures at the Azuma Cinema Theatre. He loved the cowboy and vaudeville silent pictures and soon began imitating these cinema shows. Williams and his friends studied dancing from the movies and books and then began staging their own variety shows at the Merry Villas in the early 1920s. When Ocansey built the Palladium in 1923, he invited Williams to "come 'round with your men and put up your performance, every Saturday night" (Amartey and Williams #95.51). So Williams and his partner, Joseph Tetteh Marbel, agreed. The two became known as "Williams and Marbel." They performed short comic sketches, popular songs, and tap dance numbers while wearing bowler hats, blackface makeup, tailcoats, and tattered trousers (fig. 15).

Like concert performances in Cape Coast, those of Accra drew liberally upon Western theatrical practices. The Palladium's former pianist Robert Jamieson Amartey recalls that actors "took the form of these Negro performances in America. They blackened their faces with the white here" (*points to his mouth*) (Williams and Amartey #95.51). Augustus Williams remembers singing Al Jolson's famous song "Yes, We Have No Bananas," accompanied by the "Jazzlanders"— a small dance orchestra comprised of brass instruments, an acoustic bass, drums, and piano—as well as a chorus of young men and women. Williams describes a typical comedy sketch:

> One man was the ghost and two of us, myself and Marbel . . . were sitting down and I was telling him that if a ghost came I wouldn't fear. Then all of a sudden a hand taps me on the shoulder—it was a ghost and I started shaking and then Marbel turned around and we ran away. The ghost was left on stage shouting, "I'll kill 'em kill 'em." Then I come in backwards and Marbel is coming backwards, we bang into one another and run away. I was thinking he was the ghost and he was thinking the same, but there were only two of us. For this show, I

wore a short white pique coat with bow-tie and cummerbund and with white around the mouth. We used the Palladium's band, and later when the Accra Orchestra was formed, Yeboah Mensah came in on trumpet. (quoted in Collins 1994a, 152–153)[13]

Early concerts at the Palladium were generally light-hearted sketches with physical comedy and simple plots. Williams got ideas for such routines from imported play books, sheet music, and movies. He also studied with foreign performers whom A. J. Ocansey brought to the Gold Coast from England. In the mid-1920s, Ocansey invited two Americans to the Palladium, Mr. Hoyte and Gene Fineran. Fineran, a "first-class" tap dancer, taught Williams new dance steps and shared his stage makeup and wigs (Amartey and Williams 95.51). Around 1924, Ocansey brought a husband-and-wife team from Liberia known as "Glass and Grant." Grant was a tall slim woman, and Glass was a noisy, boisterous man (Williams #95.52).[14] According to Augustus Williams, Ocansey did not pay his performers very well and "monetary affairs" drove Fineran and other foreign performers away from the Gold Coast after only a short stay (Williams #95.52).

Entertainment at the Palladium attracted a large, boisterous, and socially mixed crowd. The hall was often filled to capacity, standing room only. The cost of admission varied, depending on where spectators sat or stood, ranging from 3 shillings to 6 pence (*Gold Coast Independent* 1924a). The most expensive seats were those in the balcony, in areas known as the "upper circle" and "dress circle." Only European expatriates and wealthy Africans such as lawyers and doctors could afford balcony seats. The rest of the seating was on the main floor with varying ticket prices depending on proximity to the stage (Amartey and Williams #95.51). The least expensive seats, those closest to the front, were cheap enough that "everybody could afford to come to the Palladium," not just the so-called elite, according to Amartey and Williams (#95.51). While audiences were separated within the theatre space according to their admission fee, such economic divisions were suspended at the close of the variety entertainment or cinema show, at which time all chairs were removed from the main floor so that all patrons could come to dance. Many colonial Ghanaians in coastal cities had learned foreign dance steps by reading books on dancing, studying at formal and informal dance schools, or even reading the local newspapers which carried regular columns teaching new dance steps. The Palladium dance floor provided patrons with an opportunity to practice the fox trot, waltz, blues,[15] quickstep, tango, Charleston, and highlife steps to the accompaniment of the Jazzlanders Orchestra. Amartey recalls that the dance floor was an exciting venue for personal display: "We will shake ourselves with dancing, show them that we are doing something!" (Amartey and Williams #95.51). Even the Europeans and wealthy Africans came down from the balcony to dance. The majority of expatriates were "without wives," explains Williams. "They left their wives at home and come here. So they mix up" (Amartey and Williams #95.51). Apparently, the socio-economic divisions which so polarized and disrupted concert performances in Cape Coast were largely unknown in Accra venues. This may be due both to the commercial nature of Accra performances and to the fact that Accra was a much "newer" town than Cape Coast. While traditionally belonging to the Ga, that ethnic group was already by this time far outnumbered by the ethnically heterogeneous migrants who came to seek their fortunes in Accra's growing economy. Cape Coast, by way of contrast, was overwhelmingly Fante and had well-established and powerful social factions that extended back for many generations.

While Western-style theatrical activities thrived in the cities of Cape Coast and Accra, concerts in Sekondi, a city 140 miles west of Accra, ultimately had the greatest impact on the history of the concert party. It was here that the pioneers of the concert party form as it is known today in Ghana got their start in the late 1920s. Sekondi was an important trading center because, unlike Accra, it had a natural port in which large ships could dock. Sekondi was also the headquarters of the Gold Coast Railway Administration, and the city's advanced transportation and communication infrastructure was of crucial importance to the mining and timber industries developing inland. From the 1910s onward, Sekondi attracted a migrant population of clerical, skilled, and semi-skilled laborers who worked for the railways (Jeffries 1978, 13).[16]

Prior to the construction of Takoradi Harbor in 1928, "Sekondi was considered the most festive town in the country," according to long-time resident Lawrence Cudjoe: "To spend Saturday night in Sekondi was like celebrating Christmas. . . . It was so lively that many people from all parts of the country preferred to come and work or stay in Sekondi" (1995, 2). During their leisure hours, Sekondi citizens could enjoy Western-style amusements such as ballroom dancing, religious cantatas, cinema, plays such as Shakespeare's *Macbeth,* and magic acts (Cudjoe #94.25, 1995, 1; *Gold Coast Nation* 1914a). Social life in the town was generally segregated according to class and race. "Europeans and Africans virtually spent their leisure separately," says Lawrence Cudjoe. "It was only in the railway that the senior African officers spent their leisure with the Europeans" (Cudjoe 1995, 2). Sekondi had two main entertainment sites for the African population: the Optimism Club and the Palladium.[17] The former was for "very big people," according to Bob Johnson, such as lawyers and other men of social standing (quoted in Sutherland 1970, 6). The Palladium, on the other hand, was open to the public, so that "anybody of any character could attend," says Lawrence Cudjoe (#94.25).

Founded by affluent African citizens of Sekondi 1915, the Optimism Club was intended to "cultivate hope for the best of everything, seek development in the study of literature, promote cultural and healthy social intercourse and recreational activities, and to impart optimism to others and to aim at higher virtues" (Optimism Club 1915, 1).[18] The only explicit requirement for membership was that an applicant deliver a lecture to the club in English on "any subject chosen by themselves." After each lecture at the Optimism Club, a man appointed as the resident "critic" would "detect and expose for discussion and correction all grammatical, logical and other errors committed by members" (Cudjoe #94.25; Optimism Club 1915, 5). The Optimism Club constructed a clubhouse in 1923, and there they began to host social events. Dance bands such as the Railway Silver Band, the Nanshamaq Orchestra, and the Cape Coast Sugar Babies came to provide musical accompaniment for these high-brow affairs, at which attendance was restricted to Optimism Club members and their invited guests (Cudjoe #94.25).

The Optimism Club even formed its own orchestra in May of 1923, comprised of club members who were "philharmonic and possessed fiddles of their own" (Ruhle 1925). A report on this enterprise adds, "In conduction with the Orchestra, a section entitled 'BOBS' was also formed in order to play the part of Actors during the concerts and some willing members joined that section with enthusiasm." The report went on to say that "the composition of the 'Bobs' is indefinite, as members of that section have not shown stability." This amorphous group of comedians appears to have been the first in the Gold Coast to use the name "Bob," which later became the stock name for all concert party comedians or "jokers" throughout concert party history, from Bob Johnson in the 1930s through Bob Ocala in the 1990s.[19] The Optimism Club "Bobs" were also among the first comedians to perform with dance bands, a tradition that continued when the Axim Trio toured Nigeria with the Cape Coast Sugar Babies in 1935 and when Bob Cole performed with the Broadway Dance Band in the early years of independence (NCC 1993; *Sunday Mirror* 1960c).

In addition to private club-sponsored social events, the Optimism Club rented its facilities to cinema operators, other clubs, individuals, church groups, roving magicians, and other entertainers. With a raised stage and excellent electric light fixtures, the Optimism Club was a particularly attractive site for performers. The conjurer and illusionist Professor E. C. Otoo rented the hall in 1927 at a rate of 2 pounds and 2 shillings per night, which he paid out of box office receipts (Otoo 1927). The Roman Catholic Sunday School used the Optimism clubhouse for a "Fanti Sacred Cantata" (Ruhle 1927). Frank Krakue wrote the club secretary in 1926 requesting permission to use the hall on December 30th "for the purpose of a Concert by Mr. Yalley the Laughter Maker of Tarquah" (Krakue 1926). Yalley is an important figure in the history of the concert party because he has been credited with inspiring the first generation of itinerant concert comedians. Yalley was a teacher at the A.M.E. Zion school in Abontiakoon, a mining town near Tarkwa, and he often came to Sekondi to stage shows at the Optimism Club.[20] Yalley's shows at the Optimism Club were one-man affairs, in which he sang, danced, and "talked a lively patter to the accompaniment of jazz music from a snare drum and organ" (Sutherland 1970, 7). Bob Johnson remembers Yalley wearing huge shoes, false mustaches, raffia skirts, wigs, and blackface makeup (Sutherland 1970, 6–7).

Yalley's performances fascinated some young students at the Methodist School in Sekondi, located directly across the street from the Optimism Club. Three students in particular—Bob Johnson, Charles B. Horton, and J. B. Ansah—studied Yalley's shows and began performing similar comic sketches of their own (Sutherland 1970, 6–7). Johnson, Horton, and Ansah introduced several innovations to the Western-style concert performances that had developed in the cities of Cape Coast, Accra, and Sekondi: They mixed the Fante language into the concert's usual English-language songs and dialogues, established a conventional three-part dramatic structure, and invented three stock character roles that came to be known as "trios." But their single most important innovation was taking concert shows on the road, making these performances available for the first time to working-class and agriculturally based audiences living outside of the major coastal cities. During school vacations they traveled to mining towns such as Tarkwa and Obuasi and to market centers located along the railway lines and major roadways. "The Two Bobs and Their Carolina Girl," as this group eventually named themselves in the 1930s, are now generally credited as the originators of the concert party genre as it known today.[21]

As *The Blinkards* so vividly dramatized in 1915, the ideology of colonialism became popularly accessible to Africans in the coastal cities of colonial Ghana through embodied manners of dress, eating, and speech. Through these practices, coastal populations came to perceive a stark dichotomy between "civilized" and "savage" cultures. By putting the excesses of Western behaviors on stage and creating satirical sketches about drunken Englishmen, mock trials, and playing at parliament, concerts created a space for critical evaluation of Western behaviors even as they modeled these behaviors for spectators to emulate. While performances from this period never seem to have directly criticized colonial rule, they capitalized on the extravagances of colonized behavior and created a space for public laughter at behaviors that people adopted to achieve power within the colonial social order.

"Ohia Ma Adwennwen,"
or "Use Your Gumption!"

THE PRAGMATICS OF PERFORMANCE, 1927–1945

Whereas concerts from 1895 through the mid-1920s were consumed largely by Western-educated audiences residing in coastal cities, concerts from the 1930s onward attracted working-class audiences and farmers from coastal, inland, and northern areas. The most formative years for Ghana's popular theatre were between 1927 and the end of World War II. It was during this period that Bob Johnson, E. K. Dadson, and other young men from the Western Region introduced concerts to new social classes and geographic regions. By incorporating African languages, blending imported characters with homegrown tricksters, and taking their shows on the road, pioneer actors of the 1930s made concerts a genuinely popular and profitable theatre form. The sociology of actors and troupes and their experiences of everyday life while on trek reveal the many ways that concert practitioners used their ingenuity to manipulate the established social and cultural order. Out of a leisure activity, they invented full-time jobs. Rather than work for large organizations, they founded lucrative, independent entertainment businesses. Concert practitioners exploited the colonial infrastructure of roads, railways, mines, and formal education in ways that engineers, commercial developers, and colonial administrators never anticipated.

These early pioneers of the concert party form transformed a ritual of colonial power—variety shows that they performed as schoolchildren on Empire Day—into a successful commercial enterprise and opportunity for personal advancement. While Empire Day shows were intended to celebrate the joys of being a colonial subject, school boys from Sekondi such as Bob Johnson and Charles

Horton appropriated these performances for very different purposes.[1] According to Johnson, "It was after Empire Day parade in my school days, when my fellow mates and I would entertain people in the school compound" with "mock performances" (*Sunday Mirror* 1960c). Johnson and his cohorts infused English songs and dialogues with Fante, and they created a stock comic persona known as "Bob," a character with a bulging stomach who, like the trickster Ananse of Akan folklore, lived for his appetite and survived by his wit (figs. 16 and 17). Finally, Johnson and his friends took their shows on the road, touring local villages and towns in order to collect money.

In addition to Empire Day theatricals, concert party actors of the 1930s and 1940s appropriated and refurbished a wide range of available cultural idioms, be they of local or distant origin, from recent times or the historical past. In her survey of popular arts in Africa, Karin Barber argues that the method by which modern syncretic arts combine old and new sources is neither automatic nor random: "It is the result of conscious choices and combinations" (1987, 39–41). The concert party is an example of what Michel de Certeau identifies as an "art of combination," a collage of "this and that," an art of "making do" in which consumers transform the dominant cultural economy for their own interests and their own uses ([1984] 1988, xiii, xv). Like "silent discoverers in the jungle of functionalist rationality," concert actors used British colonial culture and American mass media to form what de Certeau calls "unforeseeable sentences," indirect trajectories propelled by "interests and desires that are neither determined nor captured by the system in which they develop[ed]" ([1984] 1988, xviii).

By what grammatical rules did concert practitioners create these "unforeseeable sentences"? What principles guided their process of invention? This chapter and the one that follows explore the principles that guided the process of selective appropriation and incorporation among concert innovators. I will first address the pragmatics of life on the road, examining the sociology of actors and troupes and their experiences of everyday life while on trek during the period from 1927 to 1945. The subsequent chapter addresses the creative process by which early concert party practitioners poached from sources ranging from *anansesɛm,* a storytelling tradition with deep roots in Ghanaian culture, to the comic cinema of Charlie Chaplin.

Rather than automatically imposing interpretive categories generated from outside Ghana onto the concert party, my objective in this chapter is to discern the discursive principles operative *within* this tradition itself, to uncover the theories implicit in the concert party's production and consumption. One of the driving questions of Africanist research in recent years has been whether epistemologies, conceptual systems, and interpretive categories derived from Europe and North America are adequate for the study of African culture.[2] While many scholars have questioned the hegemony of North American and European paradigms, few have moved beyond a critique of the Western epistemology to identify and use a more Africa-centered framework. Such, of course, is the trap of a counter-discourse. Margaret Thompson Drewal has noted that V. Y. Mudimbe's *Invention of Africa* is "powerfully persuasive precisely because [Mudimbe] has successfully inhabited the space of the Western episteme, dismantling it and thereby contesting it *in* and *on* its own terms." However, deconstructive critiques such as Mudimbe's raise a fundamental question. As Drewal puts it: "How can African traditional systems of thought be made explicit within the framework of their own discourse and rationality?" (1991, 33). This chapter proposes to do just that: analyze the fundamental principles of concert party performance and, in a more general sense, Akan creativity in and on their own terms.

In looking for theories that are germane to Ghanaian popular theatre practices I am also following the lead of Henry Louis Gates Jr., who identifies a theory of criticism inscribed within African American vernacular and literary traditions in *The Signifying Monkey*. Gates says he wants to "allow the black tradition to speak for itself about its nature and various functions, rather than to read it, or analyze it, in terms of literary theories borrowed whole from other traditions, appropriated from without" (1988, xix). Just as Gates perceives the tale of the signifying monkey as a metaphor for intertextuality in African American literature, I see the Ghanaian proverb *"ohia ma adwennwen"* as a generative principle of the concert party tradition. This proverb, memorably recorded in song by the famous concert party musician Kakaiku, approximates "necessity is the mother of invention." The phrase also contains an imperative command that some concert artists translate as, "Use your gumption!" Resourcefulness and ingenuity are central to concert party history, both onstage and in the everyday life of troupes on trek. In the 1930s, actors artfully manipulated and altered the colonial infrastructure and Western cultural practices. They transformed sheds used for cocoa storage into performance spaces. They observed costumes, characters, dance steps, and music portrayed in Hollywood films and gramophone records and then imitated these performance ideas on local stages—with a critical difference.

The interviews upon which this chapter is based were conducted with the oldest surviving concert actors in Ghana, all of whom began their careers between 1923 and 1948. According to the wishes of individual actors, all our interviews were either in Fante, Twi, or English. However, this older generation of performers typically preferred English, for they were keen to demonstrate their sophistication, education, and ease with foreign culture. Most concert party elders had formal education through the primary level known as Standard VII. These men are members of intermediate classes who would have worked, had they not gone into show business, as teachers, tailors, skilled railway or mine workers, drivers, clerks, or petty traders.[3]

Ohia Ma Adwennwen

I first learned the proverb *"ohia ma adwennwen"* from the Kakaiku song of the same name. Its irresistibly catchy tune invaded my head, prompting me to ask people what the lyrics meant. The song tells a story about how Tortoise, a slow and land-bound creature, managed to ascend high into the trees in order to attend the funeral of his friend Monkey's late mother. Ingenuity is the vehicle by which Tortoise rises into the trees, and cleverness also brings him safely down again. The song's refrain is:

> Ohia ma adwennwen
> *Me nyɛnko pa*
> Cleverness is what is needed
> My dear friend
> Use your ingenuity
> My dear friend
> Necessity is the mother of invention
> My dear friend. (Kakaiku's Band #95.37)

Just as the concert party form itself uses proverbially based highlife songs and thematically related stories to explicate a moral, Kakaiku's song taught me an Akan proverb through music and narrative: The melody first captured my attention, then the tale about the Tortoise sustained my interest. Through melody and story, a deceptively simple proverb made its way into my daily consciousness. Once I understood the proverb, I began to see its relevance to the entire process of concert party creation and production. Unlike questions about identity, race, gender, nationalism, or postcolonial "hybridity" which have great currency in the Euro-American academy of the 1990s, questions about *ohia ma adwennwen* led organically through this research material. The proverb opened up whole new areas of conversation among concert practitioners and provoked colorful anecdotes, impromptu performances, and animated dialogues.

As a theory of daily practice and creative process, there are several important dimensions to this proverb. First, *ohia ma adwennwen* is a discourse on power that illuminates how subaltern individuals assert their agency and autonomy within a hierarchically organized social order. Second, the proverb connotes a very particular type of mental acuity, one which can be contrasted with the related Akan concepts of wisdom, as will be examined in this and the next chapter. *Ohia ma adwennwen* is a specific means used to achieve specific ends. Finally, the proverb is essentially about *performance,* how individuals use a whole range of embodied skills and knowledge—from verbal wit and vocal intonation to gesture and kinesthetic parody—to negotiate the challenges of performance on stage and in everyday life.

Like many proverbial expressions, *"ohia ma adwennwen"* has multiple meanings. The proverb connotes a dynamic oscillation between forces that act upon and overwhelm individuals, and the active assertion of will and personal agency in response to those forces. According to J. G. Christaller's *Dictionary of the Asante and Fante Language* ([1881] 1933), the Akan word *ohia* means "poverty, indigence, want, necessity, straitened circumstances, straits."[4] Rather than say "I am poor," Akan speakers say *"ohia de me,"* which literally means "poverty has overtaken me." Destitution is thus linguistically constructed as an active agent and human beings as passive recipients. Poverty is said to bite people (*"ohia aka no"*), or to stare them in the face (*"ohia rehi ato no"*). Such grammatical constructions resemble those used to talk about other negative states of being such as cold, hunger, and thirst. Rather than saying "I am hungry," Akan speakers say "hunger has seized hold of me" (*"ɔkɔm de me"*).

Other layers of significance in this proverb derive from the grammatical properties of *ohia ma adwennwen*. The word *"ma"* means "to make" and *"adwennwen"* means "thought, deliberation, reflection." So the proverb can be translated "necessity makes thought" or "poverty makes you think." But *"ohia ma adwennwen"* is open to other interpretations, ones that cast human beings in active, rather than passive, roles. The word *"ma"* can transform a sentence into an imperative command, such as *"ma wo nan so"*—"make your feet go" or "hurry up!" Interpreted in this imperative form, *ohia ma adwennwen* means "use your wit!"

The concert party leader Kakaiku popularized *"ohia ma adwennwen"* through music. Kakaiku's song tells a story, an *anansesɛm,* about the friendship between Tortoise and Monkey, two creatures from different strata of the animal kingdom.[5] Tortoise can only roam on land, while Monkey can move freely between the ground and the trees. Monkey intimates that Tortoise's physical attributes are a liability, a serious impediment that he will never be able to overcome. His "poverty" or necessity is his lack of substantial arms and legs. During the course of the story, Tortoise uses his ingenuity to disprove Monkey's estimation of him.

One day Monkey asked his intimate friend Tortoise if he would be able to attend the funeral of Monkey's mother when she dies (Kakaiku's Band #95.37).[6] He was teasing Tortoise, for he knew that without substantial arms and legs, a tortoise would never be able to climb into the trees where monkeys live. Yet Tortoise answered Monkey's query enigmatically, saying *"Ohia ma adwennwen."* Not long afterward this encounter, Monkey's mother died, so Monkey sent a messenger, Vulture, to inform Tortoise about the funeral. When Tortoise heard the news, he said, "My friend Vulture, have a short walk and come back. I will leave my bag here. Whether I am here or not, take the bag to Monkey and tell him I will soon be up." When Vulture returned from his walk, Tortoise was gone, but the bag was there. So Vulture carried the bag to the trees and told Monkey that Tortoise would soon come. Monkey became very angry and said, "I detest lies. I detest arrogance. Tortoise, as he is, he has no hands, he has no legs. How then can he turn up for the funeral?" Monkey then decided to look inside the bag. When he loosened the strings, Tortoise came out and asked, "Haven't I turned up? I have already told you that in this world, *ohia ma adwennwen.*"

After the funeral, Monkey asked Tortoise how he would return back down to the land. Once more, Tortoise said what was needed most in life was cleverness. The next day, Tortoise told Monkey, "You live up in the trees, and I live on land. At funerals on the land, baskets are always involved. All refuse made by people at the funeral is put in a basket." Tortoise continued, "By that act, you make it possible for the dead to go straight to God. So if you would like your mother's spirit to go to God, then you must provide a basket." Monkey wanted his mother's soul to go to God, so he provided a basket. Tortoise then instructed him to put all garbage into the container, and at exactly five o'clock in the morning he should take it to the dumping grounds. He added, "If I am still asleep at the time you take the basket, please don't wake me up. If you wake me up, the ritual will be of no use."

Nobody knew that Tortoise's instruction about that basket and its ability to help a soul to enter heaven was a complete fabrication. In the night, Tortoise went secretly and hid under the refuse. In the morning, Monkey came with all his family members to perform the ritual. They gradually lowered the basket to the ground. As soon as the refuse was dumped, Tortoise emerged saying, "Haven't I come down? I have told you that in this world *ohia ma adwennwen.*"

At the beginning of the story, Tortoise could have simply asked Vulture to transport him to the funeral. But instead of asking for help, which would confirm Monkey's opinion of his inferiority, Tortoise found a solution that asserted his autonomy through mental acuity and resourcefulness. He used his wits to put himself, quite literally, on the same level as an animal of supposedly superior physical ability and rank in the animal kingdom. Tortoise's success was especially impressive in light of the fact that monkeys are, by reputation, very clever animals. Akan elders say, "One cannot deceive the chimpanzee by tricks" (Christaller [1879] 1990, 13).

Ohia ma adwennwen can be read as discourse on how the weak work *within* an order established by the strong.[7] Tortoise manipulates existing social conventions. He uses the Vulture's role as messenger to convey a parcel. According to custom, Vulture presumes the parcel to be either personal effects or a gift of food to help with the funeral.[8] Vulture is obliged, as Monkey's messenger, to carry the package up to him. Later in the story, Tortoise again manipulates custom and social mores. Akan funerals are elaborate rituals, the details of which people learn gradually over a lifetime as they bury deceased family members. The Monkey must perform the burial rituals properly if his mother is to have a safe journey to the ancestors, and he is dependent on those around him for instruction. Tortoise exploits Monkey's vulnerability by fabricating a ritual. He prefaces his instruction by highlighting the cultural differences between tortoises and monkeys. He says, "You live up in the trees, and I live on land. At funerals on the land, baskets are always involved." Tortoise capitalizes on Monkey's prejudice and his ignorance about the customs of a subaltern "other." Thus the very attitudes by which Monkey judged Tortoise as inferior earlier in the story become the means by which Tortoise proves him wrong.

In Kakaiku's song *"Ohia Ma Adwennwen,"* Tortoise accomplishes his ruse through performance. In order to ascend into the trees, he *acts* as though the parcel which he asks Vulture to carry is a small detail of his journey. Vulture falls for his con and thus unwittingly provides Tortoise's transportation. When Tortoise later wishes to descend from the trees, Tortoise *enacts* the role of a ritual "expert," giving such precise instructions about the basket ritual that Monkey never thinks to question their veracity. Simply having wisdom, cleverness, and strategies for survival is not enough; one must be able to enact those strategies, to put them into motion, by means of persuasive performance.

Ohia ma adwennwen is a particular type of trickery. The proverb does not valorize all scheming and manipulative behaviors, such as those done to exploit or harm others. Nor does it promote selfish opportunism. Such behavior is pejoratively described in Akan as *kokotako.* Concert practitioners taught me this word when we discussed the opportunistic way some people in Ghana tried to manipulate foreigners (like me) who were perceived to have money. I asked if such behavior was an example of using one's gumption. Concert elders said it was not, that such people were rather *kokotako,* manipulative in a negative sense. They were like the *ohuri,* the stinging tsetse fly or gadfly, and if I was not careful, my *mogya bɛsa,* my blood would soon be finished.

The Tortoise is a weak creature who "gets even" with a powerful animal through a benign manipulation of established conventions and attitudes. His critique of Monkey's arrogance is indirect, phrased as a rhetorical question, "Haven't I come?" His wisdom, or *adwennwen,* cannot be characterized as profound insight into human character or the nature of existence. Such insight is described in Akan as *nyansa* or *nimdeɛ* (Ephirim-Donkor 1997). *Adwennwen* is rather the prosaic ingenuity by which ordinary people address the problems of daily life in a hierarchically ordered universe. As a discourse about performance, power, and social inequality, *ohia ma adwennwen* can be provocatively extended to analyze the practices and procedures by which concert party actors pursued their profession and toured trio shows during a period of intense colonial development in the Gold Coast.

Sociology of Performers and Troupes

Nearly all concert party pioneers grew up in major cities of southern Ghana. Their mothers and fathers migrated from villages and small towns to urban centers, seeking to take advantage of new occupational opportunities within the growing cash economy.[9] Bob Johnson's family migrated from their hometown village of Nyanyaano to the city of Saltpond, where Johnson's father worked as a cooper with the Swanzy trading company and his mother traded beads (Johnson Family 1985; Sutherland 1970, 5). E. K. Dadson's father was an independent merchant in Axim (Zynenwartel n.d., 1). Bob S. Ansah's father was a bookkeeper with the United African Company, a large general merchant trading company. Ansah's father frequently changed jobs or his employer transferred him, so Ansah spent his childhood moving between the towns of Sekondi, Saltpond, Bekwai, and Kumasi (Ansah #94.14). Jimmy Narkwa's father worked with the railways in Sekondi (Narkwa #94.26). I. K. Ntama's mother was a baker, and his father worked as a fisherman, a post office stationmaster, and a railway worker. In 1925, Ntama's family migrated from Dix Cove to the mining town of Tarkwa where

Ntama's father worked as a photographer (Ntama #95.41). Y. B. Bampoe was born in Suhum in the Eastern Region of Ghana, a "stranger town," meaning one established by migrant cocoa farmers and traders in the early twentieth century (Hill 1963, 228–230). Bampoe's mother, a Fante woman from Shama, was a trader, and his father was a migrant cocoa farmer originally from Akuapem. K. Acquaah Hammond's parents were Fantes from the coastal village of Kuntum who migrated inland to Koforidua, a major trading center in the Eastern Region, where his father traded cocoa and his mother worked as a seamstress (Bampoe and Hammond #95.55).

These families participated in the major economic transformations of the Gold Coast during the nineteenth and early twentieth centuries: the growth of merchant trade, the cocoa industry, railways, roadways, mines, and the development of a communication infrastructure. Large-scale commercial trade was the first of these major innovations. According to historian Kwame Arhin, the period between 1831 and 1896 saw a commercial revolution in the coastal Fante regions of the Gold Coast and a consequent rise of a genuine mercantile class (1983, 15–16). Arhin divides this incipient Fante class into three groups: a) independent traders; b) agents or employees of commercial houses who had specialized skills; and c) less skilled peddlers and laborers who were dependent on large operators (1983, 16). The father of pioneer actor E. K. Dadson was a merchant from Axim and can thus be placed in the first category, while the fathers of Bob Johnson and Bob S. Ansah belong to the second category, skilled employees of large commercial houses.[10]

Industrial and agricultural transformations in the twentieth century followed the mercantile transformations of the nineteenth century. David Kimble identifies two periods of intensive, revolutionary development between 1897–1907 and 1919–1927 (1963, 58). The most remarkable features of this period were the growth of the cocoa and mining industries and the planned development of railways, harbors, roads, and communication.

The development of the cocoa industry is most striking for the degree to which small-scale African farmers founded it and kept it in their hands (Kimble 1963, 35). Economist Polly Hill calls the Gold Coast cocoa industry "one of the great events of the recent economic history of Africa south of the Sahara" (Hill 1963, 1). Exports of this cash crop grew from 0 in 1892 to 50,000 tons in 1914 (17). By 1930, exports exceeded 200,000 tons per year (Bourret 1949, 26). In 1911, the Gold Coast became the world's largest cocoa producer, and the colony experienced a phenomenal cocoa boom after World War I (Kimble 1963, 49–50). Hill's excellent history *The Migrant Cocoa-Farmers of Southern Ghana* (1963) charts the impact of the cocoa industry on migration, land tenure, the cash economy, and "traditional" organizational structures in the Gold Coast. Hill calls the expansionary processes of small-scale cocoa farming "creative, adventurous, and all absorbing" (1963, 180). Much as concert party actors later adapted African social, artistic, and economic structures to meet new needs and desires, the inception and development of the cocoa industry was improvisational. Farmers and traders worked within established family, ethnic, economic, land tenure, and distribution structures to create new variations that suited their needs at that particular historical moment.

Rail construction began in the Gold Coast in 1898. Goods and minerals carried by rail—such as cocoa, timber, manganese ore, gold, diamonds, wood fuel, and shea butter—expanded from 24,000 tons in 1904 to nearly 700,000 tons two decades later. Railway revenue grew from £148,000 in 1904 to £1,080,000 in 1924 (British Empire Exhibition 1925).[11] According to Richard Jeffries, the Railway Administration represented one of the largest single concentrations of manual workers in the Gold Coast. By 1936, the Railway and Harbour Administration employed almost 6,000 Africans in clerical, skilled, semi-skilled, and unskilled positions (1978, 13–14).

However, in terms of the number of wage laborers it employed, the mining industry far surpassed the railways. The Gold Coast got its name from its rich deposits of gold, but the country also had an abundance of other minerals, such as manganese and diamonds. Technological limitations, labor shortages, and market forces made mining an economically unstable activity during the early twentieth century, but with innovations and persistence, this industry grew, attracting a steady stream of migrants to towns such as Nsuta, Tarkwa, Aboso, Dunkwa, and Obuasi. According to Jeff Crisp, "By 1917 migrant workers accounted for over 47 percent of the industry's 19,000 strong labour force and over 64 per cent of the 8,600 underground employees, an increase of more than 20 per cent since 1911" (1984, 42).[12]

Large-scale economic activity in mining, railways, and export cash crops instigated drastic changes in Gold Coast society in terms of urban migration, wage labor, formal education, social mobility, and new indices of social status. From Obuasi to Tarkwa, from Takoradi to Accra, from Nsawam to Konongo, the cities of the southern Gold Coast expanded with migrant workers in the early twentieth century. Polly Hill describes the migratory process as essentially "forward-looking, prospective, provident, prudential—the opposite of hand-to-mouth" (1963, 179). Whether people migrated to work in cocoa, mining, railways, or mercantile trade, they did so with the hope of moving onward and upward economically. Urban centers brought together people of disparate social, ethnic, and political backgrounds (Kimble 1963, 59). Unmoored from hometown constraints, workers experimented with new lifestyles. Many of them had, for the first time, ready cash to spend on imported goods, alcohol, and leisure activities such as cinema shows, dances, gramophone music, and concert parties (Akyeampong 1996c).

While some migrants maintained close ties to their home towns, traveling home frequently, others started families in the new cities to which they had migrated. When their children were of age, they sent them to government, missionary, or independent schools. Formal education was more readily available in the larger towns than in villages, and city children were free from the agricultural responsibilities that often kept rural children at home.[13] By educating their children, urban migrants hoped to improve their family's financial condition and social status. Many parents wanted their children to work as clerks, one of the most prestigious and highly valued occupations within the colonial status structure, and education was a necessary prerequisite for such jobs (Foster 1965, 89–91).

From among the offspring of urban migrants came the first generation of professional concert party performers. Actors who began their careers between 1930 and 1946 were children of miners, merchants, and railway workers. They generally had formal education through the level known as Standard VII, which meant they had at least ten years of schooling (Foster 1965, 118). In the late colonial period, this was considered to be a very good education.[14] This first generation of concert actors belonged neither to the elite nor to the peasant extremes of the socio-economic spectrum, but were rather drawn from the large, amorphous intermediate sectors.

Concert actors could speak, read, and write English quite well. Their facility with the English language and ease with foreign culture greatly enhanced their performing careers. Concerts in the 1930s and 1940s often shifted between English and Ghanaian languages and between various African and Western manners, dances, and songs. Kwame Mbia Hammond told me, "While nowadays many performers are illiterate, formerly, if you don't go to school, you can never be a comedian" (Hammond #93.6). When asked what they remember about concert shows from this period, former spectators, such as Nelson Saidu, comment on the actors' exquisite command of English language and manners, performative skills acquired through formal Western-style education (Saidu #94.19).

Why did the children of urban migrants, who had been educated and socialized to assume clerkships or skilled labor positions, choose instead to become professional performers?[15] Such a career choice was especially radical in light of the fact that prior to this time, making a living through entertainment was virtually unknown in the Gold Coast. While "traditional" drummers, dancers, and storytellers received some remuneration for their art, they generally did not charge admission fees for their performances, and thus had to provide for their financial sustenance through other occupations (Arkhurst #95.58).

Concert party elders explain their career choices both in terms of economic and qualitative issues. Though they had sufficient education to assume clerkship positions, unemployment in this sector of the economy was extraordinarily high. Concert veterans found acting professionally to be far more desirable than other occupations, such as skilled labor, for they could make more money, had more autonomy, and were free from the time-regimented work climate of the mines, railways, and mercantile companies. Some actors expressed sheer pleasure in and love of performance as a factor in their career choice. Others used concert parties as a way of either circumventing or relieving the hardship of military service during World War II. By entertaining the Royal West African Frontier Forces (RWAFF) stationed in the Gold Coast, members of troupes such as the Gold Coast Two Bobs and the Dix Covian Jokers managed to avoid enlistment themselves. Among actors who did enlist in the RWAFF—such as Bob Cole, Bob

Vans, and I. K. Ntama—performing gave them new options and creative outlets. They staged shows for other soldiers stationed in Burma during the war.

To understand the many reasons why concert artists chose acting as a profession, one must consider the employment alternatives available to them. While Standard VII graduates may have aspired to clerical employment, such positions were in fact quite scarce (Foster 1965, 94). Africans with formal education generally ended up doing semi-skilled labor, working as drivers and mechanics in the mines, railways, or the Public Works Department. According to Bob S. Ansah, wage labor was generally available in the 1930s, but most people preferred self-employment over wage labor positions:

> Anybody who wants a job can get a job to do. Any type of job: you will study, you will learn, you become apprentice, then you will get a job to do. But at that time there were a lot of people who didn't want to work under anybody. They prefer to work on their own, by themselves as a farmer, fisherman, a driver, a mason, a carpenter. All of these artisans didn't want to work for government or large company. They wanted to work on their own. Experienced people prefer that because they get more money like that, working on contract rather than on salary or wages. (#95.34a)

Polly Hill's account of cocoa farming (1963) and A. W. Cardinall's review of conditions in the Gold Coast in 1931 (1931, 114–117, 169–177) confirm that many Gold Coast Africans preferred independent occupations over wage and salary labor.

Early concert party practitioners can be divided into two categories: those who held down full-time jobs while moonlighting as actors and those who abandoned wage labor positions altogether in order to pursue acting as a full-time profession. Among amateur concert practitioners who did not pursue acting professionally was Charles Horton of the Two Bobs and Their Carolina Girl. He worked as a meter reader with the railways in Sekondi (Ansah #93.10). Many of his colleagues in that group also had full-time jobs: Mr. Nseidu was a draughtsman, and Messrs. Last and Archer were road overseers with the Public Works Department. The amateur nature of the Two Bobs and Their Carolina Girl frustrated Bob S. Ansah. Because so many members of this troupe held full-time jobs, they could only perform on weekends. Work obligations also prevented this concert party from touring far from Sekondi (Ansah #95.34c). So Ansah and some other performers split off to form their own professional company. Ansah recalls:

> Horton, the founder of the Two Bobs, had permanent work, you see. He was not a professional actor. He was acting, and he was working. So we find it difficult. We who had love for show business broke away from Horton. Then we formed the Gold Coast Two Bobs with professionals. We acted and did no other work. (#94.14)

In narrating concert party history, Ansah placed great emphasis on distinguishing professional performers from amateurs. He himself first worked as a railway coach attendant earning 1 shilling, 6 pence a day. But when he went into show business, Ansah discovered he could make 3 pounds a night. "So I had no interest in my [railway] work anymore" (Ansah #93.10). Concert work was simply far more lucrative than other full-time occupations available to him.

Professional comedians organized their groups into shareholding "clubs" (Ansah #95.34a; Ntama #95.41). Each of the three principle actors shared equally in both the profits and losses of their enterprise. On bad days, they might receive as little as 9 pence per share or simply foodstuffs (CPMR #95.27)[16] But other times, their earnings far exceeded that of a company manager (Ansah #95.34a). Concert parties also had non-shareholding participants, such as guest artists who did not pursue concerts as a full-time profession but only made occasional appearances. According to Bob S. Ansah,

> If you are a worker and you come to join us with the show, we like it. But you don't have any account with us. We only give you your transportation costs, and some small allowance. Then we shareholders take our shares, because we don't do any work besides acting. We took this work as professional comedians. (#93.10)

Every troupe employed an organist and a trap drum player called a "jazzer," each of whom received a small allowance. Musicians were non-shareholding members (Ansah #95.34a). Their allowance was substantially less than that of actors because, according to Jimmy Narkwa, they didn't "suffer much" on the platform (#94.26). "When I would get 1 pound and 6 shillings, the organist would get 1 shilling," explained Narkwa. Concert parties thus apportioned shares according to one's level of commitment and participation.

The motivations of concert party practitioners for pursuing acting professionally also included qualitative issues. Y. B. Bampoe said when concert parties such as the West End Trio visited his home town, he and his friends "became so interested in these shows we had no time for our books. . . . I swear to God, we were extremely interested in the West End Trio" (CPMR #95.27). Jimmy Narkwa quit his job as mail clerk for Shell Oil Company in Takoradi in order to pursue the concert business full time. When I asked why he left his job, Narkwa responded, "Oh, I never enjoyed it very much. Hence I fall out" (Narkwa #94.26). I. K. Ntama told me he left his job at the Nsuta mines and took up acting both because he loved the concert profession and because he preferred the pay schedule: "In the mines, you work for one good month before you get your pay. But in this acting profession, if God permits and there is no rain, then you get something every day" (Ntama #95.41).

Frequently, actors' parents objected to their profession because concert acting was not considered to be a respectable occupation. "When we started this concert business," explained I. K. Ntama, "people regarded it as foolish work. They didn't admire it at all" (Ntama #95.41). Kwame Mbia Hammond concurred, "When I was performing, my parents did not like it. They said I was a vagabond. Formerly, if you make this concert, when you come home, your family will beat you. They will flog you" (Hammond #93.6).[17] Bob S. Ansah said when he informed his parents he planned to act professionally, "They didn't talk to me for three years. They didn't want me to do that job, because they thought I was only moving about with no fixed position or address. When I came home, my mother wept bitterly" (Ansah #93.10). In order to persuade his family acting was a valid profession, Ansah did two things: He came home one night dressed in the attire of a lady impersonator. This made his mother stop crying and become curious about his work. Ansah then paid his sister's boarding school fees with money he earned on trek. Many veteran actors tell similar stories about how they overcame family objections to their concert work through their earnings (CPMR #95.27, Ntama #95.41). Kwame Mbia Hammond said, "When the family saw that money was coming home, they appreciated it" (Hammond #93.6). Parents who invested in their children's education had hoped their offspring would follow more stable, conventional, and respectable career paths than concert party acting. However, when young actors were able to pay school fees and contribute to household expenses, they usually won the support of their families.

Y. B. Bampoe's uncle so vehemently disliked the concert business he forbade his nephew to perform. However, Bampoe disobeyed his uncle, went on tour with a concert anyway, and earned so much money he was able to buy a pair of very expensive Achimota sandals. According to Bampoe,

> Achimota sandals cost 1 pound, 7. It was the wish of every young man to own a pair. As soon as we returned from trek, I overlooked all other personal needs and bought a pair of Achimota sandals from Koforidua. My mother wanted to know where we had been all those ten days. We told her that we went places to stage shows. I told her that I had been able to purchase a pair of those Achimota sandals that cost 1 pound, 7 shillings. I showed them to her. She said, "Fine, fine, fine. If you would like to take to this concert business, then do it with all seriousness." (CPMR #95.27)

Just as Tortoise surprised Monkey when he ascended into the trees by hiding himself in a bag, concert artists astonished their parents by making so much money while standing on a platform, singing songs, and enacting comic sketches. Like Tortoise's rhetorical question, "Haven't I come?," Bampoe's presentation of his Achimota sandals to his mother was a subordinate's assertion of autonomy and agency.

Pioneer actors used their "gumption" to transform the concert party, a colonial school diversion, into a full-time profession. Like Tortoise in the song *"Ohia Ma Adwennwen,"* concert comedians were people of modest means who worked *within* an order established by colonial powers in order to achieve individual objectives. While the government and large commercial firms strategically developed Gold Coast mining, railways, roads, and public works in ways that profited non-Africans and a few elite Africans far more than the workers on whose labor they depended, concert practitioners tactically exploited the opportunities that wage labor, a cash economy, and their own formal education made possible. The creation of time-regimented work schedules meant that people in the cities had non-working hours specifically designated as "leisure." Due to the development of wage labor and large-scale cash crop farming, they also had surplus income to spend on entertainment. The new infrastructure of roads and railways provided transportation for concert troupes as they circulated between cities, towns, and villages. And the embodied skills and knowledge actors learned from foreign movies, colonial schools, Akan storytelling, and the competitive, entrepreneurial nature of life among urban migrants provided the creative resources and practical training out of which concert parties fabricated novel and eclectic shows.

Life on the Road

"We know exactly the time when people get money, and when they haven't got money. Based upon that, we draw up our itinerary," said Bob Ansah of his group the Gold Coast Two Bobs (Ansah #95.57). Concert actors knew the economic cycles of every important industry and crop in the Gold Coast, and they set up their travel itineraries based upon market forces, seasonal conditions, and cyclical festivals. When workers received their wages, what time of year farmers harvested particular crops, and when various towns held their market days and important annual festivals all influenced scheduling of major concert tours.

I. K. Ntama and his concert party the Burma Jokers found that most wage laborers received their pay at the end of the month. So the Burma Jokers would tour from the 28th of the month, when people got paid, through the 13th of the following month, by which time workers had usually exhausted their salary (Ntama #95.41). However some mines, such as the diamond mine at Akwatia, paid their workers every Friday. So if a concert party on tour was short of cash, they knew they could dash over to Akwatia virtually any time of the month and stage a profitable show (Ansah #95.57).

When cocoa was harvested in the Volta Region or yam was harvested in the Northern Territories, concert parties toured those regions, staging every night for six weeks or more. They continued until either the rainy season came or the expendable cash of farmers dried up (Ansah #95.57). Concert parties also timed their performances to coincide with cyclical festivals. Bob S. Ansah told me he and his fellow actors did research on each region's holidays so that "during Easter holiday, we know where to go. During Christmas, we know where to go" (#95.57). Some concert parties went to Krobo areas during the annual Dipo ceremonies.[18] Other groups went to Winneba for the annual Deer-Catching Festival (*Gold Coast Spectator* 1936).[19] In the town of Larteh, concert parties always came to celebrate the New Year's Day festival (Ansah #95.57). Easter was the best time to stage in Kwawu. Many Kwawu people are traders whose work requires them to travel. "But during Easter," according to Bob S. Ansah, "everybody goes home" (Ansah #95.57).[20] They would return to Kwawu with cash to spend and an appetite for entertainment—needs concert artists gladly satisfied.

The rhythms and cycles of touring routes developed gradually over time, as more and more concert parties entered the field. However, the earliest itinerant troupes quickly identified the importance of festivals and mining towns. As early as 1934, the Two Bobs and Their Carolina Girl staged a series of concerts in Akropong during Easter (*Gold Coast Spectator* 1934a). During that same year, the Two Bobs toured the mining cities of Aboso, Tarkwa, and Nsuta (*Gold Coast Spectator* 1934g).

The mining industry instituted a number of programs in the late 1930s and early 1940s that had a dramatic impact on concert party tours. The labor force in the mines expanded from 12,500 men in 1930–1931 to approximately 40,000 in 1938–1939 (Crisp 1984, 56–93). Along with this expansion in size came a growth of political consciousness and collective action among the workers. Between 1930 and 1937, there were at least twelve major strikes in the mines of the Gold Coast, several of which led to violence. Low wages combined with a sharp increase in food prices, housing shortages, and a huge influx of aspirant wage earners into urban centers created a volatile political climate, making both the colonial government and mine management nervous.

The government tried to quell unrest through wage control and labor legislation. But the mining industry came up with a new strategy: paternalistic initiatives aimed at controlling labor. Management reduced their workers' living costs through subsidized food and improved health and housing conditions (Crisp 1984, 72–75). They instituted planned activities for leisure time, established music bands and sporting teams, hired welfare officers, built African clubs, and provided cinema and other forms of amusement. According to one manager at the Ashanti Goldfields Corporation, such programs were intended to "make our labour more dependent on us for social services."[21] In Jeff Crisp's opinion, such paternalistic strategies tended "to check the decline of the mine workers' real earnings, to increase the workers' 'job satisfaction,' and thereby counteract the strikes and the upward pressure on wages that were threatening the industry's profits" (1984, 72). While subsidized living costs, health care, and planned leisure activities certainly improved the standard of living of workers, these initiatives were not instigated for purely altruistic reasons.

As part of this pacification strategy, the mines hired concert parties to entertain their workers. Nelson Saidu, a former employee of the Ariston Gold Mines in Prestea, remembers attending concert parties in the company yard and social club (Saidu #94.19). Clubhouses at the mines were racially segregated, so when concert parties came to perform, they did one show for the European club and another for the African club (Ansah #94.14). Bob S. Ansah recalled that concert troupes would tailor their shows to suit each audience. At the European club, the Gold Coast Two Bobs "would do everything in English. We feel that they must understand what we are doing, so they would appreciate our show" (Ansah #94.14). Audiences of laborers at the African clubs were extremely diverse ethnically, so the Two Bobs would mix English with several different African languages.[22] Sometimes concert troupes would give a third performance for the general public in the mining towns. This would be staged in the city's town hall and performed entirely in the "vernacular."

The gate fee in the 1930s and 1940s was usually 6 pence for children, 1 shilling for adult general admission, and 2 shillings for reserved seats (Ansah

#94.14; K. Acquaah Hammond at CPMR #95.27).[23] But when mining companies invited concert parties to perform, they paid the troupe directly and invited the workers to attend free of charge. According Bob S. Ansah:

> We gave them [the mines] a fixed charge, and they paid. They paid us real, real well. The money given to us was sometimes just as high as the gate fee we charged in the city. Sometimes too, the Europeans gave us clothing, a complete suit and dinner jacket to fit our show. They just presented it to us. Most of our costumes were donations from these people, because it was costly to buy dinner jackets, ladies' dresses, and top hats. (#94.14)

Because the mining companies paid so well and provided concert parties with so many added perquisites, performers found mines to be very attractive venues.

During World War II, the RWAFF appropriated the strategy of the mining companies of using concert parties to improve morale. Army welfare officers commissioned concert parties to entertain troops stationed in the Gold Coast and overseas in Burma during World War II. The RWAFF included soldiers from Nigeria, Sierra Leone, the Gambia, and the Gold Coast, many of whom trained in the Gold Coast before being shipped overseas (Haywood and Clarke 1964). In 1939, the British government approached the Gold Coast Two Bobs and asked them to put up a show to raise money for a special wartime Spitfire fund (Ansah #95.34a). Soon after, the army invited the Two Bobs to move from unit to unit, entertaining the armed forces. At first the army wanted concert performers to enlist as soldiers. But Bob S. Ansah pleaded personal hardship. His father was dead and his brothers were all in the army. So if he too enlisted, there would be no male in his household to deal with important family affairs (Ansah #95.34a). Rather than enlist, Ansah became attached to the army as a civilian entertainer. His group, the Gold Coast Two Bobs, along with the Dix Covian Jokers, moved from unit to unit, among the fifty-nine units stationed throughout the Gold Coast. They performed 45-minute shows and sometimes staged as many as three or four shows a day. According to Ansah, the army paid performers £3 for each performance, so each actor's income would average £48 per month. This salary far exceeded what they would have made as soldiers.

Performers who actually enlisted in the RWAFF and served overseas also began to entertain the troupes. Bob Vans, one such actor, enlisted in 1942. After his army training, Vans was sent to India with the 81st Divisional Battalion to fight in the Burma Campaign. Vans arrived in India on Christmas Day, and "the officers invited people to come and sing. So I went and sang" (Vans #95.31). Vans did a rendition of "Stormy Weather" and danced with a walking stick like Charlie Chaplin. He imitated shows he had seen by the Axim Trio when they toured his home town of Aboso. "Later, I was called to the office," said Vans. "When I went, they told me they liked the way I sang. They told me I had been selected to train some people in order to entertain the soldiers." So Vans gathered twenty-five actors representing each of the West African countries in the RWAFF. He broke them into smaller groups based upon their country of origin and had them create shows from their respective traditions. The Nigerian, Gambian, and Sierra Leonean groups generally only sang and danced. But the Gold Coast group performed musical theatre shows in the style of the Axim Trio.[24]

Whether staging for military or civilian audiences, all concert parties performing between 1930 and the end of World War II utilized a tremendous range of performance spaces. Sometimes they transformed sheds used for storing cocoa or merchandise into theatres (Ansah #93.10; Sutherland 1970, 16). When the Axim Trio appeared in Suhum in 1934, they held their show in the shed of W. Bartholomew & Co., a major trading company (*Gold Coast Spectator* 1934f).[25] When the Gold Coast Two Bobs helped the government raise money for the wartime Spitfire fund, they performed in lorry parks (Ansah #95.34a). The actors who entertained the RWAFF performed in army camps, often joining two army trucks together to make a raised platform (Ansah #95.34a). The Optimism Club, which had a permanent raised stage, was a favorite commercial venue in Sekondi.[26] Although membership in the Optimism Club was exclusive and restricted to "very big people" (Sutherland 1970, 6), once a concert was going to be staged there, "anybody could buy a ticket and attend," according to club rector Lawrence Cudjoe (#94.25). Concert parties appeared at other private clubs in the Gold Coast, such as the Rodger Club in Accra, the Domarch Club in Nsawam, and the many African and European clubs at the mines.[27] They also performed in cinema halls such as the Palladium in Sekondi and the Merry Villas and Ocansey's Palladium in Accra.[28] On a few rare occasions, the High Court in Cape Coast and Parliament House in Accra served as performance venues (Ansah #93.10; Sutherland 1970, 16). While concert parties used town halls in large urban areas, in smaller villages they used schools, chapels, open yards, and large family compounds.[29]

From 1930 onward, a defining characteristic of the concert party was its itinerant nature. Whether traveling by train, lorry, or foot, comedians were always on the move (map 1). Their touring routes took them from Accra all the way to Jasikan, a city in the Volta region. From Jasikan, they moved north to Yendi, and onward to such remote northern cities as Bawku in the east and Wa in the west. Concert troupes would descend back south from Tamale, stopping in major trading centers from Kintampo to Sunyani and Kumasi. They traveled by rail from Kumasi to Sekondi, performing in all the mining centers en route. From Takoradi, they headed east along the coast toward the capital city of Accra by lorry. After performing in and around Accra, troupes would travel northwest through the cocoa-rich towns of the east and the trading centers along the Kumasi road, from Nsawam to Nkawkaw and Konongo.

With such an active and wide-ranging touring schedule, concert parties depended on the roads and railways built by the colonial government. According to a 1931 government report, the 1920s saw a "complete revolution in the carrying trade" (Cardinall 1931, 106). Whereas there were only 2,241 miles of motorable road in 1921, by 1931 that figure had tripled. A large and complex system of privately owned buses quickly developed to move passengers to their various destinations along these roads (Cardinall 1931, 107, 114–117). Railway travel

MAP 1. Map of routes commonly used by touring concert troupes from the late 1930s through the 1950s. (Inset: Ghana.) Map drawn by Nathan Kwame Braun.

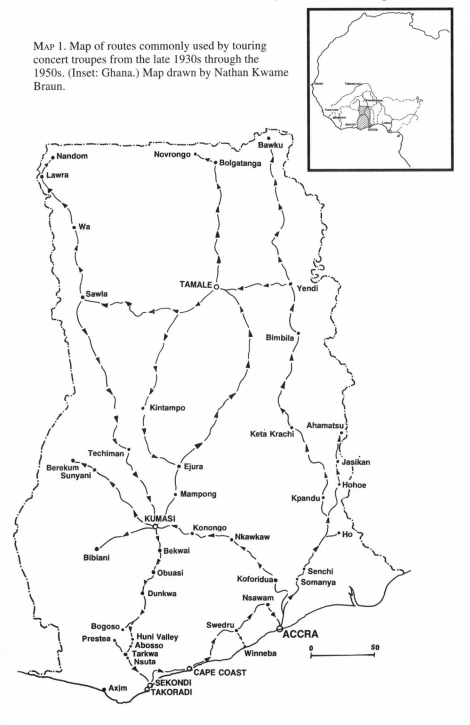

also improved during the 1920s. Colonial Governor Sir Gordon Guggisberg over-
saw the installation of better equipment, an increase in the total miles of rail, and
the construction of more stations.

Concert practitioners exploited the opportunities capitalist and colonial transportation development inadvertently made possible for them. They learned how
to profit from a system that generally favored the demands of large-scale commerce over passenger needs. Census figures from 1931 indicate most African
passengers preferred lorry over train travel (Cardinall 1931). In his assessment of
transportation in the Gold Coast in 1931, A. W. Cardinall offered several economic and subjective reasons why passengers favored lorries over trains. He cited
the entrepreneurial nature of private lorry services as evidence that the "African
in spite of his rapid development during the past few years retains the age-old
manner of commercial thinking common to traders. . . . He has not yet passed
beyond the stage of barter" (1931, 114). Independent lorry owners' supposedly
backward barter system of credits and exchanges with traders and petrol dealers
was, in fact, fantastically successful at keeping overhead costs down (Cardinall
1931, 114). Small private lorries could charge much less than state-owned rails
and transport firms. Also, since private lorries expressly served the needs of African passengers, their routes and schedules were flexible and accommodated the
changing needs of passengers, such as the rhythm of local markets and regional
festivals.

The routes for railways were, on the other hand, quite rigid, serving the needs
of industry and international trade rather than private passengers. A brief glance
at a rail map (map 2) reveals whose interests the trains were built to serve. Trains
carried cocoa, manganese, timber, bauxite, rubber, and gold from the mining and
harvesting areas in the southern part of the colony to the Takoradi Harbor, where
these valuable goods were shipped overseas (British Empire Exhibition 1925).
Passenger service on Gold Coast railways was an afterthought, and domestic agricultural trade does not appear to have been a factor in railway planning at all.[30]
Trains did not serve yam traders, for instance, who needed to move heavy produce from the north to the main Kumasi market. Nor did rail routes have the
capillaries necessary to help coastal fisherman distribute their produce among
consumers in the hinterland.

However, trains did meet the transportation needs of concert practitioners,
for it connected them with an important audience sector. Cities along rail lines
tended to be full of migrant workers who had expendable cash and a desire to
experiment with new lifestyles, such as attending drinking bars, dances, and concert parties (Akyeampong 1996c). Such towns had money expressly *because*
they were exporting goods by rail to serve an international market. The railways
were arteries serving new capital-based relationships. They transported large-
scale mining and agricultural products to Takoradi for export and brought cash
back into the local economy. Concert actors literally moved with these goods, as
when they traveled by the "goods train," or night train. A troupe staging in Bekwai

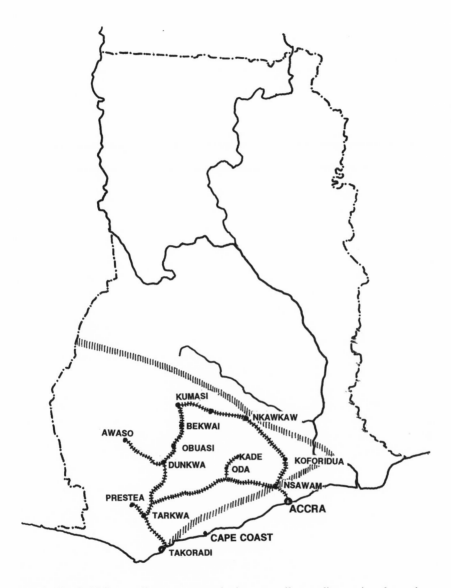

MAP 2. The Gold Coast railways connected mines as well as trading stations located within the cocoa-producing area (enclosed by hachured line). Map drawn by Nathan Kwame Braun.

might catch, for instance, the late-night goods train to Obuasi after their show closed, thus arriving in Obuasi before dawn. By traveling this way, actors could spring into action at daybreak, promoting their show in the city and gathering the materials they needed for the evening's performance (Ansah #95.34c).

Occasionally concert parties traveled outside of the Gold Coast altogether. The first record of such a journey was when the Axim Trio toured Nigeria with the Cape Coast Sugar Babies dance band in 1935 (Sutherland 1970, 16–20).[31] This trip showed the Axim Trio they could expand their audience to non-Akan-speaking areas of the Gold Coast. Shortly after they returned from Nigeria, they went on trek to Tamale and the Northern Territories. In the 1940s, the Axim Trio also went to the neighboring West African countries of Ivory Coast, Liberia, and Sierra Leone (Sutherland 1970, 20, 23).

Once a concert party's itinerary was set, they had to publicize their shows. "About two or three weeks, or even a month, before a concert party comes," according to I. K. Ntama, a troupe advance man would "file posters in the town. And the date of performance is on the posters. So we know when they will come by train" (#95.41). When the concert troupe finally arrived, they would use various techniques to announce their presence in the town and promote the evening's show. First thing in the morning the troupe would walk around the town wearing special hats so that market women setting up their stalls, laborers on their way to work, children walking to school, and travelers waiting for transport in the lorry park would all know the concert party had arrived. Bob S. Ansah explained, "We are hailed upon our arrival at any station we go to. We would all put on uniform straw hats so that upon our arrival, people will shout, 'Oh, the concert people have arrived! The concert people have arrived!'" (#95.34c). Another technique used for promoting their shows was to hire the local church or school brass band to parade through town playing highlife music (CPMR #95.27).

As soon as young school boys learned a concert party had come, they would run from school to the train station. According to Bob Vans:

> During those days, a small boy can't get money to attend the show. So what you do is that you run away from school to the railway station. Immediately the concert party arrives, you will try hard, very hard to get one of their luggage boxes and carry it to the place of performance. And then they will write down your name. Then you don't go any place. You will stay there and hang around. By 7:00 or 7:30 P.M. you go in to the concert house. They allow you to go in for free. (#95.30)

Concert parties traveled with as many as nine boxes containing costumes for the stock roles of boy actor, gentleman, lady impersonator, and cloth woman. Special boxes were needed for the lady impersonator's hats and the Petromax (kerosene) lanterns used to illuminate concert shows (Ansah #95.34c). The lantern mantles were extremely delicate and expensive to replace. Bob S. Ansah said, "We wrapped the lantern with newspapers, packed them decently, and handled them with care so that we can be using them continuously" (Ansah #95.34c). The swarm of children who came to the train station not only helped convey all this luggage to the concert house, but their excitement and network of friends also helped publicize the show in the town.

In addition to carrying a concert party's boxes from the station to the performance venue, children who wanted to gain free admission to the show served in many other capacities. K. Acquaah Hammond told me:

> We helped them too much! We would go to them, "What do you want us to do for you?" We wash their clothes, fetch water for them to bath. And in those days too, there was no pipe-borne water, so you must go far away to fetch water from the stream and give it to them. We iron their clothes. We help them, and we like them too. In order to get free entry to the show, we help them too much. (Bampoe and Hammond #95.55)

One of the most coveted jobs a small boy could do for a concert party was to be the *Yefun Pee* (big stomach) promoter, also known as "O Charlie, Mask Man." A child would dress in a mask and Charlie Chaplinesque outfit, sometimes stuffing his stomach to give him a comically big belly (Hammond #93.6; Sutherland 1970, 16). He would wear a sandwich board with the troupe's posters plastered on it and walk through town, ringing a bell and announcing there would be a show that night. All the other children would parade behind this Pied Piper–like character, rhythmically chanting (Ntama #95.41; Sutherland 1970, 16). Y. B. Bampoe remembers performing as the Mask Man:

> You put on mask with costume, go round the town, and ring the bell, with posters on your back saying, "Tonight there will be a show by the Axim Trio. Rate: penny." You would go around town about two times. Then the concert party would write your name down. That meant that you have passed your entrance [earned your admission]. Then you know you are okay. (Bampoe and Hammond #95.55)

When the Axim Trio came to Tarkwa in the early 1940s, I. K. Ntama would fight with the other boys and young men over who would play O Charlie. "We small boys, we fight on this. If I come to the concert house and I see you are getting dressed as the Mask Man, I have to pull you down, take the dress, and put it on myself" (Ntama #95.41).

Children were so preoccupied with finding ways to get into the show for free they would hang on the actors' coattails all day. Y. B. Bampoe told me that if you were a child,

> you won't go home. Your mother and father will search for you. But the concert people have arrived, so you have no mother, no father. The concert people are you parents. You don't care whether you have eaten any food or not. Not unless your name is written, proving that you are one of the concert party workers . . . then you go home. (Bampoe and Hammond #95.55)

The competitive environment in which young males vied for the privilege of serving itinerant concert parties fostered an informal apprenticeship system. Nearly every professional concert party actor from the 1930s through the 1960s began his career by serving his concert elders. As a school boy, Bob Johnson helped Teacher Yalley cart chairs for his shows at the Optimism Club (Sutherland 1970, 6). Kwame Mbia Hammond, I. K. Ntama, and Bob Vans all helped the Axim Trio by carrying their boxes and playing "O Charlie" (Hammond #93.6; Ntama #95.41; Vans #95.30). When Y. B. Bampoe was young, he fetched water for Jimmy Narkwa of the Dix Covian Jokers (CPMR #95.27; Narkwa #94.26).

Out of the horde of young boys who besieged a concert troupe at the train station, a few would distinguish themselves as being the most ingenious and talented. Such individuals would be given special tasks that involved performance skills. Concert actors occasionally selected one or two boys to make cameo appearances on stage. Charles Horton of the Two Bobs and Their Carolina Girl trained Jimmy Narkwa. According to Narkwa:

> Horton started teaching me ragtime songs. So I felt interest in him. That was the beginning of my show business career. When we went to the Optimism Club, he would arrange for entertainment. We would go there and he would say, "Go to the stage and sing. I am coming." When you go to the stage, he wouldn't come! He would waste time. So it's for you to use your brains, your wits to do something to entice the audience. (Narkwa #94.26)

Abandoning a fledgling performer on stage was a way of forcing him "to add some variation," according to Narkwa. It was a test. If the boy used his gumption under such stressful conditions, he had a future in the concert business.

Being a professional comedian took ingenuity. A performer had to be a hustler offstage and a witty improviser onstage. The young Y. B. Bampoe had a healthy dose of both qualities. When the Dix Covian Jokers came to Suhum to perform, Bampoe devised a strategy for getting the actor Kwamena Dadzie to teach him new songs:

> Dadzie was a heavy smoker. So whenever I obtained one pence from any source, I used it to buy a cigarette for him. He was a good singer. One of his songs was "In the Mood." I liked it very much, so I asked him to teach me how to sing it. He said, "Give me one gasper." I would buy one straight away. He would then sing the song. I asked him to write down the song for me, which he always obliged. As soon as I could sing the song well, I would go teach it to my brother, Kofi Bɔndze and my other friend. If we could sing the new song well, our next line of action was to give a concert ourselves. (Bampoe at CPMR #95.27)

Bampoe used the economy of service established between young boys and professional actors not only as a means of gaining admission to shows but also of obtaining creative material for his own budding career. Even as a boy, Bampoe had already started his own group. Whenever a professional concert such as the Axim Trio came to town, Bampoe's group of friends would stage a show the very next day, shamelessly appropriating and reformulating their predecessors' ideas. "In fact, we were imitating them," said Bampoe:

> I played the part of E. K. Dadson, my brother played Bob Johnson, and Kofi Bondze played the part of Charlie Turpin. We would do exactly what they had done the previous night. We wrote our posters and filed them on walls using starch. They read, "Concert Tonight." Instead of gate fees, we accepted plantains. We also accepted fish. By the end of a play, we might have collected plenty of these items. I gave my share to my mother. (CPMR #95.27)

Bampoe was not the only young man with entrepreneurial spirit and raw acting talent who was inspired to mount amateur shows imitating the concert greats. I. K. Ntama did the same thing with his friends in Tarkwa (#95.41). Bob Cole also traveled with his amateur group of schoolmates during school vacations in the 1930s. Emulating the Axim Trio, they toured similar performances from Abosso, Cole's hometown, to Prestea, Obuasi, and even Kumasi (Vans #95.31).

When a concert party arrived in a new town, each member of the troupe had different responsibilities in terms of making arrangements for the evening's performance (Bampoe and Hammond #95.55). One actor would borrow or rent two gas lanterns for illuminating the show. Lanterns were placed on two pedestals at the foot of the stage. Another actor would go to the police to obtain a permit for the show. And the third actor would borrow boards and cement blocks to make the stage and benches on which the audience would sit. The flock of school boys who trailed concert actors helped transport these items to the concert house. Young men helped assemble the platform by stacking the bricks and carefully laying the boards on top of them. Concert party stages were very small, roughly 10 feet wide and 7 feet deep. Neither the boards nor the bricks were fastened with any nails or adhesive, but concert actors knew exactly how to balance these materials so they could withstand the rigors of concert party dancing and acrobatic physical comedy. In addition to borrowing lanterns, boards, and benches, some troupes needed to borrow a bass and side drum "jazz" trap set from the local school.[32] Sometimes they would have to borrow costume items as well (CPMR #95.29).

Once the actors in a touring concert party had arranged publicity and performance details in a particular town, each was free to socialize and make hospitality arrangements for the evening. Sometimes entire troupes would lodge in one family's compound. Most concert pioneers were Fante, so they often stayed with Fante migrants. For instance, concert parties that toured Suhum usually stayed at Y. B. Bampoe's family compound (Bampoe and Hammond #95.55). Bampoe's maternal relatives are Fante, and they felt a particular affinity with concert groups from the Western Region. Sometimes actors would split up and lodge with individual friends or relatives. Others formed romantic liaisons with women, who would see that their accommodation and catering needs were met. According to Y. B. Bampoe, "We concert actors had girlfriends wherever we went" (CPMR

#95.27). If a woman was interested in an actor, she would prepare food and send it to the concert house. The actor and the woman might then meet to make further arrangements. "The women who willingly helped the bandsmen on tour with food and so on, we refer to them as 'orchestra wives,'" Bampoe told me (CPMR #95.27). Such women were like musical instruments among bandsmen: One instrument could have many players. "We don't trust the orchestra wives," said Bampoe, "because today when you are in, you are her friend. But tomorrow when the next band comes. . . ." Such women were particularly fond of concert party lady impersonators (Narkwa #94.26; Ntama #95.41). J. E. Baidoe, the lady impersonator of the West End Trio and the Axim Trio, has a scrapbook from his concert years full of photographic portraits from women who adored him.

If concert actors did not make any special arrangements for their accommodation, they would simply sleep in the open yard of the compound or town hall where they performed (Ansah #93.10). An actor would push three benches together, use his bag for a pillow, and wrap himself in his sleeping cloth to protect him from mosquitoes (Ntama #95.41). When I asked if such a bed was uncomfortable, actors answered with the Akan proverb, "One who is not tired complains he has nowhere to sleep." After touring day after day, rising early in the morning and working late into the night, actors were usually tired enough that they could fall asleep anywhere.

Concert party veterans belonged to a burgeoning intermediate sector of the Gold Coast population. Their parents were employed in new industries such as railways, mining, export cash crops, and large-scale commercial trade. Many of their fathers had migrated to southern towns and cities to seek new employment opportunities, bringing their wives and families with them to settle in these towns. They sent their children to colonial and mission schools, believing that education would enhance their progeny's employment opportunities and thereby help their extended family improve their material circumstances. However, aspirations did not always match opportunities. As in much of colonial Africa, the rhetoric of "civilization" diverged from the material realities. Colonial infrastructures were ultimately meant to serve international interests much more than African ones. Development rarely served Africans to the degree that it exploited their labor and their country's natural resources. Unemployment, low wages, and transportation systems that failed to serve local needs were common features of colonial life. In the Gold Coast throughout the 1930s, low wages were a frequent source of conflict, leading to strikes by miners, railway workers, and government employees (Crisp 1984, 56–93). With the minimum wage for government workers in 1939 at only 1 shilling, 4 pence, even the governor privately admitted in 1939 that it was "almost impossible to justify the low wages at present paid to labourers" (Crisp 1984, 69).

The first generation of professional concert party actors faced discouraging economic prospects when they completed their Standard VII education. Upon graduation they discovered that being able to read, write, and speak English was not, contrary to what they had been led to believe, any assurance of secure employment. Rather than abandoning hope of finding fulfilling and lucrative work and settling instead for underpaid semi-skilled work in the mines, these young men invented a new profession. They capitalized on the embodied skills they had learned in Western-style schools. They performed Western culture—for a fee—to migrant populations in the new mining towns, cocoa trading centers, and international ports created by colonial development. While many colonial Ghanaians scoffed at their career choice and considered such itinerant entertainment frivolous and undignified, concert actors eventually won respect through their financial success. From their earnings, they could pay siblings' school fees, buy expensive shoes, and bring home wages equal to or surpassing that of a company manager.

"Poverty makes you think," says the Akan proverb *ohia ma adwennwen.* Whether the difficulty one faces in life is being a land-bound creature with short legs in a world run by those who live in trees or being an urban youth with education and no viable employment prospects in a world run by powerful colonial interests, *adwennwen* can turn obstacles into opportunities. I suggested earlier that *ohia ma adwennwen* is a discourse on power that illuminates how subaltern individuals assert their agency and autonomy within a hierarchically organized social order. Rather than a deliberate form of resistance aimed at overturning that social order, *adwennwen* is a means of survival. It is the prosaic ingenuity by which individuals address the problems of daily life in a socially stratified universe. Concert party pioneers of the 1930s and 1940s were people with limited socio-economic means who faced numerous obstacles while trying to survive in an economy that was built to serve interests other than theirs. Just as Tortoise transformed Monkey's prejudices into opportunities, concert actors used *adwennwen* to exploit the very infrastructure that exploited them.

Performance is essential to the proverb *ohia ma adwennwen.* One must be able to think on one's feet and play-act convincingly. The following chapter will explore the performative nature of *ohia ma adwennwen* in more detail by concentrating on the poetics of concert party invention, the use of stock characters, and the role of improvisation. It will also implicitly use the concept of *ohia ma adwennwen* by manipulating theories espoused by the powerful—scholars based in the Euro-American metropoles who set the agenda for much contemporary research—in order to assert Akan precepts that have not heretofore received much scholarly attention.

5

Improvising Popular Traveling Theatre

THE POETICS OF INVENTION

Concert parties occupy a nebulous position in Ghana's cultural hierarchy. Lacking the prestige of scripted dramas written in English and the "authenticity" of so-called traditional cultural practices such as *odwira* festivals or *adowa* dancing, concert parties fall into that vast, amorphous terrain of African popular culture that has fallen outside the purview of dominant cultural paradigms (Barber 1987, 1997). The concert party's historical roots in cultural syncretism are in part responsible for its ambivalent status. Shows of the 1930s and 1940s, much more so than those of subsequent decades, drew liberally upon Western sources. They featured plot scenarios from American films such as *Sonny Boy* and *On with the Show;* foreign dance steps such as the waltz, quickstep, and foxtrot; and songs such as "Stormy Weather" and "Don't Fence Me In." Some observers point to this history as evidence that the concert party began as a merely derivative performance form, a pale imitation of Western vaudeville, far too hybrid to be considered genuinely African.

The concert party's ancestry is certainly complex and heterogeneous. Yet, as I will argue in this chapter, the creative ethos from which it springs has deep roots in Akan culture. While concerts were a novel innovation of the twentieth century, they utilized techniques of creativity well-established in traditional Akan performing arts such as festivals and storytelling. Akan festivals have certain key structural elements that are always repeated. However, every expression of a set of patterns always involves "the principle of *variation* to greater or lesser degrees," according to art historian Herbert M. Cole (1975, 22). "No two chiefs or priests dress or embellish themselves identically nor do their entourages include exactly the same numbers of people or the same decorations" (22). This principle of repetition and revision so central to Akan festivals, storytelling, and proverb usage is also fundamental to the creative process of making a concert party.

A related dimension of Akan artistry that concerts share with "traditional" cultural practices is the high value placed on performance, on the imagination and skill with which individuals embody ideas and enact them in front of spectators. Akan notions of performance are not bounded by proscenium staging or particular venues labeled as "theatre." For instance, when concert actors on trek in the 1930s would arrive at a new town and parade through the streets wearing straw hats, they were purposefully performing a role, just as they would later in the day when they staged their show "on the platform."[1] In the folktale of Tortoise and Monkey analyzed in the previous chapter, Tortoise uses his ability to act, to role play and persuade through embodied simulation, in order to both dupe Vulture into carrying him up to the trees and to trick Monkey into assisting him down to the ground again. Proverbs, another "traditional" Akan performance genre, achieve meaning not merely through words but also through the poetry of action: a speaker's style of communication, use of tone, elision, paraphrasing, and personalization (Yankah 1989b, 247–260).

Whether one is invoking a proverb, telling an Ananse tale, or assuming a role for strategic purposes, performances within Akan culture are as likely to be impromptu, constituted in the everyday interactions of social life, as they are to be planned and circumscribed by temporal and spatial markers framing the event as extraordinary. For instance, proverbs can be spontaneously invoked during court proceedings, domestic quarrels, and informal conversations among friends and acquaintances. Similarly, an incident in daily life can trigger an *anansesɛm,* especially if the storyteller wishes to communicate indirectly a message to the listener. Once while I was waiting at an electronics shop in Osu for my tape machine to be repaired, everyone in the shop gathered around the doorway to watch a young woman try to coax a drunk relative back into the family compound. The intoxicated aunt was verbally abusive and uncooperative, which provoked commentary and laughter among spectators. One person in the shop remarked, *"ɛnɛ concetfoɔ aba!"* or "Today the concert people have come." Everyone nodded in assent. The scene was not merely *like* a concert party, it *was* a concert party inasmuch as it incorporated the same domestic conflicts and dynamics of audience commentary and interaction that one finds at commercial concert events.

Akan understandings of performance are far more fluid and dynamic than bounded Western definitions of theatre generally allow. Whether performances happen on a physical stage and are clearly separated off from "real" life or whether they transpire in more mundane contexts is of little consequence. Such a liberal conception of performance is consonant with theories recently advanced in the academic field of performance studies. Margaret Thompson Drewal defines performance as "the praxis of everyday social life; indeed it is the practical application of embodied skill and knowledge to the task of taking action" (Drewal 1991, 1). This is an extension of Richard Schechner's theory of performance as being restored, or twice-behaved, behavior (1985, 35–116) and is an elaboration of the ideas about performance in everyday life advanced by sociologist Erving Goffman (1959).[2]

While many in performance studies have been reluctant to delimit the field's boundaries or define what exactly "performance" might be, most agree that performance is a far more inclusive concept than theatre. Peggy Phelan summarizes the questions that have driven the evolution of performance studies:

> Was "theatre" an adequate term for the wide range of "theatrical acts" that intercultural observation was everywhere revealing? Perhaps "performance" better captured and conveyed the activity that was provoking these questions. Since only a tiny portion of the world's cultures equated theatre with written scripts, performance studies would begin with an intercultural understanding of its fundamental term, rather than enlisting intercultural case studies as additives, rhetorically or ideologically based postures of inclusion and relevance. (Phelan and Lane 1998, 3)

An expansion of terminology from "theatre" to "performance" became imperative when Euro-American theatre scholars moved into non-Western areas, for many cultures do not share Europe's tradition of logocentrism, the West's fascination with and privileging of written texts, its tendency to separate drama from dance and music, and its bifurcated understanding of the boundary between theatre and reality.

Akans have been using expansive conceptions of performance to tell stories and proverbs, enact rituals and festivals, and strategize solutions to the problems of everyday life through *adwennwen* since long before the academic field of performance studies was even a twinkle in some disaffected American theatre scholar's eye. However, until now there have been few occasions for Euro-American and Ghanaian discourses on performance to interact. A premise of this book is that there is something valuable to be gained on both sides of the Atlantic precisely through such transcultural intellectual interactions.

Akan notions of performance have much in common with poststructuralist understandings of performativity.[3] Implicit in Akan storytelling, proverb usage, and festival enactments is an assumption that stylized gestures, embodied behaviors, and verbal expressions do not merely reflect reality: They *create* it. How concert parties participated in the construction of reality in colonial Ghana during the 1930s and 1940s is the subject of this present chapter. I will first explore the poetics of invention by which concert practitioners drew inspiration from various traditions and identify some of the key creative principles that guided their process of inclusion, exclusion, and revision. I will then analyze the dramaturgy and structure of concert shows from the 1930s and 1940s. The final section interprets the social and political significance of the stereotypes and stock roles that were so prevalent on concert stages. I argue that the concert party's self-conscious theatricalization and deliberate foregrounding of the difference between the ontological status of stock characters and their assumed social identities subverted, or at least performatively disrupted, the compulsory Anglophilia that was so rampant in colonial Ghana.

Just as concert parties incorporate ideas from Akan folklore, Yorùbá pop music, American movies, and British music hall, my method here involves combining ideas from disparate intellectual traditions and reformulating them to meet my needs. In reading the concert party's use of female impersonation and stereotypes, I have found Euro-American theories of drag and gender performativity to be both enlightening and limiting: enlightening because these theories led me to recognize the centrality of "civilization" as a master discourse of colonialism; yet limiting because these theories too often presume gender to be of primary, universal importance, superceding all other categories of identity. Such presumptions, as Oyèrónké Oyêwùmí has so compellingly argued, are particularly problematic in the case of Africa (1997).

In my repetition and revision of Euro-American drag theory, I argue that all of the characters in concert party "trios" were in drag, not just male actors who appeared in female roles. What made these performances "drag" had much more do to with *how* the characters were constructed—the self-conscious use of role playing and the overall presentational theatrical style—than with the fact that men in frocks played women's roles. North American performance scholars often interpret cross-dressing to be a technique for subverting dominant gender roles and contesting "compulsory heterosexuality." However, colonial Ghanaian concert parties used drag to contest and undermine the master narrative of "civilization," the foundational discourse of colonial rule.

Euro-American drag and gender performativity theory presumes, by the very abstraction of its language, universal applicability. This chapter concludes by suggesting how such theories might be productively extended and revised not only to become more genuinely inclusive of non-Western performance practices but also to be more effective in analyzing drag performances closer to its "home" turf, such as female impersonation in nineteenth-century American minstrelsy and the Harlem drag balls depicted in the film *Paris Is Burning* (Livingston 1992).

Traditions of Invention

I once asked concert party veterans Y. B. Bampoe and Acquaah Hammond, "If someone who is not from Ghana were looking at the concert party, and they saw that in the early days you spoke English, sang American songs, and wore this blackface like they had in America, that person might say, 'Oh the concert party is not real African culture.' What would be your response?" Hammond and Bampoe replied:

> *Hammond:* Oh, I think it's not an African culture. It's something imported.
> *Bampoe:* Imported, but we have (*gestures as though slipping something in an envelope*) put in African culture . . .
> *Hammond:* Yeah . . . yeah
> *Bampoe:* . . . side by side.
> *Hammond:* Yeah.
> *Bampoe:* . . . to tell African stories.
> *Hammond:* Yes. Tell African stories by way of staging, or by way of performing . . .
> *Bampoe:* But . . . so people take it to be our own origin.
> *Hammond:* But if you ask anyone who doesn't know the details, he will tell you it's African culture. But it's an imported thing.
> *CC:* So you took it and then you changed it.
> *Bampoe:* (*Teasing me*) That's as you are doing: You are going to change it! (*Motions with his hands as if turning the steering wheel on a car. Laughs.*) *Oburoni ɔkorɔmfo!* [Thieving foreigner!]
> *CC:* We are thieves!
> *Bampoe:* Yes!
> (*All laugh*)
> (Bampoe and Hammond #95.55)

Bampoe and Hammond responded to my question about who really owns the concert party by asking who really owns my research. In reply to either question, no simple answer will suffice.

What most interests me at present is the gesture Bampoe used when explaining how actors changed imported ideas by putting in African culture "side by side," the way he motioned with his hands as if slipping something into an envelope. What techniques does this gesture signify? By what process did concert party pioneers transform "imported" ideas into something that was perceived as African? What overall principles guided the creative process of practitioners as they gathered ideas from disparate sources?

Creating a concert party, both in the 1930s and in more recent times, requires an active manipulation of resources from everyday life. Ideas are seized "on the fly" and rapidly refurbished. The consumption of an idea is never passive but is an active process of tactical maneuvering. Whatever a tactic wins, as Michel de Certeau has argued, "it does not keep. It must constantly manipulate events in order to turn them into opportunities" ([1984] 1988, xix). Concert actors gather material from dreams, personal experiences, movies, newspapers, historical events, folklore, novels, and local scandals. "In the night, you'll get some pictures," Y. B. Bampoe told me. "You think of something, and then you put it into operation. You master it. That's how I used to get my plays and my songs" (Bampoe and Hammond #93.11). While some ideas come in dreams, others come from chance encounters on the street. I. K. Ntama gives an example: "When I was coming from the station, I saw two women fighting. And one said this, and one said that, one said that. And I will pick something out of it" in order to make a play (#95.41).

Previous scholars have identified Ananse storytelling as an inspiration or precursor of the concert party. Adelaide Amegatcher says "concert parties found the form [of *anansesεm*] most suited to the type of audiences they aimed at and accordingly modeled their dramatic form after that of storytelling, with the dance and music forming an integral part of the whole drama" (1968, 28). Kwabena Bame concurs, suggesting that Ananse is the prototype for the concert party joker, the "Bob" (1985, 10). John Collins also believes that storytelling was "particularly important as a formative agent on the Ghanaian concert party" (1976a, 50; 1994a, 190–206). While many scholars allude to a connection between concerts and *anansesεm,* none have analyzed in detail the relationship between these two genres.

The concert party and Akan storytelling share techniques of creation, presentation, and reception. Both *anansesεm* and concert parties convey stories through a combination of song and narrative. Nearly all Ananse stories and concert party narratives conclude with a moral lesson. In performance, both genres incorporate cross-gender impersonation and doubling of character roles, and they elicit and capitalize upon audience participation. Neither is formally dominated or controlled by institutions such as chieftaincy, family lineages, or religion. Both concerts and *anansesεm* are "popular" in the sense that they are very well liked and accessible to people at all levels of the socio-economic spectrum.

Concert parties and Ananse storytelling also share a creative process of repetition and revision. *Anansesεm* are comprised of an established repertoire of characters and narratives. However, each storyteller transforms received material by adding idiosyncratic expressions and variations to the tales. According to Efua Sutherland, a storyteller "tries to prove his artistry by refreshing and up-dating his story by spontaneous improvisation as he tells it" (Sutherland 1987, 3–4). This is why one finds so many different versions of the same tale in various collections. Compare, for example, the versions of "How the Spider Got a Bald Head" in the collections of R. S. Rattray (1930, 119–123), Peggy Appiah (1966, 97–104), and Peter E. A. Addo (1968, 33–34). Each time a tale is reproduced, it is made new through the innovations and personal style of the storyteller. A performer adds her own embellishments, reshapes the tale to communicate some particular message, or introduces topical references that will engage her immediate audience.

This tradition of reproducing received ideas and adding idiosyncratic revisions is not only essential to storytelling performance but is also imbedded in the character and temperament of Ananse himself. All folktales told among the Akan are called *anansesεm.* This term literally means matters or stories relating to Kwaku Ananse, the fabled trickster spider. Like most animals in Ghanaian folktales, Ananse has distinctly human characteristics. He is a trickster, an opportunist. Cleverness is sometimes the solution to Ananse's problems, though as often as not it leads to his own undoing. Not all *anansesεm* feature Ananse, but all folktales belong to him because, according to legend, Ananse was greedy and smart enough to steal all the world's stories from Ɔnyame, the sky god.[4]

Ananse is a small animal, described as a mere "bushman," a "neck standing all alone" (Rattray 1930, 55, 179). However, despite his limitations, Ananse is fantastically successful at exploiting opportunities. He often takes some small substance such as a slice of yam or some gunpowder and, through ingenuity, transforms it into something grand, such as a baby, an elephant, or a cow.[5] In one story, Ananse boasts that if God gives him a single grain of corn, he can bring a whole village in exchange. So God gives Ananse a kernel of corn. Ananse takes it to a man's house, where he spends the night. Ananse tells his host that he has a special grain of corn from God and that it must be stored overnight with the fowls. However, in the morning the grain of corn is gone, consumed by a chicken. In restitution for Ananse's loss, the host gives Ananse the chicken that ate the corn. Then Ananse goes to the next village, and he pulls the same trick. He says his chicken—a special chicken from God—must sleep with the sheep. But in the night the chicken is trampled. So Ananse is given a sheep in exchange. He proceeds in the same manner to two more villages, where he is given a cow and then a corpse. Ananse goes to the final village and visits the chief's palace, where he pretends the corpse he is carrying is the sleeping son of God. He says God's son is very tired and must not be disturbed. God's son is put in the children's room where he is to sleep. In the night, the children detect a bad smell, and they think God's son has broken wind. So they beat him. In the morning God's son is found dead, his body covered with bruises. Ananse says the chief and all the people of his town must go before God to plead their case. So they all go to God. When they arrive, Ananse says, "A single grain of corn I received, saying I would come with the inhabitants of a town. There are the people of a town standing there" (Rattray 1930, 261).

Like Ananse, concert actors in colonial Ghana made formidable creations primarily through resourcefulness and performance skills rather than material wealth. The everyday lives of concert actors on trek, the conditions under which they worked, and the characters and situations they portrayed on stage all demanded cleverness, for an inspired "touch of mind" often had to compensate for an empty pocket. Just as Kwaku Ananse transformed a kernel of corn into a chicken, or a sheep into a cow, concert actors transformed cooking charcoal into pancake makeup and burnt matchsticks into eyeliner. One lady impersonator had an ingenious method of using blackboard chalk to create jewelry: He would grind a stick of chalk into powder, make a paste, dab the powder on the end of a comb, and then carefully imprint the teeth of the comb on his neck. Voilà! A beaded necklace.

Colonial-era concert actors took ideas from movies, gramophone records, songbooks, migrant workers, local rumors, and international scandals and then turned these "borrowed" sources into something new. Veteran artists often use the verb "to pick" when describing their creative process.[6] Bob S. Ansah told me he would read music albums and watch religious cantatas and the movies of Charlie Chaplin, Al Jolson, and Sammy Davis Jr. in order to "pick something out of it" and then "we form a play" (Ansah #93.10). Ansah explains, "Whenever you have love for something, immediately you see it, you pick it. Then we try to make something out of it."

The process of making a concert involves not only "picking," but choosing. According to I. K. Ntama:

> We start by rehearsing. Kwaku will bring a story, Acquaah will bring a story, and I will bring a story. Now, you have to narrate your story, and Acquaah narrates his. And then we pick, you see? Anything that has happened before, any story. . . . We join it, you see. We put pieces together so that it becomes one good story. If it isn't good, we have to delete it. But if it's good, then we put it in. (Ntama #95.41)

Once ideas have been picked, then actors' roles are cast according to their individual talents and character types. Kwame Mbia Hammond explains:

> We copy some of the plays from books, you see. . . . We take some act, then stories of Charlie Chaplin. We grab in general from anybody called comedians. Then we ourselves, we sit down and then we share the characters. "You are fine, you take this part. You are ugly, take this part. You resemble a female, you take this part." Because if there is one fit for the old man, and you give him the part of the woman to play, it's not natural. See? You will spoil the whole show. (Hammond #93.6)

A concert party is thus a collage of sources and a collaboration of talents. Practitioners make deliberate choices of inclusion and exclusion. Good ideas are appropriated and incorporated, while unsuitable material is "deleted." While few actors articulate the aesthetic basis upon which such choices are made, most have great clarity about their personal distinction between "good" and "bad" material.

Before actors put a particular idea on stage, they would "polish" it. Augustus Williams learned foreign dance steps by reading newspapers and books on dancing. "After reading them, I had to change them, to polish them up," said Williams (#95.52). When an important event happened in colonial Ghana, such as a murder trial or chieftaincy dispute, Bob S. Ansah and his colleagues would "polish it in a way, then form a dialogue with it, and put it up. So it becomes natural" (#93.10). Polishing source material is more than a process of refinement: Polishing produces a fundamental transformation. A borrowed idea is reborn as a unique creation.

"I will see people who dance," recalled Augustus Williams. "And I was a dancer. So I tried to copy them. I took all. Then I *put in my own!*" (emphasis mine; #95.52). "Putting in one's own" was an essential part of the process, for it was the means by which imported ideas became domesticated, personalized, and original.[7] Bob S. Ansah would "put in his own" whenever he learned new dance steps. As a child, Ansah helped his uncle when he threw parties: "I took the business of playing the gramophone for them. I changed the records: fox trot, blues, waltz" (Ansah #93.10). After learning foreign songs and dances from the gramophone, he "tried to coin a lot of different dances. All types of dances, such as even native dances. I coin it, polish it, and then you see me using it on stage." When Ansah "coined" his dances, he was remaking received African, American, and African American dance steps into distinctive, personalized choreography.

Like the jazz musicians interviewed by Paul Berliner in his book *Thinking in Jazz: The Infinite Art of Improvisation,* concert actors filter through their imaginations myriad inflections, personalities, voices, and techniques (1994, 204). Each performance is part of an extended conversation, layered with associations which may be known only to the performer, and even he himself may forget what inspired a particular gesture, joke, or facial expression. The degree to which concert parties are embroidered with fragments of conversations long forgotten was clear when I worked with the Jaguar Jokers on transcribing the lyrics to their "signature tune." Y. B. Bampoe and K. Acquaah Hammond were unable to remember the lyrics without actually standing up and doing all the hand motions and dance steps of their routine. Their embodied knowledge of the song was far more reliable than their oral recollections. When we finally did piece together the lyrics, I discovered that the song was peppered with expressions from different cultures and historical eras: a fragment from a Ga *kolomashie* song from the 1940s, private expressions known only to the Jaguar Jokers, slang from India that Bampoe's uncle learned when he served in Burma during World War II, and Kru expressions from Liberian stevedores.

Inasmuch as polishing involves an incremental repetition of tropes and idioms, it is a form of signifying, a cultural practice common among African Americans. Like the artists studied by Henry Louis Gates Jr. in *The Signifying Monkey,* concert party practitioners stress not *what* they borrow, but rather *how* they transform it, for play and individual artistry are often far more important than the ostensible "meanings" embedded in content (1988, 70, 52). In concerts, the play *is* the thing. Consequently, among many concert actors, my scholarly project of carefully parsing out their sources was really beside the point. Indeed, actors often deliberately obscure their sources. When I asked Y. B. Bampoe if he studied the films of Charlie Chaplin, he said, "Yes, I am staging in his line. But I don't tell people" (Bampoe and Hammond #95.55). When I asked Bob S. Ansah *how* he incorporated Ananse stories into concerts, he said these stories underwent such a radical adaptation that "when we come out with it in a play, it becomes different. You will never know that it's an Ananse story we are forming" (#93.10).

For a more detailed examination of how the practice of repetition and revision actually works, I turn now to the character "Opia," the signature persona of Y. B. Bampoe (fig. 18). Bampoe is among the second generation of professional concert party performers, since his career began in the 1950s. However, Bampoe was trained by concert pioneers of the 1930s and 1940s such as Bob Johnson and Charlie Turpin of the Axim Trio. Since performance techniques used by this earlier generation were never documented and most of them are now deceased, recollections by their apprentices such as Bampoe are a primary link to this important aspect of concert history.

In order to create the stock persona Opia, Y. B. Bampoe, leader of the Jaguar Jokers, says he combined Charlie Chaplin, Bob Johnson, and Ananse (Bampoe and Hammond #95.55). Like a resourceful chef, Bampoe cooked up his signature character out of ingredients readily at hand: He took some ideas from Hollywood's Little Tramp, whose movies were often screened in Bampoe's boyhood town of Suhum during World War II. He was most impressed by Chaplin's physical comedy, his ability to convey humor through expressive eye movements and subtle body language. Bampoe plundered additional creative material from concert elder Bob Johnson, who developed the stock persona Bob, the houseboy in concert plays who usually appeared in blackface makeup (fig. 19). Although "Bob" was illiterate, he would usually turn out to be the most clever character in the show. Finally, Opia lifted character attributes and even whole stories from Ananse, the fabled Akan trickster.

Although elements of Opia can be traced directly to Charlie Chaplin, Bob Johnson, and Ananse, Bampoe so reformulated his sources that his public does not recognize Opia as anything other than Bampoe's own creation. Indeed, Bampoe deliberately obscures his sources. In the first two years I knew him, Bampoe never mentioned Ananse in connection with Opia. But when I studied Ananse tales, the affinity between the notorious Akan spider and Opia became clear. Both characters are driven by selfish appetites which have anti-social consequences. When Opia first appears in the Jaguar Jokers play *Onipa Hia Moa,* he is fleeing his wife, who is chasing him with a stick because he stole their children's food, a crime for which Ananse is frequently found guilty. Later in the play, when Opia meets a drunkard, he regales him with a drinking song in the hopes of getting a free drink. And when Opia's friend Kofi is on the brink of death, he literally steals food from a dying man (Jaguar Jokers 1995a and 1995b).

Like Opia, Kwaku Ananse is notorious for his obsession with food. Sandy Arkhurst of the School of Performing Arts at the University of Ghana says, "As far as food is concerned, [Ananse] has no consideration for his family. He will work [on the farm] with his family, wife, and children, and when the food is ready to be harvested, he will scheme nicely and eat everything. He will pretend he is dead. [His family will] bury him on the farm. Then in the night he will get up and prepare food and eat. He will finish everything [all the food growing on the farm]. Ananse is like that" (#95.58). Ananse is, by nature, greedy and ravenous. He will satisfy his own desires, even to the detriment of his family. In another story, Ananse attends the funeral of his mother-in-law, and he publicly pretends to fast in observance of mourning custom. But surreptitiously he hides boiled beans under his hat for occasional snacking. As the hot beans begin to scorch him, Ananse shakes his head. When his wife asks what is wrong, Ananse makes up an preposterous excuse about having to rush off to a "hat-shaking festival" in his father's village (Rattray 1930, 118–125).

While I was in Ghana in 1994–1995, I saw this Ananse "hat-shaking" story appear in a much altered form in a concert party called "The Wedding Day," which Bampoe's troupe, the Jaguar Jokers, performed at the National Theatre. In this play, Opia disgraces himself on his wedding day by hiding fish, pepper, *kenkey,* and ice water in his suit and under his hat.[8] When *kenkey* rolls on the floor in the middle of the ceremony and Opia is caught, he defends himself by saying to the congregation and minister that he knew they were going to sing Twi hymn number 264, which is very long, and surely he would get hungry before it was over. Bampoe derived this story idea from *ananseɛm,* but he changed the Ananse "hat-shaking" story so radically that spectators would not recognize the connection.

I once directly asked Bampoe if Opia was based on Ananse. Ever the trickster, he diverted the whole conversation by *telling* me *anansesɛm.* He told various Ananse stories and then condemned Ananse for his greediness (perhaps commenting through Akan *akutia,* or indirection, on my own ravenous appetite for information).[9] I brought the conversation back to my original question: "Is Opia the same as Ananse?" I asked. Bampoe and his stage partner Acquaah Hammond burst into laughter.

> *Bampoe:* Opia is there, but I have some difference.
> *CC:* Some difference.
> *Bampoe:* Some difference.
> *Braun:*[10] What is the difference?
> *Bampoe:* Opia is a human being. And Ananse is an animal.
> (*Bampoe and Hammond laugh*)
> *Braun:* That's the only difference.
> *CC:* That's the difference.
> (*All laugh*)
> *Bampoe:* And I'm not greedy.
> *CC:* You're not greedy?
> *Bampoe:* No.
> *CC:* But you like food?
> *Bampoe:* Yes. I like food. But I'm not greedy. I like food on the stage. But I . . .
>   Ananse . . . it's his character . . .
> *Hammond:* . . . habitual . . .
> *Bampoe:* . . . character. He always cheats.
> *CC:* He always cheats. Does Opia cheat?
> *Bampoe:* Opia cheats, but not as Kwaku Ananse.
> (*Hammond laughs*)
> *CC:* Kwaku Ananse is bad.
> *Hammond:* Oh yeah.
> *Bampoe:* Kwaku Ananse!
> *Hammond:* Kwaku Ananse! Greedy! With sense.
> *CC:* Ohia ma adwennwen.
> *Hammond:* Ohia ma adwennwen paa. (Bampoe and Hammond #95.55)

While Opia is very much like Ananse, there are important differences. Akan traditions of creativity emphasize not where ideas come from but how well the artist manages to put in his own unique variations. Bampoe is widely recognized as a master of such innovations. Like Ananse himself, Bampoe has a voracious appetite for ideas that belong to others. He is greedy for such material, but he uses it with sense, transforming something borrowed into something new through *ad-wennwen*.

Making a concert party is a fundamentally improvisational process, requiring an in-the-moment manipulation of received structures and idioms and a personal expression of wit. A concert depends upon "actions from the actor's own initiatives," according to comedian Waterproof (GCPU #95.54). Hammond and Bampoe concur that actors must bring "variations":

> *Hammond:* There are some jokes which you will bring in, of which it's not in the show, but with a touch of mind, you will bring it in.
> *CC:* So you will be doing the show, and then the idea will come.
> *Hammond:* Yes!
> *Bampoe:* By itself. Variation.
> *Hammond:* Touch of mind. Your mind should work fast, fast, fast. (Bampoe and Hammond #95.55)

"Variation" is the word actors use to describe live, spontaneously inspired improvisations. They contrast this creative process with that used by actors who work from written scripts. Actors in "dramas"—as written plays are called—"must conform to the writer's directives," according to Bob S. Ansah. "If the writer directs that you must move the left leg at a given time of the show, and you move the right leg, you spoil the whole show" (GCPU #95.54). Concert actors believe that their form of theatre requires far more ingenuity on the part of every participant than does scripted drama.

In the realm of textuality, the Ghanaian concert party contrasts markedly with similar theatre in Nigeria. According to Karin Barber, Yorùbá popular traveling theatre, while largely improvised and unscripted, nevertheless aspires to the condition of writing (1995). When actors from the Adéjọbí company talked to Barber about the production process, none of them "stressed the oral, improvisatory, collaborative and expansive aspects of their work. Instead they all insisted on the idea of authorship and writing" (1995, 17). Ghanaian concert party actors, on the other hand, eschew writing, for they say texts inhibit their creative process. Scripts are believed to reduce an actor's freedom to make "additions and subtractions here and there to suit the taste of the audience" (Charlotte Obeng Kakra at GCPU #95.54). Like the Yorùbá traveling theatre studied by Karin Barber (1995, 12, 18), concert parties do sometimes use a one-page plot synopsis during rehearsals. Concert actors also use an educational vocabulary of instruction and correction in perfecting their plays. For instance, if a performance is not "correct," then "mistakes" must be identified and "deleted." Such schoolroom-inspired English words are frequently inserted into Twi sentences.

Among concert actors, writing has many negative connotations, some of which emanate from experiences in colonial classrooms. An instructor from the Presbyterian Girls' School in Aburi wrote in 1934 that the school's most successful dramatic "experiments" were those in which

> pupils were given a story and asked to dramatise it, either in the vernacular or in English. It was found, naturally, that they are apt to enlarge and elaborate the play in a disconcerting manner when they are on the stage. For this reason, it is advisable that plays should always be written out. This provides a good composition exercise, whether in English or in the vernacular, and the acting is more controlled. (McKillican 1934, 219)[11]

In colonial schools, dramatic texts were used as a means of control, a way of curbing the alarming propensity of students to embroider and elaborate on the platform, for such flourishes were seen by instructors as aesthetically undesirable. Ironically, it is precisely this tendency to improvise and extend ideas that is highly valued among the Akan.

The dichotomy that developed in the colonial years between improvised concert parties and scripted drama has had a long-lasting insidious impact on theatre in Ghana through today. In 1994–1995, there were two actors' unions in Ghana: the Ghana Concert Parties Union for actors who do non-scripted plays in Ghanaian languages, and the Actors Guild for those who do written plays in English. One concert actress told me she had initially joined the Actors Guild, but the union alienated "those of us who perform plays in Ghanaian languages because their shows were in English. Even at our meetings, the only language used was English, and they look down on those of us who spoke Ghanaian languages" (GCPU #95.54). Language was at the heart of the colonial enterprise and the power hierarchies embedded in colonial languages continue to have a palpable impact on artistic practices in Ghana even forty years after independence.

Concert artists do not hold actors of scripted Anglophone dramas in high regard, for these actors can only "chew, pour, and forget," as Moses K. Oppong explained to me. "You will learn the thing from the book. According to what they have written in the book. You don't leave [out] even one word. You chew in your mind, and you go to the stage, and you pour it to the people. Then off . . . you forget" (Oppong and Oppong #95.40). Not only will an actor who has learned her lines from a book forget at some later date what she said, but the audience will also forget. To illustrate this point, Oppong pointed out that when I came to visit him in Aboso, the people of the town recognized me from a televised show in which I had appeared with the Jaguar Jokers Concert Party. Townspeople of Aboso identified me with my most memorable line, *"Opia ɔnyare! Ɔnyare koraa!"* ("Opia is not sick! He's not sick at all!"). Mnemonic tags such as *"Opia ɔnyare!"* not only help performers navigate through complex and changeable plots, they help spectators to remember and repeat what they have seen. The Jaguar Jokers had very consciously crafted this line knowing that *"Opia ɔnyare!"* would become the landmark phrase by which my character and the play would be remembered. Such phrases are crucial to a concert troupe's word-of-mouth advertisement when spectators later discuss the show at school, in the market, or in the office, at the beauty salon, in the fitter's shop, or at the lorry park.

Among concert artists in colonial Ghana, embodied, spontaneous, improvised innovations were essential not only to performances on stage, but also to the challenges of everyday life. When troupes went on trek in the 1930s and 1940s, in each town they would devise ways to borrow boards from a lumber yard to build a stage, secure free food from adoring women, and elicit complimentary services from the school brass band who would "campaign" for them in town. Performance was a strategy for survival, for the very same skills actors used on stage they also used to negotiate the pragmatics of life on trek.

One veteran performer, Bob S. Ansah, had an ingenious strategy for obtaining the school band. Whenever he set out on that particular errand, Y. B. Bampoe recalls, he would dress neatly: "He put on a suit and walked majestically to the school. Teachers and pupils alike took him for a school inspector" (CPMR #95.27). School inspectors were dreaded and powerful colonial officials. In the novel *This Earth, My Brother,* Kofi Awoonor writes, "The history of colonial education is one long war between the young and arrogant white school inspector and the teachers" (1972, 37).[12] When Bob Ansah reached the schoolgrounds, he would ask some child in English, "Where is the schoolmaster?" He would be taken to the schoolmaster, and the two would sit across from each other at a table. Ansah would then explain his mission using highly mannered and peculiar English: "Weeee thu goco too baaaabs, 'n' we puddin' 'p a shoooo t'naaat. . . ." The school master would say nothing, but just stare, for he had no idea what Ansah was saying. The schoolchildren would watch closely to see if their master could understand English. After a pause, the schoolmaster would say, "Pardon?," which provoked titters and whispers among the schoolchildren: *"Hwε! Teacher no ɔnti borofo!"* ("Look! The teacher doesn't understand English!"). Ansah would repeat his bizarre sentence, and the teacher would again be forced to beg his pardon. Finally Ansah would speak in perfectly clear English: "We are the Gold Coast Two Bobs, and we're putting up a show tonight, and we need the school band for concert." The schoolmaster would be so relieved to understand Ansah's English and to save face in front of his students that he would immediately summon the band and offer their instruments for the concert party, free of charge.

Like Tortoise in the song *"Ohia Ma Adwennwen"* analyzed in the previous chapter, Ansah assumed a role in everyday life for strategic purposes. Whereas Tortoise pretended he was a ritual expert in order to trick Monkey into transporting him back to the ground, Ansah assumed the role of a school inspector in order to con the headmaster into lending his concert party band instruments. Both Tortoise and Ansah played upon the prejudices of those with whom they were negotiating: Tortoise capitalized on the distinction Monkey habitually made between animals who live on the ground and the supposedly superior beings who live in trees. Ansah likewise exploited the headmaster's desire to privilege English culture and language over Akan.

Whether performing on the "platform" or in life on the road, concert actors utilized well-established conventions of Akan creativity and invention. They used performance skills, improvisation, repetition, and revision to transform existing structures, idioms, narratives, prejudices, and tropes into fresh material. Any aspect of life in colonial Ghana was grist for their creative mill: comic scenarios from American movies, arguments encountered by chance in the street, habitual behaviors of school inspectors, music riffs from popular ballads, makeup from everyday household items, and story elements from *anansesɛm*. By way of performance, concert artists refashioned eclectic source material into shows perceived to be original creations. Each artist would "put in his own" unique variations and improvisational inspirations, "just to make the whole thing interesting." While the source material used in concert parties was far more wide-ranging than what one might have found in "traditional" performance genres, the creative principles guiding the process of invention of concert actors were entirely consonant with those used in storytelling, proverb usage, and festival celebrations. This is why most people in Ghana today interpret the concert party to be a genre "of our own origin," as Y. B. Bampoe argues (Bampoe and Hammond #95.55). Inspiration for early colonial-era concert parties clearly came from imported as well as domestic sources. But throughout concert history actors have "put in" African culture side by side with imported material "to tell African stories by way of performing" (Bampoe and Hammond #95.55). Like practitioners of fújì music and praise poetry in Nigeria, concert artists domesticated difference so thoroughly that their source material was fundamentally altered in the process, rendering all simplistic binary models of analysis utterly ineffectual (Barber and Waterman 1995).

Creating Trios in the 1930s and 1940s

Keeping these general principles of Akan creativity in mind, let us now consider a particularly formative moment of concert party history, the time when the "trio" format of concerts appeared in the 1930s and 1940s. While amateur concerts had been performed in the coastal cities of the Gold Coast for the first three decades of the twentieth century, it was not until school boys from Sekondi and Axim took to the stage in the 1930s that concerts underwent a thorough renovation. The students, now perceived to be the "founding fathers" of the concert party form as it is known today, highjacked the amateur theatricals they learned in school and turned such entertainments into a viable profession. To the conventional English songs and dialogues, they added African languages. They blended imported characters from England and Liberia with homegrown tricksters. And when they took their shows on the road, these young men made concerts available for the first time to working-class and village audiences as well as to the educated urbanites who had patronized amateur concerts during previous decades. The two most famous troupes from the 1930s were the Two Bobs and Their Carolina Girl, based in Sekondi, and the Axim Trio from Axim. These two groups created the "trio" format that was to dominate concert party stages for the subsequent thirty years.

The Two Bobs began with Bob Johnson and his classmates at the Methodist School in Sekondi. When they first formed in 1927, they were known as the "Versatile Eight." The idea for this group sprang not only from impromptu restagings of Empire Day concerts but also from an itinerant solo comedian named Teacher Yalley who performed at the Optimism Club in Sekondi, an African establishment located directly across the street from the Methodist School. By watching and assisting Yalley, Johnson and his mates learned new routines. "My friends and I were very thrilled with those performances," said Johnson. "C. B. Hutton [*sic*] was given a chance to play the drum. Very soon we decided to start performing ourselves and did" (Sutherland 1970, 7). The Versatile Eight appeared at the Optimism Club on several occasions (Versatile Eight 1929a, 1929b, 1930). They soon got the idea of taking their shows on the road. Bob Johnson recalls, "During the holidays we would go as far as Axim, forty-seven miles west of Sekondi, and give performances for which we charged entrance fees of 6d and 3d" (Sutherland 1970, 7).

Meanwhile, in Axim, a similar group known as the Six Stars also began doing concerts for profit. Comprised of students from the Axim Methodist School, the troupe's core members were Charlie Turpin, known as "the Charlie Chaplin of Axim," E. K. Dadson, who had "a voice like Jimmy Rodgers," and a man named Abraham (Zynenwartel n.d.; *Gold Coast Times* 1932a). Like the Versatile Eight, the Six Stars toured neighboring towns. They "stormed Axim, Esiama, Atwabu and Half Assini constantly with their usual enchanting shows" (*Gold Coast Times* 1932a). The Six Stars eventually dwindled to three members, and around 1931 they renamed themselves the Axim Trio. Also at this time, the membership of the Versatile Eight shrank to three key actors: J. B. Ansah, Charles Horton, and Bob Johnson, and they too changed their name, calling themselves The Two Bobs and Their Carolina Girl.

The Axim Trio and the Two Bobs and Their Carolina Girl created the classic "trio" format which consisted of three stock roles: the Lady, the Gentleman, and the Houseboy (fig. 16).[13] The Lady was a "school girl," an African woman with formal education whose breeding, refinement, and exposure to Western ways often initiated the central conflict of the play (Ansah #93.10). Her husband, the Gentleman, was also an affluent African with formal education. The Houseboy was an illiterate whose comic antics undermined his master's pretensions. From 1930 through 1950, every concert party was a trio. Among them were the Gold Coast Two Bobs, Happy Trio, Dix Covian Jokers, West End Trio, Keta Trio, Saltpond Trio, Jovial Jokers, Burma Jokers, and Yankey Trio (Collins 1976a, 52). Even when troupes expanded from three to more than twenty actors in the 1950s, many concerts continued to incorporate the original three stock characters into their plays.

Trio shows would begin around 8:00 P.M. and typically had a three-part structure. They commenced with an opening chorus in which the three actors sang their group's signature tune, followed by a short duet or comic monologue. Then came the "dialogue," or the main dramatic sketch. The whole evening lasted somewhere between forty-five minutes and two hours, depending on the venue and circumstances of performance.[14] For the opening chorus, two men appeared on stage in uniform costume with the lady impersonator positioned in between them (figs. 20 and 21). The trio sang three-part harmony songs they called "ragtimes," meaning in this context tunes from abroad, accompanied by a trap drum and a pump organ. The Gold Coast Bobs sang:

> Good even', mame ooo
> Good even', papa ooo
> Down deep way by the moonlight bay,
> By the moonlight bay,
> On the evening I heard
> By the moon, love made it play . . .
> Yokahuna, yokadoo, yokahuna, yokadoo.
> Yokahuna, yokadoo, yokahuna, yokadoo. (Ansah #93.10)

The Gold Coast Two Bobs had special choreographed movements to accompany this trademark opening chorus. When the opening chorus was over, one of the actors would go offstage to change costume while the other two sang a duet to a tune such as "The Cat and the Fiddle" (Ansah #93.10; Hammond #93.6). These opening numbers were occasions for actors to display their talent at foreign dance steps. What was prized even more than talent was mastery. Audiences flocked to see E. K. Dadson of the Axim Trio because he was known as a "first class" ballroom dancer, a master of "ballroom etiquette" (Adams and Amoah #93.8; Vans #95.33).

The dramatic "dialogue" came next. Trio concert parties had a very limited repertoire of characters and scenarios, with some actors doubling in more than one part. The plots usually revolved around either the husband's or the wife's infidelity. In the play *Afei Menu Moho* (*Had I Known*) performed by the Two Bobs and Their Carolina Girl in 1934, the husband takes up with a "good-time" girl when his wife travels to visit her family (Sutherland 1970, 13–14). Another play portrayed the plight of an illiterate man who marries an educated woman. When he is at work, his wife entertains a lover in the house. But one day her husband unexpectedly comes home at midday, and the woman frantically hides her lover. A comic farce ensues in which the husband eventually discovers the hidden boyfriend.

There were many variations of this story, as each troupe "picked" and "polished" the core idea.[15] Sometimes the woman hid her boyfriend under a table, which she then covered with a cloth. When the husband asked what was under the table, the woman said it was a new radio. The husband was delighted. According to Adelaide Amegatcher, he would then say he

> wanted to listen to his new radio. But since he did not know how to operate it, he
> left that to his wife to do. The girl bent over and whispered to the lover under the
> table "radio speak," and immediately the man under the table started running a
> football commentary. After the commentary, he read the news, and followed
> this with a series of songs. The husband was very thrilled; he was so thrilled that
> he decided to spend half of his time around the house listening to the radio.
> (1968, 36)

However when the husband later tried to move the table, he discovered the boy-friend and his wife's infidelity.

In other versions of this story, the boyfriend hides in a water barrel, a cocoa sack, or a laundry basket. In the water barrel version, the husband inadvertently pours water on the boyfriend. In the cocoa sack and laundry basket versions, the husband unknowingly carries the boyfriend on his head. As the husband, who is a washman by trade, struggles to carry the laundry basket to the river, he cries out in pidgin English, *"Woman palaver e hard oo!!"* ("Women's problems are difficult!"). Then the boyfriend on top cries out, *"Ay be so, I dey for top o!"* ("This is why I am on top here!").[16] This call and response happens several times. The husband, mystified, keeps asking, "Who is responding to me?" He finally lowers the laundry basket and uncovers the boyfriend hidden inside.

Concert party trio scenarios were highly formulaic, varying only slightly from one troupe to the next. Many of the stories revolved around issues of infidelity, changes in family life due to Western influences, and conflicts endemic to the three key characters—the Lady, Gentleman, and Houseboy. Since these stock roles were so consistent from one troupe to the next, and so central to concert party plays, their significance and the self-consciously presentational style in which they were performed on stage demands further scrutiny. Why did concert parties of this period so explicitly emphasize role playing? Why these particular stereotypes? What did African audiences get out of watching these shows?

One of the most important characters in concert trios was the Houseboy, a role historically associated with its best-known innovator, Bob Johnson. According to Johnson, the Houseboy was a servant who would "make trouble" between his masters (Sutherland 1970, 8). A notoriously troublesome figure, he was nicknamed "Master *no deh*" ["Master not there"]. K. Acquaah Hammond explains, "When the Master is in the house, the Boy obeys him. When the Master is out, and the Madam tells him anything to do, he refuses. So we start singing, 'Master *no deh,* Boy *e deh!*'" (Bampoe and Hammond #93.11).

The Houseboy's insolent and mischievous temperament can be seen in the following trio story.[17] A man marries an educated Lady, and since "Ladies" do not do housework, the couple decides to hire a Houseboy. The husband instructs the Boy to cook and fetch water for the woman's bath. But when the husband leaves for work and the wife orders the Boy to prepare her bath, he refuses. The Boy says, "If the master is not in the house, then *I* am the master of the house." He tells the Lady to go fetch her own water. The two quarrel, and during the argument, the Boy insinuates that she is only a housemaid, that her husband has a real wife elsewhere. The Lady becomes furious. When her husband comes home, she accuses him of infidelity, storms out of the house, and returns to her family. Meanwhile the actor playing the Houseboy changes costume and becomes the wife's aunt, a "Cloth Woman," that is, a woman who wears Ghanaian cloth in a *cabah* or simple wrap style rather than a Western-style dress. Her clothing was supposed to indicate her illiteracy and lack of formal Western education.

The aunt advises her niece to return to her husband. The wife complies, returns home, and everything is peaceful for a time. But soon the Houseboy sows new seeds of discord. One day the wife goes out to collect a dress from her seamstress. When the husband comes home from work and finds his wife gone, he asks the Houseboy where his wife has gone. With feigned reluctance, the Houseboy answers, "Oh, I'm very, very sorry. A gentleman with a Pontiac car has taken her away. Master, don't you know that she is having another husband. They always come here and they go. They always come here and then they go. But I'm afraid to say anything. I'm afraid to report." The husband is furious. When his wife returns, he angrily confronts her. A heated argument erupts between them, but their disagreement cannot be resolved because each has an entirely different perception of what is going on.

So they call the Houseboy. The wife asks him whether anybody came to the house to pick her up in a car. The Boy says, "No." Then the husband asks, "Isn't it you who told me that somebody came here to pick my wife away?" The Boy answers, "Yes." The husband and wife press him further: How can he answer both "no" and "yes"? Then the Houseboy tells the couple that he has got two mouths: "The upper one says 'yes' and the down one says 'no.'" Exasperated with his doublespeak, the couple chase the Houseboy away from their house.[18]

The actor playing the Houseboy then changes costume and becomes the old aunt again. The aunt advises the couple that the only way they will have a successful marriage is if they "dispense" with houseboys. She counsels: "You are a woman; do a woman's thing. You are a man; do the man. So you, woman, you are to go to the kitchen and do all your things yourself. And you man, go to your job." The play concludes with the song "*Skuul maame* no good o!":

Wɔnhwɛ, skuul maame no good o.	Look, an educated woman isn't good.
Wɔnhwɛ, skuul maame no good o.	Look, an educated woman isn't good.
I tell you,	I tell you,
Wɔnhwɛ, skuul maame no good o	An educated woman isn't good.
If you follow them,	If you follow them,
They no go follow you.	They won't follow you.
I tell you,	I tell you,
Wɔnhwɛ, skuul maame no good o.	Look, an educated woman isn't good.
I tell you,	I tell you,
Wɔnhwɛ, skuul maame no good o.	An educated woman isn't good.[19]
(CPMR #95.28)	

A *skuul maame,* a woman with formal education, is not good because she is fickle in love. The song admonishes, "If you follow them, they won't follow you." This advice seems somewhat misplaced in the case of this play since the wife was not, in fact, guilty of any romantic infidelity. The problem of the play emanated rather from the Houseboy who invented tales that created misunderstanding and animosity between the husband and wife. The aunt, who represents the play's moral, says that in order to restore matrimonial peace, the couple must get rid of the Houseboy and conform to expected gender roles: The man should go to his job and the woman should work at home.

So what message did this trio play convey? Was the aunt advocating a return to pre-colonial traditions? In Akan culture, which is matrilineal, the family is defined based upon blood rather than marriage. Within this system, women traditionally have had much more financial autonomy than have women in the West. Husbands and wives generally do not pool their monetary resources, and many Akan women invest their money in independent business ventures such as trading foodstuffs in the market (Clark 1994). Thus, there is nothing necessarily "traditional" about a woman staying home to do housework. But when an Akan woman works outside the home, she is still expected to provide for her husband domestic services such as cooking, washing, and cleaning. As a woman matures, some of these tasks can be delegated to children and maids (Clark 1994, 108). In the "Pontiac car" concert party, the wife's failure to do her own domestic chores was morally reprehensible because she is too young to delegate these duties. Ladies in concert trios were notorious for adamantly refusing to do housework, and such refusals did indeed fly in the face of Akan conventions.

At first glance, such trio plays may appear as allegories of colonial power. The Lady and Gentleman seem to represent British identity, and the Houseboy could be read as the voice of the colonized, oppressed "subaltern." Yet such a reading misses deeper issues of significance. Concert trios were indeed subversive of colonial ideologies, but their subversions were indirect, realized by means of performance rather than explicitly stated in narratives, dialogue, and dramatic structure.

Concert trio scenarios have several parallels with the African American signifying monkey tale analyzed by Henry Louis Gates in *The Signifying Monkey* (1988). Just as the Monkey is the smallest animal in a triadic relationship with the stock characters Lion and Elephant, the Houseboy appears to be the least powerful figure in a trio with the Lady and Gentleman (Gates 1988, 56). Both the Monkey and the Houseboy undermine the power of their superiors by inciting them to fight. Whereas the Monkey uses verbal tricks to reverse the Lion's status (he repeats insults that the Elephant supposedly spoke against the Lion's closest relatives), the Houseboy uses innuendo. In the "Pontiac car" trio scenario analyzed above, the Houseboy insinuates to both the Lady and the Gentleman that the other spouse is having an adulterous affair. In the signifying monkey tale, the Monkey undermines the Lion by using what Gates calls "double-voiced" discourse. He uses figurative statements that the Lion interprets literally. The Houseboy, on the other hand, escapes from his situation by explicitly claiming to have two mouths, "the upper one and the lower one." The Houseboy is "double-voiced" on another level as well, inasmuch as the actor playing this role doubles as the aunt, the voice of the play's moral message.

Gates argues that it is a mistake to interpret the signifying monkey tales as a simple allegory about black political oppression because this imposes a binary opposition on a tale with the trinary forces of the Monkey, the Lion, and the Elephant. Gates asserts that signifying "encompasses a larger domain than merely the political. It is a game of language, independent of reaction to white racism or even to collective black wish-fulfillment vis-à-vis white racism" (1988, 55, 70). I would submit that we should similarly resist reading the concert party trio as a straightforward allegory about colonialism. The Houseboy cannot be read as the colonized Gold Coast "native," for this character was actually a Kru from Liberia, a character more "alien" to Gold Coast audiences than either the Lady or the Gentleman. The Lady and Gentleman, however Anglicized, were at least Akans, and therefore far more "native" to the Gold Coast than the Houseboy. In order to interpret the significance of the three stock trio roles, we must pay attention to *how* these roles were performed, for the style of enactment by particular actors conveys deeper meaning.

When concert parties incorporated the Kru Houseboy into their shows, they used a familiar imported stereotype. The Liberian Kru are a seafaring ethnic group, and their labor was essential to West African maritime commerce in the nineteenth and early twentieth centuries (Brooks 1972). All along the Guinea Coast, Krus worked as sailors, carpenters, cooks, stevedores, traders, and artisans. Coastal cities such as Sekondi and Accra had neighborhoods designated as "Kroo Towns." Dennis Kemp, who lived in Cape Coast in the late nineteenth century, wrote that Krus were so ubiquitous and essential to the coastal economy that it was difficult to imagine "what would become of the West African trade if these labourers went out 'on strike'" (1898, 207). Kru men were known for speaking Pidgin English, eating rice, making music, cracking jokes, and carrying night soil.[20] Kru laborers reportedly insulted Gold Coast Africans by saying in Pidgin English, *"You be bushman too much, you 'chop' kassada and koko; me no be bushman, me chop lice (rice)"* (Kemp 1898, 207–208). The stereotypical Kru man's predilection for Pidgin English and rice was often satirized in concert trios. When the Gentleman would shout, "Boy, where are you?" the Houseboy would answer in Pidgin, *"Me, I deh come!"* (Bampoe and Hammond #93.11). A sketch by Two Bobs and Their Carolina Girl featured two Liberian stevedores who would come on stage with a huge iron pot of rice. They would place the pot between them, and they would eye each other suspiciously across the pot:

> Each Bob carried an oversize spoon which was well worn to show much use. The pot is supposed to contain rice. The Two Bobs know their audiences are very familiar with the jokes about 'kroo boys,' that is Liberian stevedores, and their passionate love of rice. Rice eating was supposed to be such a serious business among them that even friendship was in danger should eating partners not keep strict rules for eating one's fair share only (Sutherland 1970, 10).

The two Bobs would then sing a version of Cab Calloway's song "Minnie the Moocher," with lyrics in English, Fante, and Calloway's scat phrases.

	Cab Calloway's version	Two Bobs' version
Call:	Ho de ho de ho	Ho di-ho di-ho
Response:	Ho de ho de ho	Yiidzi yiidzi emo
		(*We're eating eating rice*)
Call:	Rah dah dah	Ra da da-a
Response:	Rah dah dah	Ra da da-a

Call:	Tee dee dee	Tsi-bi-dzi (*Eat your share*)
Response:	Tee dee dee	Woso tsi-bi dzi
		(*You too eat your share*)
Call:	But Minnie had a heart	But Mini had a heart
	as big as a whale.	as big as a whale.
	(Warner Brothers	(Sutherland 1970, 10)
	1985, 343)	

The last two lines would be sung with exaggerated grins, as each Bob tried to discourage the other from being too greedy. This "Minnie the Moocher" sketch captured and domesticated difference: The characters were Liberian, the song they sang was African American, and some of the lyrics to their song were in English. But concert actors also put in Fante variations, transforming nonsense scat phrases into meaningful Akan sentences.

The Houseboy, or "Bob," character has been a standard feature of concert parties from 1930 to the present. Over the years, actors interpreted the Bob differently, as they took received ideas from Ananse, Al Jolson, Kru migrants, and Charlie Chaplin and rendered them "anew in unexpected ways" (Gates 1988, 61). Bob Johnson performed the Houseboy by wearing highly idiosyncratic makeup: He painted a white line down his nose, white circles on his cheeks, and a white rim around his lips (fig. 16). He had a long mustache that jutted out from his nose like whiskers on a cat. Johnson wore a tail coat, a scarf, and loose calico pantaloons. His shoes were of two different colors and his belly bulged like a pregnant woman's. Johnson's shoes were inspired by Charlie Chaplin.[21] Johnson's stuffed stomach may very well have derived from *anansesɛm;* for Ananse is said to have a big belly both because he is a spider and because he is so obsessed with food. In 1946, Y. B. Bampoe and his friends imitated the performances they had seen by the Two Bobs, the Axim Trio, and other touring troupes (fig. 12). Bampoe and his brother stuffed their bellies, as Johnson had done, and they wore bow ties, like the Axim Trio. But their makeup was inspired by the Dix Covian Jokers, who, in turn, seem to have copied from Al Jolson (figs. 6 and 7).

This photographic genealogy of the "Bobs" between 1930 and 1946 demonstrates the creative process of repetition and revision through which concert artists made their art. They selected elements from Ananse, American movies, and fellow performers, and then added their own variations. A reviewer for the *Gold Coast Spectator* objected to a performance by Augustus Williams in 1932 because he did not use enough variation:

> I consider that a young artist must imitate one greater than himself, but should exhibit little of the imitation. This accounts for the trouble I have with Mr. Williams regarding his Glassian ways and make-ups. . . . One hopes the real Williams will be revealed to us some day. (*Gold Coast Spectator* 1932h)

When a concert actor borrowed conventions, narratives, or motifs, he had to "put in his own" in order to satisfy the tastes of his audience and critics. Williams, it seems, followed the footsteps of his master, J. C. Glass, too closely.

The creative process by which concert artists appropriated ideas and then added idiosyncratic variations meant that how a particular actor repeated and revised concert conventions was as important as what the characters said. Concert parties were indeed subversive of colonial ideologies. But their subversion arose indirectly by means of performance, in the theatrical style of presentation, and in the underlying logic upon which each figure in concert trios was based.

Gender and Other "Troubles" from the Motherland

From the time when concerts first became a profession in the 1930s through the early years of independence in the 1960s, the concert party was exclusively a male performance genre. Concert practitioners invariably explain the absence of women during this time as the result of public prejudice against women touring and performing on stage. The itinerant, rootless nature of concert acting and its association with frivolity made men who chose the concert profession morally suspect. A woman on stage would have faced additional censure, presumed to be a prostitute or at least sexually available. She would also come under scrutiny for her reproductive choices. Akan culture places a high value on progeny, and the daily responsibilities of rearing children generally fall upon women. Given the rigors of life on the road, it would have been difficult for an actress who was a mother to care for her children while on trek. The gender dynamics of concert party acting began to change in the 1960s when the Workers' Brigade Concert Party was formed under the auspices of Kwame Nkrumah's government. The Brigade, developed to address issues of unemployment, was an initiative that included farming and manufacturing work camps, with concert acting as just one of the vocational outlets available to recruits. Under the auspices of the Workers' Brigade, women such as Essi Kum and Margaret Quainoo began to enter the ranks of concert performers, their reputations protected by fact that they were somehow doing "government work." But before the development of the Workers' Brigade in the early 1960s, and indeed well into subsequent decades, female impersonation was a standard and central part of concert party performances.

In North American scholarship, cross dressing and gender performativity have been the subject of much recent theorizing (see Butler 1990; Davy 1990; Garber 1992; Meyer 1994; Newton 1972; and Phelan 1993, 93–111). Since men routinely play women's roles in Ghana's concert party theatre, it is tempting to apply gender performance theory to Ghanaian praxis. Yet unlike Charles Ludlam's The Ridiculous Theatre, or the butch-femme aesthetic of the WOW Cafe, or Oscar Wilde's manipulation of Delsarte's poses, or the Harlem drag balls depicted in the film *Paris Is Burning,* concert parties happen near the equator in a continent visible to most North Americans only as a dark and enigmatic sign, a place that is mysterious, exotic, and ultimately irrelevant. Africa is neither central nor peripheral to contemporary Euro-American gender performance theory: it is completely off the conceptual map. The role of the lady impersonator was a standard element of the concert party from 1927 through the 1970s. Figures 6, 9, 10, 12, 16, 20, 21, 22, and 23 depict African men in drag—or so I have been telling myself. But I have begun to wonder if the theories of "drag" developed in the West can, really encompass what these West African performers were doing. Can drag, camp, queer, and gender performance theory really stretch this far?

Each of the characters in the classic trios of the 1930s and 1940s was built upon fundamental contradictions within colonial ideology. The Gentleman, depicted on the left in fig. 16, purported to be a wealthy, educated, "civilized" African man, but he never seemed to have enough money, and he had trouble speaking English. The Houseboy appeared to be an illiterate, "uncivilized" Liberian immigrant, yet he was far more clever than his masters. And the Lady—while performing the quintessence of English femininity with a graceful gait, lilting voice, and refined English speech—was in fact an African man in women's clothing. What ideas about gender did the transvestism of the lady impersonator role express? In trying to interpret concert transvestism, I turned to contemporary gender performance theory generated in America for some guidance about what sorts of issues should be considered when thinking about the gendered aspects of this colonial art form.

Is it possible that somewhere in the picture of the Jaguar Jokers lady impersonators depicted in figure 10—perhaps in the hand gesture evoking Diana Ross and the Supremes or eyes that look directly at the camera or a head tilted just slightly to the side—is it possible there lurks a "camp" sign? Is the concept of camp even available to West Africa? Theorist Moe Meyer emphatically tells me it is not, for he says, "There are not different kinds of camp. There is only one. And it is queer" (1994, 1–22). So much for camp theory: "Queer" is neither central nor peripheral to colonial Ghanaian culture; it is completely off the conceptual map.

I try drag theory next. Esther Newton says that drag is a double inversion that suggests that appearance itself is an illusion (1972, 103). In her book *Gender Trouble,* Judith Butler says that drag, through its imitation of gender, "implicitly reveals the imitative structure of gender itself—as well as its contingency" (1990, 137). Butler's confidence in the subversive potential of drag is tempered by Kate Davy's qualification that "both female and male impersonation foreground the male voice and, either way, women are erased" (1994, 133). Each of these theorists articulates a different perspective on what drag is and what it is not. And through the abstraction of their language, each presumes universal applicability.

Since the label on drag theory has no precautionary warnings such as "for internal use only" or "do not use in Africa," I have tried applying it to the Ghanaian concert party. I want to share here some of the insights drag theory has given me into the concert party. I also want to describe what drag theory looks like from the perspective of Africa and suggest ways that gender performance theory might be productively extended and revised to be less ethnocentric.

Of the three stock roles in the concert party, I will focus on two. First, the Lady. Concert party practitioners make a point of saying "lady" instead of "female" impersonator. They do so for good reason. The "Lady" was a well-known stereotype in colonial Ghana. A report by the Wesleyan Methodist Synod from 1892–1893 describes the categories of "native" women from a colonist's point of view: "At present time there are two classes of females in the district—the 'lady' and the 'cloth woman.' The former is supposed to be 'educated,' and adopts English dress, and is above menial occupation; the latter is generally, though not necessarily, illiterate, and consequently becomes the drudge" (quoted in Kemp 1898, 189). While the range of gender roles within Akan culture was multiple and wide-ranging—shaded by issues of seniority, reproductive status, and position within the extended matrilineage—colonialism reduced African women's gender roles to just two types: the lady and the cloth woman. And it was the Lady that concert parties put on stage.

On concert stages, the Lady wore a European-style frock, a pearl necklace, earrings, spectacles, lipstick, gloves, shoes, and a purse. The Lady was African, but she represented white femininity. The Lady spoke English, only rarely reverting to Twi or Fante (Vans #95.33). She was a "school girl" who did not know how to cook and would not lift a finger to do household chores (Oppong and Oppong #95.40; Vans #95.30). The Lady was fickle in love, and her infidelity was the moral focus of many concert plays. Prior to 1950, concert party ladies were always played by men.[22]

The Gentleman character was also a familiar cliché in colonial Ghana. Wesleyan minister Dennis Kemp wrote in 1898 that "among our Gold Coast people there are distinctions greater than those which wealth can create. We have the unsophisticated bushman, and the coast man; the illiterate, and the scholar" (1898, 58). The Gentleman was marked by distinctive ethnic qualities. He was known as a "coast man" and thus associated with the Fante ethnic group who live along Ghana's coast. Whereas an admirable man among the Asante who lived inland would be praised for resembling a chief (*ose ohene*), among the coastal Fante he would be praised *oye krakye dodo,* literally he is very well educated, or "too much like a clerk" (Arhin 1983, 2). The stereotypical Fante gentleman also had particular class affiliations. He had formal education, earned his living through trade or government work, was fond of Western clothing, and despised manual labor. Unlike the Lady stereotype, colonials saw the African gentleman as a buffoon. Colonists criticized him for succumbing to the "habit" of grandiloquent language and wearing ridiculously flamboyant clothing.[23]

The ethnic stereotype of the Fante gentleman was a trope readily available to Ghanaian theatre practitioners. They put this character on stage as the husband of the Lady. But unlike the Lady impersonator, whose convincing embodiment of white femininity so fascinated spectators, audience interest in the Gentleman's role arose from the exaggerated and grotesque way in which the gentleman filled his position. A photograph of the Two Bobs and Their Carolina Girl taken about 1934 depicts the Gentleman as a buffoon (fig. 16). Although he wears a Western hat, tail coat, and covered shoes, his face paint is clownish and his shirt and trousers ludicrously ruffled and baggy. The Gentleman's makeup, derived partly from Al Jolson's minstrel blackface, served as a kind of mask, highlighting the gap between who he was and what he was trying to be.[24] Although the Gentleman feigned affluence, he had no cash. And while he pretended to be fluent in English, he was really far more comfortable speaking Fante. According to Bob S. Ansah, when an actor appears as a Gentleman, "you have to put on dinner jacket, you see, with a voice of smooth English, acting even as if you don't understand Fante, until it comes to a point then you'll come up with it" (#93.10). The Gentleman would "come up" with Fante when he became very angry or agitated and could not express his emotions in English. His anger would expose his "essential" character, revealing the absurdity of his pretensions.

Spectator interest in the Gentleman character arose from an obvious dichotomy *within* the character between his ideal and real self. Audiences enjoyed the Gentleman because he imitated English manners so imperfectly. The appeal of the Lady impersonator role, on the other hand, came from the barely perceptible, yet profound, discrepancy between the sex of the character and that of the actor. Lady impersonators played their roles with such understatement and fidelity that audiences often mistook them for the "real" thing (*Gold Coast Spectator* 1932i). The Lady appeared "real" and the Gentleman was grotesquely exaggerated, yet each of these characters shared an underlying contrast between surface and substance, between their performed exteriority and their interior ontological status.

I want to make several arguments about the concert party in relationship to drag: First, I assert that *all* actors in concert party trios, not just the lady impersonators, were in drag. In reading this performance form, it simply does not make sense to single out gender as an isolated category of analysis. Whatever the lady impersonators were doing with gender, they were also doing with race, class, and ethnicity. The Gentleman was an upwardly mobile Fante from the intermediate classes. The Lady was not just a woman: She was an African woman who performed British femininity.

The Gentleman and the Houseboy were in "drag" in as much as they were playing with categories of identity, using precisely the same dichotomy between appearance and ontology that informed the lady impersonator's role. Each character signaled a distance between the limited, circumscribed roles that colonialism created and the African people who tried to fill them. What united the stock characters was a style of performance that was two-dimensional and self-consciously presentational. The plot scenarios and character types portrayed on concert party stages were so familiar to spectators that their pleasure in these shows was derived from watching *how* a particular actor would play a stock role, or *how* some particular troupe would re-invent a familiar play. (I would argue that this very same emphasis on extraordinary enactments of familiar types and structures is central to audience pleasure in the Harlem drag balls depicted in the film *Paris Is Burning*.) Style and the emphasis on role playing, rather than cross dressing per se, is what leads me to interpret the entire concert party performance as a kind of drag ball.

I would also argue that by imitating and exaggerating colonial stereotypes, concert party drag revealed the imitative structure of colonialism itself, as well as its contingency. Concert party drag disrupted what was at the time a rampant Anglophilia among colonial Ghanaians. Rather than address compulsory heterosexuality, as cross-gender drag in the West often does, concert parties took issue with compulsory civilization. I am adapting here ideas about drag and performance developed by Judith Butler, but I substitute "colonialism" in places where she says "gender." Butler asserts that gender is a *doing* rather than a *being,* and that drag reveals the imitative structure of gender (1990, 134–141). In applying this idea to the concert party, I am stretching Butler's concepts to fit a context for which they never were created. However, I find that Butler's underlying idea about the performative nature of identity is supple enough to address race and class issues in West Africa with the same sophistication Butler and other scholars have brought to the analysis of drag and gender performances in New York, London, and other Western venues.

Whereas gender and heterosexuality are central to Western drag theory, "civilization," the authorizing fiction of colonialism, was central to concert party drag. Within this grand narrative of civilization, race, gender, class, and ethnic assumptions played out like so many sub-plots and minor themes in a sprawling Victorian novel. Concert parties demonstrated that although one might dress, move, and speak within the regulatory fictions of compulsory civility, civilization was something one *did,* rather than something one *was* or was not. The stock roles emphasized the artifice of colonial behaviors. Concert parties exposed civilization as a performative strategy available to all rather than a birthright and entitlement of God's select few. Perhaps this is why the Akan Trio always began their shows by singing;

> We are the Akan Trio
> We come from Ghanaland
> The Mother of civilization all over the world.

In order to use Western drag theory, which never imagined African performance as a possible site of application, I have had to modify it in some fairly substantial ways. Such adaptation is nothing new to Africa, where irrigation systems, telecommunication equipment, and computers manufactured abroad routinely have to be re-configured to meet African needs never anticipated by product engineers. I believe Eurocentric designers of technology as well as theory could benefit greatly from seeing how their creations have to be adapted to fit African contexts. It is in this spirit that I offer the following suggestions.

I have argued that drag in Ghanaian concert parties was about much more than gender, and that to focus on gender in isolation from or as more important than race, class, ethnicity, and other relevant categories of identity flattens and distorts a complex and highly layered performance practice. I would also submit that gender myopia is a problem for studies of Western drag as well. Drag performances in America and Europe might also be *as much* about class and race as they are about gender. When white men in minstrelsy and vaudeville dressed as ballerinas, they were certainly "crossing-dressing" in the most conventional sense, inasmuch as they crossed the gender line between male and female. But when they wore blackface makeup and referenced through their costume a high-culture art form within the context of lowbrow popular theater, their "troubles" extended far beyond gender (fig. 24). Can we even say that gender was of primary importance to this performance?

This analysis of concert party drag has several implications for drag and gender performativity theory: Does one have to cross the binary gender line to be "in drag"? This seems to be the assumption of many Western gender performance theorists. One of the most striking aspects, for me, of the Harlem drag balls depicted in *Paris Is Burning* is the profusion of "categories" in which the performers compete: pretty girl, luscious body, school boy, school girl, town & country (male and female), bangie boy, bangie girl, high-fashion evening wear (male and female), and so forth (Livingston 1992). And yet Jeanie Livingston, the filmmaker, and her critics gravitate to one particular category: the femme realness queens such as Octavia and Venus Extravaganza, thereby implying that this one category is the essence of drag. Peggy Phelan says as much when she opens her critique of the film with the disclaimer that while the balls are also aimed at "other idealized images—such as male business executives and military men—I am concerned here primarily with drag" (1993, 94). So what about all those other categories? When a gay black civilian man dresses as a straight military officer in the Harlem drag balls, is he not also in drag?

If we were to theorize the whole range of categories performed in the Harlem drag balls, it would be difficult to argue, as bell hooks does, that the aspirations expressed by the performers always reveal a longing to be in the position of the ruling-class woman (1992, 148). The femme realness queen Venus Extravaganza may have expressed such desires, but what about the men who pose as straight male African American urban gangsters? What do they want? Neither the film *Paris Is Burning* nor its many critics ask this question.

Judith Butler, in her reading of *Paris Is Burning,* says "it would not be enough to claim that for Venus gender is *marked by* race and class, for gender is not the substance or primary substrate and race and class the qualifying attributes" (1993, 130). Butler's essay suggests that the foundational assumption of the entire psychoanalytic paradigm that sexual difference is primary, prior to race or class, in the constitution of the subject must be thoroughly revised. I would agree, as would, I suspect, the critical legal theorist Kimberlé Crenshaw (1992), whose work on the intersectionality of race, class, sexuality, and gender has so profoundly revolutionized my thinking on gender that I am entirely unsatisfied with the current trend of "marking" whatever the critic inadvertently left out of her analysis. "Marking" our blindnesses does little to address or exempt us from the underlying problems of institutionalized prejudice.

On a superficial level, what is most noticeable about concert trios of the 1930s and 1940s was their eclecticism, their voracious appetite for material that was novel and topical. What is much less readily apparent are the deeper principles of creativity that guided concert actors of this period as they wove together such wildly divergent elements. As with more established Akan performing arts, concert parties of this period were constructed out of a standard repertoire of landmark phrases, tropes, and conventions. They had three stock character roles, a three-part dramaturgical structure, and predictable plot scenarios. However, just as no two chiefs in Akan festivals dress or parade through town in an identical fashion, no two trios repeated received ideas without adding variations, idiosyncratic revisions, and personal expressions. Concert artists would "pick" elements from local, national, continental, diasporic, European, and American sources, and then "polish" and reshape them. As with Akan storytelling, festivals, and proverb usage, the "play" of ideas was the thing, for *how* ideas were performed in a given context was often far more important than *where* those ideas came from or even *what* those ideas seemed to signify at the level of literal content. The poetics of invention in concert trios reached full fruition in the body and in the moment through live, improvised performance. It is for this reason that one must analyze the concert party's "poetry of action" in order to discover its social, political, and cultural significance.

Operating within a social order that was at once hierarchically organized and in a state of tremendous flux, concert parties participated in the construction of reality in the Gold Coast in the 1930s and 1940s. Colonialism and its attendant institutions such as churches and schools propagated in Akan culture a stark dichotomy between "civilized" and "savage." In order to partake fully in the economic advantages of "progress," Africans were told they had to learn to speak English, eat with a fork and knife, wear covered shoes and Western clothing, value the nuclear family over the extended matrilineage, marry only one spouse, stop paying homage to ancestors, and attend Christian churches. Concert parties drew upon, exploited, and performatively re-invented such untenable dichotomies of colonial ideology. But the critique they offered was subtle, communicated through the Akan traditions of indirection (Yankah 1995, 51–52). Rather than voicing criticisms through narrative or dialogue, concerts imbedded subversion in the *doing* of performance: in, for instance, their self-consciously presentational theatrical style and performative excess in each stereotypical trio character. By foregrounding the performative nature of colonial behaviors, concerts transformed "civilization" into a practice rather than an ontological status.

The following chapter will analyze how concert parties in the era of Ghana's independence continued to negotiate and revise colonial contradictions by means of performance. Rather than reinforcing the dichotomy between European and African cultures, between the "civilized" and the "savage," concerts created a space for critical evaluation and selective appropriation. As such, they fulfilled what political theorist and playwright Kobena Sekyi had predicted back in the early part of the century was most needed for Gold Coast Africans to survive and thrive in the modern world.

"This Is Actually a Good Interpretation of Modern Civilization"

STAGING THE SOCIAL IMAGINARY, 1946–1966

For West Africa in general and colonial Ghana in particular, World War II was a watershed experience. The war stimulated capital and administrative development, increased communication, and exposed Africans to other parts of the continent and the world. Perhaps the most dramatic and least quantifiable outcome of the war was the extent to which it revolutionized the social imaginary, the ways in which individuals conceptualized the larger collectives and communities to which they belonged (Anderson [1983] 1991). M. Fortes wrote in 1945 that the war had "engendered a new mood of increased awareness of wide horizons and exciting possibilities" among the educated urban classes (209). Likewise for the Africans who served in the Royal West African Frontier Force, the war "extended their perceptions of the world and also of British power" (Killingray 1982, 94).[1] Gold Coast newspapers provide evidence of a radical shift from local to global concerns during this period. Whereas sedition legislation, cocoa price controls, and colonial taxation measures dominated the press in the 1930s, the fate of Britain's colonies such as Singapore, Hong Kong, Malay, Jamaica, and India came under scrutiny in the 1940s.[2]

Just as colonial Ghana underwent profound transformations in the postwar years, so too did the concert party. Whereas shows of the earlier era were three-person variety shows with brief comic sketches, plays of the 1950s exploded with sprawling narratives featuring as many as twenty-seven actors portraying a huge range of characters. And while the trio plays of the earlier era had dramatized the affectations of Westernized coastal Fantes and the comic antics of "uncivilized"

Kru laborers, "troupe" shows of the 1950s onward depicted stories that were more representative of the general population. Concerts dramatized inheritance disputes, conflicts between co-wives, the problems of unemployment, the plight of orphans, and tensions within the extended family. The music changed from British and American popular ballads to highlife music, a syncretic popular music genre more closely associated with African culture. The language of the concert party, which had always been polyglot, shifted from being predominantly English to mostly Akan. This linguistic change increased the concert party's accessibility to spectators who did not have much formal Western education. Increasingly the concert party became associated with the working class.

Through their geographic mobility and widespread popularity, concert performances participated firsthand in the transformation of public consciousness in Ghana during the postwar and independence years. As concert troupes traveled in cities, towns, and villages throughout Ghana, they adapted their shows to the languages and aesthetic tastes of particular audiences. Like living magazines, they transmitted fashions, manners, dances, characters, and ideas across geographic distances. In the absence of widespread literacy, popular traveling theatre served as one of the primary mediums through which colonial Ghanaians shifted from local identifications to the more abstract realm of regional, ethnic, and national affiliation. Whereas the popular press played a central role in the formation of European nationalism, as Benedict Anderson has argued ([1983] 1991), traveling theatre performed a pivotal role among a largely non-literate population during Ghana's transition from colonialism to modern nation-state.

Troupe names give a brief glimpse into the concert party's changing relationship to the social imaginary. Groups of the 1930s and early 1940s—such as the Axim Trio, Dix Covian Jokers, Keta Trio, and Saltpond Trio—took their names from the coastal cities where these groups originated. However, from the 1950s onward, concert parties adopted names reflecting larger, more abstract affiliations based on ethnicity, region, and nationalism. Names such as Fanti Trio, Akan Trio, Ahanta Trio, and Abuakwa Trio indicated ethnic and regional identities.[3] Names such as Ghana Trio, Ethiopian Jokers, and Burma Jokers reflected an association with nationalism and countries outside Ghana's borders.[4] Downplaying discrete local identities in favor of larger affiliations based on language, nation, and Pan-Africanism was an objective the Nkrumah administration actively promoted (Hagan 1993). Due to the growing importance of band leaders as public personalities, some concert parties in the 1950s took the names of their individual leaders: Kwa Mensah's Band, Appiah Adjekum's Band, Kakaiku's Band, E. K. Nyame's Akan Trio, and Bob Cole's Ghana Trio.[5] Thus, at the very moment when concert parties began to identify with larger communities, they turned inward, aggrandizing the status of key performers. The concert party's oscillation between local and remote referents contributed to its complex and often contradictory formulation of the social imaginary.

Another expression of this social imaginary can be found in the highly disjunctive, topsy-turvy style that concerts developed in the postwar years. This era saw the evolution of a radically new aesthetic. Performances featured highly localized references as well as national and global allusions. They combined buffoonery with pathos, surfaces with substance. Plots extolled *and* ridiculed "traditional" occupations such as farming. They simultaneously embraced *and* rejected "modern" urban lifestyles. Just when concert party narratives seemed to be careening toward resolution and closure, they would take sudden never-to-be-resolved digressions. Right in the middle of the moral which concluded every show, some character would insert an amoral aside that completely undermined the play's "message." At times, spectators responded to the concert party's raucous, often incoherent style with a laugh and a shrug. At other moments, spectators wept, shouted at characters, or came up to the stage to offer money for exemplary performances. Whether weeping, rebuking, or howling with laughter, spectators intensely and actively engaged with the concert party despite—or even *because of*—its disjunctive mode of presentation.

The dynamism of the concert party in the postwar years came not just from its paradoxical style, but also from its content which was rooted in social realism. By "social realism" I mean the concert party's dramatization of issues such as inheritance disputes and family conflicts arising from migration. Socially realistic content is not to be confused with theatrical "realism," a specific style of Western theatre that developed in the nineteenth century. Theatrical realism is associated with certain formal conventions such as proscenium staging, verisimilitude, characters with psychological depth, the imaginary "fourth wall" between actors and spectators, coherent narrative, stylistic unity, and consistency of all theatrical elements. What interests me is the disjunction between the socially realistic content of the concert party and its highly presentational non-"realistic" mode of representation.

John Collins has identified the dominant themes of post-independence concert parties as urban migration, social stratification, cash crops, changing sexual norms, and generational problems (1976b, 56).[6] Concert parties invariably dramatized these issues within the context of the family, both nuclear and extended. In the estimation of Fante political theorist Kobina Sekyi, the family has long been a key site for negotiating political change with Akan culture since it is itself a political unit. Sekyi subscribed to the popular local view that the Akan state is "merely an extension of the extended family or clan; 'family' and 'state' are therefore not differentiated in kind but only in degree" (Langley 1970, 35). The prevalence of this view helps to explain how and why the domestic functions as the political in Akan popular representations. In dramatizing family problems, concert parties addressed issues that cut to the very heart of the spectacular political changes sweeping Ghana as it shifted from a British colony to an independent nation.

Concert parties fictionalized the Akan family and put their conflicts on a Western, proscenium-style stage with a bicameral separation between performers and spectators. In doing so, these performances provided a critical distance between the family and a theatre-going public which the concert party itself convened and helped constitute. Performances not only utilized Western-style stages but also exploited Akan modes of communication such as indirection (*akutia*) and the emblematic signification typical of proverbs and *adinkra* symbols.[7] These Akan conventions of communication provided the concert party with an economy of signification. Performances could achieve intense emotional engagement with their audiences through brief allusions.

By deploying such an eclectic range of styles and techniques to dramatize everyday realities and social problems, concert parties became in the postwar years a primary integrative mechanism through which Ghanaian audiences negotiated a tumultuous historical epoch. They provided a forum for audiences critically and selectively to scrutinize and appropriate colonial legacies and contemporary realities. Directly addressing their audiences and incorporating spectators into the action, concert parties invited large groups who were not inherently related by ties of clan, kin, or ethnicity to participate in domestic, personal conflicts. In concert performances, the personal became the political, and the everyday domestic sphere became a public sphere of political consequence.

This chapter focuses on the volatile years between the end of World War II through independence in 1957 and the administration of Ghana's first prime minister and president, Kwame Nkrumah (who was overthrown in 1966). Of crucial importance to my interpretation of this period is an extraordinary audio archive located at the University of Ghana's Institute of African Studies. In 1961, the Institute audiotaped several live concert party performances. This rich but overlooked resource provides unprecedented access to past performance practices, for until recently concert party performances were undocumented.

World War II through Independence

Britain's large-scale wartime propaganda efforts in colonial Ghana, the most intensive in all of Africa, contributed to a greater awareness of international affairs among all sectors of the population (Holbrook 1978, 401).[8] The British government broadcast African-language radio programs about the war over loudspeakers in city streets (Clarke 1986, 48). Mobile film units roamed the country showing footage from the front lines to crowds gathered in markets. Public rallies and press reports warned about the dangerous implications of Nazism for Africans. In addition to this mass media publicity, the army commissioned popular traveling theatre troupes to stage propaganda plays about the war, shows such as the production by the Gold Coast Two Bobs of *The Downfall of Adolph Hitler* (Ansah #95.34a; Collins 1976b, 52).[9]

As a result of this exposure to international issues and events, the Gold Coast underwent what one editorialist called a "complete reorientation of general ideas" with regard to the colonial enterprise. Through the "growing public and international interest in the affairs of the Colonies," a journalist wrote, "it has become clear that the old concepts of Colonies as possessions or personal estates of the controlling Power to be administered solely for its benefit are no longer tenable" (*Gold Coast Independent* 1943b). As colonial Ghanaians began to envision their role within communities that lay beyond local boundaries, their dissatisfaction with colonialism grew more acute and their resistance to it more concerted. The postwar years saw greater agitation for African control and representation in government. Disillusionment and unemployment among ex-servicemen, as well as frustration among businessmen over the government's restrictive licensing practices and shipping quotas, prompted many to join actively in the struggle for independence.[10]

In the years following World War II, the concert party entered a new epoch. As Gold Coast Africans struggled to define and create an independent nation, concert parties likewise burgeoned with imaginative innovations. A new generation of performers introduced more elaborate plots, an enormous range of characters, highlife music, and a diversity of themes more closely tied to the lives of ordinary people. The brief comic sketches of the trio era grew into extended and complex narratives. In addition to the Lady, Gentleman, and Houseboy characters, concert parties began depicting uncles, aunts, grandmothers, children, chiefs, traditional priests, farmers, government agents, and supernatural creatures from Akan folklore such as the forest monster Sasabonsam (fig. 23) and dwarves called *mmoatia*. While concert parties continued to dramatize the previously established themes of domestic infidelity and master/servant relationships, they added to these themes a tremendous range of conflicts with a much wider appeal. Shows depicted inheritance disputes, the problems of labor migration, infertility, witchcraft, and the fate of orphans and widows. With an increased range of characters came a massive expansion in troupe size. Concert groups swelled from three actors to large troupes ranging in size from fifteen to two dozen actors. If we think of the 1930s and early 1940s as the trio era of concert party history, the years following the war through independence can be thought of as the period of the troupe.

Shows also became more musically complex at this time. While American and British ragtime songs and sentimental ballads had previously been de rigueur on concert stages, shows increasingly incorporated proverb-laden guitar highlife music. This twentieth-century popular genre was far more closely identified with African—rather than Western—culture (Collins 1987; 1994).[11] Highlife became integral to the dramatic action of concert party plays, with song lyrics matching the emotional tone and narrative content of particular scenes.

On the surface, these formal changes in the concert party appear to express a gradual Africanization, indigenization, and domestication of this form (Collins 1994a, 1–18). However, concert party practitioners themselves narrate this historical transformation differently. According to M. K. Oppong, the son of the famous concert party impresario Kakaiku, and K. Acquaah Hammond, one of the leading actors of the Jaguar Jokers Concert Party, the changes in the concert party during the 1950s represent, rather, a process of modernization (Oppong and

Oppong #95.40). When concert artists of the 1950s introduced highlife music, Akan folklore, a greater range of characters, serious themes from everyday Ghanaian life, and greater degree of African languages, they were *modernizing* the concert party rather than indigenizing it.

This use of the term "modernization" is of particular note in light of Paul Gilroy's pioneering work *The Black Atlantic* (1993). Gilroy initiates an expansive project, the full implications of which his own work only begins to address: a reconsideration of modernity from the perspective of the black Atlantic and the African diaspora. *The Black Atlantic* incisively explores the countercultures of modernity expressed in the work of intellectuals such as W. E. B. DuBois and Richard Wright and in popular music in England, America, and the Caribbean. Yet African voices are curiously absent from Gilroy's figuration of the black Atlantic.[12] What counter-discourses of modernity have been produced on the African continent? The history of the concert party addresses this striking omission from Gilroy's book.

Concert practitioners define "modernity" not according to Western Enlightenment axiologies which dichotomize the civilized and the savage, Africa and Europe, modern and traditional cultures. Concert actors use "modernization" to describe an integrative process involving conscious, well-considered choices of inclusion and exclusion. This definition is in line with the understanding of modernization advanced by Fante intellectual and nationalist Kobina Sekyi in the early twentieth century and outlined in Chapter 3 of this book. Sekyi identified in the early colonial period the need for integrative mechanisms to help Africans participate in this "modernization" process. Sekyi thought this integrative process would most likely be facilitated by the Akan extended family and responsible leaders "capable of manipulating the integrative elements of tradition and of formulating a social philosophy incorporating the wisdom of the past" (Langley 1970, 47). But contrary to Sekyi's estimation, families and enlightened individuals could not shoulder alone the demands of integrating the disparate and conflicting elements of society that colonialism produced. I believe that the concert party developed in the 1930s and blossomed in the 1950s precisely because it fulfilled this need.

The concert party's institutional autonomy and novelty within Ghanaian culture made it a unique forum for critical reflection on present realities and inherited traditions. This performance genre's integrative role is most evident in the disjunctive style it developed in the independence era. Performances of this period maintained the farcical tone, physical comedy, and vaudevillian acting style they had inherited from previous generations. However, they grafted onto the tradition of formulaic plots and two-dimensional characters themes of social realism so emotionally affective that audiences were moved to tears and even blows because they became so carried away by the action. Such a degree of audience empathy is particularly intriguing in light of the fragmented nature of concert party style, for moments of overwhelming pathos were shot through with comic non sequiturs and pratfalls. What accounts for the concert party's unruly combination of theatrical artifice and emotional realism? Why were audiences so moved by these erratic and disjointed shows, which were alternately farcical and somber, ridiculous and pathetic, trivial and portentous? What political and social meanings can be read from such a contradictory, non-illusionistic style?

Trio plays of the 1930s and 1940s highlighted the artifice of life among the Westernized nouveaux riches. Colonial culture in these plays was a layer that appeared to be only skin deep. But in the troupe period of concert history from the 1950s onward, we see a radical shift as concert parties began negotiating the distance between rarified coastal culture rife with colonial artifice and the more widely experienced, deeply felt realities of life in Ghana. Plays during this period promoted the "correct" way to live, but their advice was neither predictable nor "politically correct." They did not, for instance, advocate a reactionary rejection of all things Western. Concert troupes often promoted their shows by bragging about how "modern," "civilized," and "up-to-date" they were. Characters modeled the latest fashions and dance steps, and could sing rock 'n' roll from America. While plays embraced and modeled foreign culture, they also ridiculed characters that were too enamored with things that came from overseas. Concert parties often promoted a "back-to-the-farm" ideology, valuing agrarian labor as the most honest and laudable occupation. But farmers were not exempt from criticism. They were often portrayed as simpletons and oafs. As concert parties played both to rural and urban audiences, they avoided categorical or unilateral definitions of the new Ghana. During a period of strong anti-colonial and pro-African sentiments, they did not follow any particular party line, but rather engaged in a more messy and complex process of cultural negotiation. While some aspects of these plays—such as use of idiom and place names—were highly localized, other aspects—such as characterization—were so generic and prototypical they could represent almost anyplace or anyone in Ghana.

A photograph of the lady impersonators of the Jaguar Jokers taken in the mid-1960s provides a vivid example of how concert parties in this period provided spectators with a range of often contradictory choices (fig. 10). The Jaguar ladies were such fashionable dressers that female spectators would sometimes come to their shows just to see, and even purchase, their dresses. All of the actors in this picture are wearing *cabah*s, an adaptation of pre-colonial attire that first emerged in colonial Ghana in the nineteenth century. *Cabah*s transformed traditional women's clothing, comprised of unsewn pieces of cloth wrapped around the bust and waist, to conform to Victorian notions of modesty. The two performers on the far right sport headwraps that became quite popular during Nkrumah's leadership. This turban-like style came to be associated with Nkrumah's "African personality," an ideology defined as "the creative expression of the African genius, the common reality behind the diversities and complexities of African cultures" (Hagan 1993, 23; Manuh 1996). However, the two impersonators in the center of the photo are wearing an accessory explicitly banned by the Nkrumah regime as colonialist: wigs of straightened hair (Manuh 1993, 113). The cloths worn by these impersonators also signify diverse cultural and geographic affiliations. The actor on the far right wears *krobo edusei,* a pattern named after a government minister in Ghana who had a terrazzo house. This highly specific local reference contrasts with the design worn by E. C. Baidoo, which is generically known as "Java" print from Indonesia. Thus, by the 1960s, concert parties provided their audiences with a much more diverse and nuanced range of female types than the sole stock female character of the 1930s and early 1940s who was a thoroughly westernized African woman.

The eclecticism of concerts from the 1950s, the genre's wide-ranging appetite for local and global culture, was also evident in dances, songs, and monologues. In the Akan Trio's play *Don't Covet Your Neighbor's Wife,* the character Koo Nimo does a comic speech about his origins. He mentions several towns near Swedru, the city where this particular performance took place:

> Just as my wife has told you, my father hails from Apam, and my mother is from Mbowire. Yes, but another secret to be revealed is that my mother was impregnated at Swedru. It just took place in the street. (*Audience laughs.*) When the time came to deliver, my mother ran very fast to Adeiso where she delivered me. Consequently, I am called Swedru-Adeiso. (*Laughter.*) Yes, that's the name my mother calls me by. (1961a, 1995a, 17)

Incorporating references to locally recognized places was one of the secrets of the concert party's widespread appeal, for shows reflected local lives with a specificity and immediacy that mass media entertainment such as movies and recorded music could not. Yet at the same time that concert parties alluded to the neighboring towns, they also signified on locations outside Ghana's borders. For instance, the Fanti Trio's play *Beautiful Nonsense* begins with a comic monologue by a character from Nigeria named "Salami" (1961a, 1995a). He speaks Twi with a thick Yorùbá accent, which provokes laughter in the audience. Salami tells the spectators he has come to challenge the musicians of Ghana. He begins singing parodies of songs by well-known Ghanaian musicians E. K. Nyame, Kakaiku, and Bob Cole. Salami concludes with a song sure to vanquish all competitors: Little Richard's "Tutti Frutti," the hot new rock 'n' roll song from America, sung with his own unique and unintelligible Yorùbá-accented version of the lyrics.

Concert plays of the early 1960s almost always valorized "traditional" rural farmers and rejected the frivolous lifestyles of urban fun-seekers.[13] However, shows also shamelessly exploited their audience's appetite for hip urban culture. Concert actors incorporated the latest dance styles into their shows, demonstrating their worldly knowledge of hot Accra dance hall numbers and North American pop music. The young suitor in the Fanti Trio's play *Man Must Work Before He Eats* spends all his time dancing at Takoradi Zenith Hall. When he meets his intended bride, they do an extremely acrobatic dance in which "you stand at one place and you whirl yourself around so fast you fall down. If you're not careful, you'll break into pieces" (1961a; 1995b, 9–10).[14] When the couple masterfully did this number during the Fanti Trio's 1961 performance, the Cape Coast audience roared in approval. The girl's father was less enthusiastic: "Oh, these ones who go to the beer bar really suffer, don't they? What kind of dance is this? . . . Oh! I was not brought up like this!" (9).

The concert party's simultaneous inward and outward movement, its oscillation between local and distant referents, its propensity to criticize and valorize the same behaviors, are consonant with what Karin Barber and Christopher Waterman perceive in the performance forms of the neighboring West African country of Nigeria. In their analysis of Yorùbá *fújì* music and *oríkì* praise poetry, Barber and Waterman identify the processes of extension, domestication, and intensification as crucial:

> *Fújì* music, *oríkì,* and other Yorùbá performance genres *extend* from a local point and traverse what lies beyond the immediate locality. Their practitioners *domesticate* difference by incorporating fragments from a multiplicity of sources into local stylistic configurations and social strategies. The ultimate goal of any performance is to *intensify* the presence, image and prospects of local actors. (1995, 243)

Like these Yorùbá performances, the Ghanaian concert parties of the 1950s and 1960s traversed across local and global spheres, dissolving conceptual barriers between such realms. They wove specific local referents together with national and international allusions according to patterns of invention established by previous generations of concert practitioners.[15] However, the ultimate aim of concert practitioners—in contrast with the individuals described in Barber and Waterman's Nigerian examples—was not intensification of their own image and prospects, but rather a redefinition of modernization along self-determined lines. Through concert parties, modernization became an integrative process of inclusion and exclusion, a performative reformulation of the many cultural forces influencing contemporary life.

Concerts and Highlife Music

One of the most profound changes of the 1950s was the concert party's fusion with highlife music. Like American jazz, highlife is a popular music genre that began in the twentieth century out of a confluence of cultures (Brempong 1986; Collins 1976b, 1992, 1994b; Coplan 1978; Yankah 1984). Highlife developed, as the concert party did, primarily among the coastal Fantes, and it is now considered to be a preeminent Ghanaian art form, the nation's most notable contribution to African pop music.

Musicologist John Collins identifies three main strands of highlife: brass bands, dance orchestras, and palmwine guitar bands (1994). Brass band highlife grew out of regimental bands stationed on the coast in the late nineteenth century. Big band dance orchestras, on the other hand, developed out of groups such as the Excelsior Orchestra which began in 1914 to entertain urban audiences in cinema and dance halls. The brother of E. T. Mensah, the "king" of dance band highlife, explains that it was from this latter strand of highlife that this music got its name:

> During the early twenties, during my childhood, the term "highlife" was created by people who gathered around the dancing clubs such as the Rodger Club (built in 1904) to watch and listen to the couples enjoying themselves. Highlife started as a catch-name for the indigenous songs played at these clubs by such early bands as the Jazz Kings, the Cape Coast Sugar Babies, the Sekondi Nanshamang, and later the Accra Orchestra. The people outside called it "highlife" as they did not reach the class of the couples going inside, who not only had to pay a, then, quite relatively high entrance fee of 7s 6d., but also had to wear full evening dress including top hats. (Collins 1994b, 42)

"Highlife" thus connoted the "high" living enjoyed by the elite classes who listened to these dance band orchestras.

The least respectable of the three styles of highlife was palmwine guitar music, which found its first audience among young men who had migrated to the cities for work. They spent their wages on alcohol, which they consumed at palmwine bars where musicians entertained patrons with guitar music. "Gold Coast young men adopted the guitar, in addition to social drinking, as their insignia," according to Emmanuel Akyeampong, so that eventually "the guitar came to be held in contempt by male elders who saw drinking and guitar-playing as a wayward sign of life" (1993, 130; 1996c, 61–62). Palmwine guitar music thus represented a relatively new and politically volatile social class.

All three types of highlife played a role in the history of the concert party. During the concert party trio era, brass bands helped concert parties promote their shows by "campaigning" in the streets on the day of performance. Dance bands in this period sometimes hired concert comedians to perform during intermissions and between songs. For instance, a group of "Bob" comedians performed with the Optimism Club Orchestra in Sekondi in the 1920s (Ruhle 1925). A decade later, Bob Johnson and the Axim Trio toured Nigeria with the Cape Coast Sugar Babies dance band (Sutherland 1970, 16–20). But it was not until palmwine guitar music combined with concert troupes in the 1950s that highlife and concerts became inextricably linked.

The popularity of palmwine guitar highlife reached an all-time high in the postwar years. Gramophone records of artists such as Appiah Adjekum, Kwaa Mensah, and E. K. Nyame made this music more respectable and accessible to a rapidly expanding audience (Collins 1994b, 12). One artist, Appiah Adjekum, approached concert party leader Bob S. Ansah in 1944 and proposed they perform together. Ansah refused, saying he already had good musicians for his concert party—a drummer and organist—and he did not want to experiment with the guitar (#93.10). Adjekum then tried to form his own concert troupe, but "he could not come up with good actors," according to Ansah.

Where Adjekum tried and failed, a former band member of his, E. K. Nyame, succeeded (fig. 25). In 1948, E. K. Nyame broke away from Adjekum and formed his own band known as "E. K.'s," which soon became one of the most successful highlife bands in the Gold Coast (*Sunday Mirror* 1960a).[16] An early composition of theirs that earned them popularity was "*Ɔnim Deɛfoɔ Kukudurufu Kwame Nkrumah*" ("Honorable Man and Hero Kwame Nkrumah"), which Nyame composed in 1950 to celebrate nationalist leader Kwame Nkrumah's release from prison (Austin 1964, 88; Collins 1994b, 16). In 1951, E. K.'s Band started making gramophone records, and soon every house had copies of E. K.'s records, according to concert veteran Bob Vans. "The whole country, every house—if you go there and you don't get E. K.'s record, then it is not a house" (Vans #95.33). E. K.'s was the band everyone was talking about, and their reputation became closely linked to the rising fortunes of Kwame Nkrumah, the emerging leader of the new nation.

Hoping to improve his group's live shows, E. K. Nyame started a concert party called the Akan Trio which staged plays together with his band's musical concerts. Rather than follow the established concert party convention of using English-language songs imported from America and England, the Akan Trio did something that had never before been seen on concert party stages: they sang highlife songs in Akan that the band leader himself had composed (Collins 1994b, 12–19; Vans #95.33). The trend spread like wildfire, and soon every concert party began to weave locally based music into the fabric of concert party narratives. Actor Kwaw Prempeh says he preferred the use of highlife over Western songs (*abrɔfo nwom*) in concert parties, because it made him "realize that highlife is our black people's (*yɛn abibifo*) greatest music" (Prempeh #95.39). The popularity of guitar highlife in the 1950s arose in part from the swelling tide of national and Pan-African sentiments.

The Akan Trio also revolutionized the concert party by dramatizing the proverbs extolled in highlife lyrics. For instance, the proverbially based song "Wusum Brɔde a, Sum Kwadu" inspired a play that dramatized this aphorism. The proverb says if you plant plantain, you should plant banana as well for you do not know which of them will save you in a time of famine (Christaller [1879] 1990, 256). Around this song, the Akan Trio created a play about a man who has two wives and favors one wife over the other. When the man later falls destitute, it is the son of the unloved wife who comes to his rescue (Collins 1994b, 15).

Bob Vans remembers vividly the first time he saw the Akan Trio perform. In the early 1950s, Vans was himself a concert party leader. His group, the Ghana Trio, was putting up a show in a cinema hall in Sekondi when they heard that E. K. Nyame's group would also be staging there within the week. So Vans and his colleagues decided to attend the show:

> We went there and occupied the front seats. They started the show. First, they came to do the Opening Chorus. It was too dull. And the audience, when they saw us, then they started shouting our names: "Ghana Trio, Ghana Trio, Ghana Trio!" We were sitting down with our girlfriends. And then another actor came on stage to perform the Duet. He came to speak this Lagos Twi, Lagos Fante [Akan with a Yorùbá accent]. That one, too, was not up to date. Then the people shouted: "Ghana Trio, Ghana Trio!" There we were . . . (*Vans chuckles.*) Now,

the third thing: We saw E. K. We saw him in a singlet, carrying this sewing machine, as Opia used to do. He came on stage, and then started to sing. Ah! Oh! He sang and sang and sang and sang! And then given some accompaniment, he whistled! (*Vans imitates Nyame singing and whistling.*) Now the audience began to cheer, "Yeaaaah!" Because what they were hearing was what had been recorded on Nyame's own gramophones. They were hearing it *live.* And then the whole place became excited. Oh, they had forgotten us—Ghana Trio, Ghana Trio, ho! Forgotten! Come and see! People went on stage giving one pound notes. That money is high! See! They go to the stage and give them one pound, ten shillings, one pound, ten shillings. Ho! (#95.33)

E. K. Nyame's live shows so captivated audiences that other concert groups, those who could only sing Western songs, soon began to suffer by comparison. According to Bob Vans, from the moment E. K. Nyame entered the concert party field, everything about the business changed: "If we, the Ghana Trio, want to go stage in Osu here, and E. K.'s are performing at Nsawam [a distance of approximately twenty miles], you will see people from Osu join a car, leave us here, and go to Nsawam, just to witness their show!" (#95.33). Nyame set a precedent for performing original highlife compositions that few other concert parties of the time could match. Although concert artists of the 1930s and 1940s were gifted comedians, actors, dancers, and singers, few were composers. Bob Vans was so troubled by the challenging precedent E. K. Nyame had set, he decided to stop performing concert parties altogether. He went off to meditate on how to "contain" E. K.'s success (Vans #95.33).[17]

Thematic and Formal Innovations

Aside from the fusion of highlife and concert parties, the 1950s brought many other changes to this performance genre, including an expansion in size from trios to large troupes, a diversification of themes, and a greater unification of theme, music, and story (Bampoe and Hammond #93.11; Vans #95.49). The person credited with introducing many of these changes is the musician, actor, and band leader Moses Kweku Oppong, a.k.a. Kakaiku (fig. 26). Although E. K. Nyame changed the concert party by introducing guitar highlife, his shows did not tamper with the basic theatrical structure established by previous concert parties.[18] But Kakaiku revolutionized both the form and content of concert party shows.

Raised in the mining town of Aboso in the Western Region, Kakaiku worked as a greaser and winding engine driver at the T & A Mines (Oppong Family 1986). During his leisure hours Kakaiku played guitar with a group of musicians who gained local fame in the late 1940s performing at funerals (Koomson #95.42). Kakaiku decided to turn his group into a professional band, which he formally founded on August 1, 1954 (Kakaiku's Band n.d.). They made their first recording with the United Africa Company that same year. One of the songs they recorded *"Sɛ Me Wɔ Me Kurom a . . ."* ("If I Were to Be in My Own Town . . . ") was soon being played on gramophones throughout the country.[19] Like E. K. Nyame, Kakaiku founded a concert party that would perform together with his highlife band. Kakaiku's concert party debuted at the Akwambo Festival in Agona Swedru in 1954. They did *School Girl,* a show about a young woman who abandons her education for a life of pleasure, falls into prostitution, returns home to ask for forgiveness, and then learns that the money for her education has all been spent (Koomson #95.42).

Unlike any concert party before this time, Kakaiku introduced plays that had a tremendous variety of characters and dramatized complex situations and themes. Whereas trios drew upon a highly limited repertoire of stock scenarios about Fante Anglophilia, class aspirations, and domestic infidelity, Kakaiku's shows focused on the extended family and the supernatural. Some of Kakaiku's most memorable plays were *Egyankaba* (about an orphan), *Takyiwa* (about a witch), *Sasabonsam Fie* (about a young girl who is to be sacrificed to a fabled forest monster), and *Siesie Wo Ekyir Ansaana Ewu* (about the importance of writing a will before one dies to avoid inheritance disputes).[20]

Y. B. Bampoe says when Kakaiku introduced the group-style concert, the quality of shows improved. Large casts "allowed every artist to play his part well. In our days, one person was a schoolmaster, a latrine boy, and what have you. Formerly we were only three artists. . . . What Kakaiku introduced was very good" (CPMR #95.28). Perhaps more significant, Kakaiku's innovations made concert parties accessible to a wider range of spectators. His shows attracted a diverse crowd because, in the words of former Kakaiku band member George Benjamin Grant, his plays dramatized "the life of the people" (#95.46). Y. B. Bampoe and K. Acquaah Hammond describe this historical change in concert party practices:

> *Hammond:* Formerly, we were performing comedy, comedy, comedy, comedy. Laughter, laughter, laughter. But later . . .
> *Bampoe:* . . . we would write our shows about what is happening generally in our houses . . .
> *Hammond:* . . . in our various homes.
> *Bampoe:* For instance, if you are having two wives, and they are having two children, one of the wives will be very cruel to the other woman's son. And this will generate many troubles in the house. . . . These are things that happen in . . .
> *Hammond:* . . . in our various homes . . .
> *Bampoe:* . . . in Africa.
> *Hammond:* Yes. (Bampoe and Hammond #93.11)

Audiences loved Kakaiku's concert parties because they depicted what was actually happening in people's everyday lives, in their homes and families. Unlike trio shows which represented the lives of only a very small minority of the Gold Coast population, troupe-style concert parties depicted the lives of the majority.

Whether rich or poor, educated or illiterate, a Fante southerner or a Hausa northerner, everyone could relate to stories about the extended family and the influence of unseen forces on everyday life.

Kakaiku's most famous play, *Egyankaba,* touched upon a common and controversial social problem concerning the status of children in Akan culture. The play is about a young girl named Mansa whose mother has died.[21] She lives with her father and his new wife and works for them doing domestic chores. However, Mansa's father and stepmother mistreat her because they consider her to be an *egyankaba,* an orphan. According to the Akan customs of matrilineage, Mansa belongs to her mother's extended family, or *abusua,* not to her father. Thus when her mother dies, Mansa becomes an "orphan."[22]

The play's most poignant scene occurs when Mansa prepares food for her stepmother and stepsisters. Rather than inviting Mansa to join the meal, the women drive Mansa from the room and order her to sweep the kitchen. When the stepmother and her daughters finish eating, they wash their hands over the remaining food, which is supposed to be Mansa's meal. When Mansa returns, she asks, "Where is my food?" The stepmother and stepsisters direct her to the bowl in the corner. Mansa lifts the cover, and when she sees the dirty water, she says, "This means my mother is dead. Oh! If my mother had not died, these people would never treat me so" (Oppong and Oppong #95.40). At this point in the show, Kwaw Prempeh, the lady impersonator who played Mansa, would break into song:

Ntsi ni na hom yɛ me sei e e	Is it me you treat this way?
cama m'enyi aber e	It has made me sad.
Ebusuafo a, merennkã hwee	My family, I am dying.
Mese minya beebi a, mobɔkɔ	If I knew a safe place, there I would go. (Kakaiku's Band #95.37)

This highlife lament tapped into the pathos of the scene, the melancholy lyrics, melody, and harmonic structure blending seamlessly with the narrative. Such a unity between songs and serious dramatic action had never before been seen on concert stages.

Kakaiku's *Egyankaba* aroused intense emotions among audience members. Spectators would weep, give money to the orphan, and even come to the stage and spit in the face of the evil stepmother (Kakaiku's Band #95.37; Oppong and Oppong #95.40). Actor David Brown recalls:

> When we stage shows such as *Egyankaba* for an audience, many spectators become so annoyed that they throw things at us. Anything they can lay hands on, they will throw it at us on the platform. One may throw a stone at you in a flash. Such a person forgets that you are just staging a play, and that you are not actually maltreating a child. That person feels so bad about how the orphan is treated. He usually has some terrible feeling for the maltreated child. Under such conditions, they forget that we are exposing to them what usually happens in some of our households. At times, we come across some audience members who refuse to accept the fact that it is just a show. (Kakaiku's Band #95.37)

Spectators recognized in *Egyankaba* a painful situation familiar to almost every Ghanaian. Housemaids are common among all social classes in Ghana, and their lot in life is a particularly difficult one, full of abuse. Most maidservants are young girls who work for extended family members either because they have lost their own parents or because their immediate nuclear families are too poor to provide for them. Both K. A. Busia's social survey of Sekondi-Takoradi ([1950] 1951, 34–37) and Ioné Acquah's survey of Accra report that maidservants in the 1950s were, in general, "inadequately fed and clothed, and grossly overworked" (Acquah [1958] 1972, 74–75).

Kakaiku's play *Egyankaba* was emotionally affective because it dramatized a ubiquitous social problem. Kakaiku's son and daughter Moses and Adom Oppong explain:

> *M. Oppong:* How the stepmother was maltreating the orphan is exactly what is happening in our various houses.
> *CC:* It happens here?
> *M. Oppong:* It happens!
> *A. Oppong: (Exclaiming)* Hey!
> *M. Oppong:* The whole country, it happens.
> *A. Oppong:* . . . *Egyankaba* is happening like that all over Africa. (Oppong and Oppong #95.40)

Many maidservants in the 1950s worked from before dawn until well into the night, performing the bulk of all household and child care chores, working conditions that prevail today for all too many women in this sector of the labor force. Not infrequently they live in substandard conditions, sleep on floors in pest-infested kitchens, and are subject to corporal punishment with little provocation (Busia [1950] 1951, 36). Working for one's relatives is no guarantee a girl will be treated well or even humanely. John Collins interprets the ubiquity of the orphan in concert party plays as representative of much more than the breakdown of family structures. He sees the orphan as emblematic of the "acute loneliness, rootlessness, and loss of primary social relations encountered by many newcomers to the city—a poetic way of expressing urban anomie" (Barber, Collins, and Ricard 1997, 90). Indeed, one might interpret the orphan as a paradigmatic postcolonial Ghanaian subject.

The name *Egyankaba* or "orphan" soon became synonymous with Kakaiku. Everywhere his band went audiences would request this show. Other concert parties were quick to copy Kakaiku's idea. Plays about mistreated orphans and maidservants sprang up everywhere and remained popular for several decades.[23] All of Kakaiku's plays dramatized familiar, ubiquitous social problems, those which reflected the tensions of social transformation in Ghanaian culture at this volatile period of history. Sometimes those tensions would be expressed through the role of supernatural forces in everyday life. But even fantastic elements such as forest monsters and witchcraft were firmly rooted in domestic conflicts. Kakaiku's famous play *Sasabonsam Fie* depicts a chief's daughter who, according to custom, is to be sacrificed to a forest monster named Sasabonsam. The daughter is a good Christian (a "chorister"), and she is rescued by a courageous young man, who eventually marries her. The play brings supernatural forces, "traditional" practices of human sacrifice, and Christian values into direct confrontation (Kakaiku's Band #95.37). Another Kakaiku play to treat the subject of the supernatural was *Takyiwa*, the story of a woman who curses her brother's children through witchcraft. One Kakaiku band member, Samuel Kwame Koomson, explains the popularity of this play: "The reason why *Takyiwa* became the hot favorite of people was the fact that witchcraft is a destructive tool in most homes and within so many families. And the way we performed it, people could identify with the various situations in the play, for many had had similar experiences in their own homes. That is why people were overjoyed with the piece" (#95.42). People flocked to see Kakaiku's plays in part because they readily identified with the conflicts and themes his shows portrayed.

Another Kakaiku play, *Siesie Wo Ekyir Ansaana Ewu (Fix Your Will Before You Die)* depicted the problems of family inheritance that arise due to Ghana's parallel legal systems of matrilineal and patrilineal descent. According to customary law, Akans inherit matrilineally. However, Christianity and colonialism introduced patrilineal inheritance. The simultaneity of these two systems creates many misunderstandings and disputes when a man dies, particularly if he does not leave a will.[24] According to traditional Akan inheritance customs, the deceased man's nephew (his sister's son) will inherit all of his possessions. Under this system, the deceased's wife and immediate children can end up penniless and even be evicted from their home. R. S. Rattray wrote in 1929, "When a man dies and leaves a wife and children, it is considered proper for his heir, *fa ne kunafo*, to take his widow (or widows); not to do so is *musuo* (an evil or unlucky thing), and the *saman* (ghost) of the late husband would be expected to take revenge. Public opinion, indeed, would be quick to condemn the man who shirked this responsibility" ([1929] 1969, 28). However, shirking customary responsibilities toward a widow and her children seems to have become much more common by the 1950s, judging from the ubiquity of this situation in concert party plays. In order to prevent disputes over inheritance, various organizations over the last few decades have actively promoted the importance of leaving written wills.[25]

Like the problems of orphans and housemaids, disputes over questions of inheritance cut across all sectors of Akan society, from the most wealthy and urbane to the poorest people living in villages. Kwame Anthony Appiah's *In My Father's House* provides an example of how inheritance questions can affect even the most elite and Western-educated sectors of Akan society (1992, 181–192). Appiah's father died leaving a codicil to his will indicating he wanted his wife and children, rather than his matrilineage, or *abusua,* to bury him. The dispute over the funeral that ensued between his paternal "nuclear" family and his matrilineage is the subject of the dramatic epilogue to Appiah's book:

> In our efforts to conduct the funeral in accordance with my father's desires—
> expressed in that codicil—we had to challenge, first, the authority of the matri-
> clan, the *abusua,* of which my father was erstwhile head and, in the end, the will

of the king of the Ashanti, my uncle. And in the midst of it—when partisans of our side were beaten up in my father's church, when sheep were slaughtered to cast powerful spells against us, when our household was convinced that the food my aunt sent me was poisoned—it seemed that every attempt to understand what was happening took me further back into my family history and the history of Asante; further away from abstractions ("tradition" and "modernity," "state" and "society," "matriclan" and "patriclan"); further into what would probably seem to a European or American an almost fairytale world of witchcraft and wicked aunts and wise old men and women. (1992, 181)

While European or American observers might classify Appiah's story as a fairy tale, I suspect most Ghanaians would be more inclined to see its resemblance to a concert party play.[26] The story's cast of characters, dramatic altercations, histrionic family meetings, spells, curses, and wicked evildoers are the very stuff of which troupe-style concert parties are made. Conflicts between traditional Akan matrilineal customs and the patrilineal practices introduced by colonialism affect nearly every Ghanaian, whether poor and entirely Akan, or as class-privileged and ethnically mixed as Appiah, a Cambridge-educated scholar who is himself half Akan and half Anglo.[27]

Historical Ethnography of a Performance Style

That concert party themes of the 1950s and 1960s were so firmly rooted in social realism, in the problems faced by Ghanaians across the socio-economic spectrum, explains in part why they became so pervasive in the independence era. But their success also arises from the paradoxical, topsy-turvy style that concert parties developed during this period. In order to analyze this disjunctive style, I turn now to several plays that were performed in 1961. In that year, the newly formed Ghana National Entertainment Association (GNEA) inaugurated their union by sponsoring a series of concert party competitions at which groups such as E. K. Nyame's Akan Trio, Bob Cole's Ghana Trio, and Kakaiku's Band performed (GNEA 1961; Nketia 1965, 42–46). The University of Ghana's Institute of African Studies recorded these shows on audiotape and preserved the tapes in their Audio Archives (UGAA). In 1994–1995, I worked with K. Keelson of the University of Ghana's Language Center to create Fante transcriptions and English translations of these plays. The resulting scripts, examined in combination with the audio recordings, afford an unprecedented opportunity for detailed analysis of concert party language, plot, themes, and character. I will focus on two episodes from concert party plays performed in 1961. The first example comes from a drama about a family dispute in the Akan matrilineage. The second example analyzes a ubiquitous concert party stereotype, the good-time girl.

The process of capturing an improvised, live performance and transforming it into a written, translated text is inherently reductive. When one experiences these plays by reading them, one must imagine the multitude of performative elements that are absolutely central to a play's overall meaning and presentation. A written text cannot easily convey the concert party's recklessly careening tempo, non-naturalistic staging techniques, ragtag costumes, verbal playfulness, and responsiveness to its audiences.[28] Embodied elements such as costume, gesture, and dance are crucial to live performance, yet difficult, if not impossible, to discern from the audio recordings. Thus I have supplemented my interpretation of the audiotapes with knowledge gained from interviews and oral histories of older performers, as well as my ethnographic experiences of present-day concert party practices, including my own performance in them.[29] According to veteran actors, central aspects of production practices of the 1990s originated in the independence period. Therefore, contemporary productions can give a reasonable indication of how shows were performed in the 1960s. This methodology of historical performance ethnography could, if overdone, lead to misleading presentist distortions of the past. But as Michel de Certeau has demonstrated, historiographical operations based solely in the archive are no less mediated ([1975] 1988). Access to the past is always shaped by the fragmentary and partial traces of that past that still happen to exist in the present, whether those traces are recorded in texts or remembered in physical gestures transmitted from a senior to a junior performer. In doing historical research on performance in Africa, one must consider the political status of writing in colonial Africa and the privileged economic status of archival preservation. By what logic would a historian dismiss the traces of performance history that exist in live performance, or rank them as inferior to written documents, when the concert party is a non-written, improvised theatre form that has been performed in African languages for which there was not until recently any standard orthography? Indeed, one could argue that the methodology of historical performance ethnography has much more veracity and persuasiveness than the written archive, which in the case of the concert party can barely testify to the existence of this theatre form at all, much less its centrality to transforming public consciousness.

Experiencing a concert party of the troupe style that developed in the 1950s and continues through today is like riding an old-fashioned roller coaster: It is a rattletrap ride along a predictable yet thrilling course of ups and downs, careening wildly from sentimental pathos to ridiculous buffoonery. Concert parties are roughly fashioned, delighting and stirring audiences in no small part because of their unpretentiousness. They destabilize ordinary life, yet one's connections to the ground, the sky, and the laws of gravity are not seriously undermined, just temporarily altered. Shows are glutted with a profusion of clownish artifice. The overall aesthetic is broad, vulgar, and makeshift. Actors' faces are sometimes cartoonishly painted. Men often appear in women's roles and speak in shrill falsetto or coarse baritone voices. The only scenery is a backdrop made from a patchwork piece of cloth strung on a line between propped-up wooden poles. The staging is flat and two-dimensional, determined not by realistic use of space, but by the position of microphones placed downstage in a line. Characters directly address the audience, confessing their problems, giving advice, or soliciting the audience's opinion about how to proceed in an interpersonal dilemma. They may even appeal to the audience for money to help solve a financial crisis in the play.

Shows typically begin with an opening chorus, followed by a comic monologue performed by a character known as "Bob," the same stock character that first developed in the 1920s and was subsequently made famous by Bob Johnson in the 1930s.[30] A Bob's outfit, while tattered and drab, is invariably decorated with colorful patches and scarves. His mouth and one or two of his eyes are rimmed with white chalky powder. Contemporary comedian Bob Okala straps an oversized alarm clock around his wrist as if it were a watch. Around his neck, serving as a bow tie, is an hourglass-shaped wooden pestle. These costumes, like many aspects of the concert party, appear hastily improvised from random kitchen utensils, sewing scraps, and discarded household items. Practitioners say conventions such as garish costumes, face painting, and female impersonation communicate to the audience that "we are coming to do something: we are doing a concert!" (Ghana Concert Parties Union 1995).

The essential nature of the concert party—what sets it apart from other Ghanaian performance forms—is a topic practitioners often debate. According to members of the Ghana Concert Parties Union, chairs, or rather lack of chairs, is what distinguishes the concert party from its sister performing art, "drama."[31] Concert party actors do not like to sit down on stage while performing. They are impatient with sedentary acting and "realistic" cause-and-effect plot development, preferring stories in which characters experience mercurial and miraculous changes of fortune. For instance, in a play performed by the Fanti Trio in 1961, a homely woman is transformed into a stunning beauty when she and her husband follow the advice of a ghost, take up farming for a living, and become rich on the profits (Fanti Trio 1961b; 1995b). In another play called *Beautiful Nonsense,* a passing stranger gives a poor man a large sum of cash. "I became rich just now!" he exclaims (Fanti Trio 1961a; 1995a, 10). Rather than take the money to search for work at Tema Harbor as the stranger advises, he falls in love with a girl at first sight, showers her with money, and posthaste proposes marriage. She immediately accepts, and the couple inform the audience they are now married. No sooner is the marriage announced than a second belle comes to the stage, the young man again falls in love, and another spontaneous marriage is performed. Then a pathetic orphan enters and she begs for help. The man relents and gives her money too. His pockets are soon emptied, and consequently his wives divorce him. All of this action happens in real time, with no attempt to convey a passage of weeks, days, or even hours. Thus within a span of twenty-five minutes, a poor man becomes rich, wins two wives, helps an orphan, loses all his money, and gets divorced.

While the narrative structure, visual style, characterization, and use of space and time in concert parties are often abrupt and non-illusionistic, audiences nevertheless experience intense emotional engagement with the dramatic action. Spectators are demonstrative, rebuking characters for their grievous deeds and waving their arms in the air when the bad guy gets his well-deserved comeuppance. Spectators frequently weep in sympathy with a character's travails and some become so engrossed in performances that they hurl objects at or even assault actors playing evil stepmothers or ruthless thieves. When Kakaiku's Concert Party performed the Cinderella-like *Egyankaba,* the actor playing the evil stepmother suffered so much abuse from spectators that the troupe had to open their shows with a disclaimer reminding the audience they were only actors and the actions on stage were not real (Oppong and Oppong #95.40).

Performances elicit such an intense degree of empathy not through subtle plot development and well-developed characters with psychological depth, but rather through dense signifiers that draw upon Akan proverbs and *akutia.* Shows are packed with allusions to a stock repertoire of conflicts and idioms that have immediate and powerful resonance among spectators. Highlife music—woven throughout every show, intensifying moments of anguish, despair, and jubilation—plays an important role in this emotional signification process. Highlife is an essential part of Ghana's daily life (Collins 1976a; 1994b). Walking down a street in Kumasi, Accra, Takoradi, or any number of smaller towns, one hears radios in beauty shops, provision stores, petrol stations, and drinking spots all tuned to highlife playing on the radio station. In the market, highlife blares from kiosks selling cassettes by the latest pop stars. People riding jitney buses listen to the distinctive rhythms and proverbial lyrics of highlife played over bus sound systems.

Song lyrics depict pitiful experiences: "When you are penniless, all of life is bitter," "If you are jobless in this world, you will never know your family members."[32] Highlife song lyrics are themselves dense signifiers as they frequently incorporate proverbs, a fundamental aspect of Akan orality. Proverbs are used in daily life as well as formal occasions such as funerals, installations of chiefs, and court proceedings. Distilled essences with multivalent and opaque meanings, proverbs are dependent on both the sender's knowledge of the appropriate occasion for invoking them and the receiver's intelligent interpretation. Direct confrontation with elders and superiors is discouraged in Akan culture, so proverbs are a means of indirect criticism and dissent (Yankah 1989a; 1989b, 86–87, 137–149; 1995, 51–52). Proverbial highlife lyrics can be used at an event such as a funeral to communicate contentious messages among disputing family members. For instance, a widow may request a song to be played that criticizes family members for being interested in her dead husband only for his estate. As the song plays over the loudspeakers at the funeral, the widow may dance in front of the funeral guests, using highly codified gestures to reinforce the song's lyrics:

> Brothers and sisters, the family honors the dead
> If you are jobless in this world,
> You will never know your family members,
> None will respond to your call.
> But when you lie dead, then they provide a coffin.
> I never knew, the family honors the dead. (Fanti Trio 1961a; 1995a, 5)

When a song such as *"Ebusua Dɔ Fun"* or "The Family Honors the Dead" appears in a concert party, as it did in the Fanti Trio's 1961 performance of *Beautiful Nonsense*, it is capable of triggering a wide range of emotions and memories among spectators who have experienced this same song in other contexts. Spectators undoubtedly will have attended or been personally involved in a funeral where opportunistic family members exploited the occasion for personal gain. By incorporating such well known songs, concert parties thus achieve an immediate emotional bond with their audiences, a connection strong enough to endure abrupt changes of tone and direction. Even as plots race forward and take improbable twists and turns, familiar motifs sustain emotional plausibility.

The proverb *ebusua dɔ fun* is a part of what Biodun Jeyifo describes as the "vast repository of expressive material so created by the popular mind and extensively quarried by the travelling theatre troupes" of West Africa (1984, 4). While the Fanti Trio used the proverb *ebusua dɔ fun* in 1961 as the basis for a song in their play *Beautiful Nonsense*, a rival troupe, the Ahanta Trio, was inspired to create an entire play on the theme of this proverb that very same year.

The Ahanta Trio's play *The Family Honors the Dead* is an extended deliberation on the complexities of family responsibilities and obligations within Akan culture (1961; 1995). One of the main characters is an *ebusuapanyin*, or head of the matrilineage.[33] In Akan culture, the *ebusuapanyin* shoulders enormous responsibilities, including settling family disputes and intervening in medical and financial crises. He presides over family funerals and other customary rites, and he advises individual family members about employment, marriage, and important life decisions. Family members also have obligations toward the *ebusuapanyin*. First and foremost, they owe him respect. They must call on him not only in times of crisis, but must also greet him and keep him informed of their activities on a regular basis. Family members are also obliged to contribute to the *ebusuapanyin* a portion of their earnings, if they can afford it. The extended family has long served as Ghana's form of social welfare and insurance.[34] In order for this system to work, all members of the family must participate according to their abilities and assigned roles.

The play begins with a woman directly addressing the audience. She says, "Well, you that have gathered here, when I came to this world, I tried my best to think less about money. . . . However, poor people rarely succeed in any endeavors they make. Whatever I say is ignored by the head of my family" (1961; 1995, 2).[35] She complains her life is hard not just because she is poor, but because she has no immediate relative among the "top men" in her *ebusua keseɛ,* her extended matrilineage. When the woman concludes her soliloquy, her daughter comes in and says, "Mama! There is a problem! My younger sister is seriously ill!" In typical concert party fashion, this plot development occurs within seconds, without illusionistic depiction of setting, character, or conflict. As soon as the mother hears this news about her sick daughter, she turns to the audience and says, "My brothers and sisters gathered here, this is an example of what I just said. I have no relative. I have just learned of my daughter's illness. From where should I seek help? I don't know where to take her. Who will help us?" (1995, 4). Although the plot develops abruptly and the characters have not been developed in any depth, audiences nevertheless immediately engaged with this play. The emotional involvement of spectators was due both to the ubiquity of conflicts within Akan matrilineages and the emblematic way in which such conflicts can be signified using Akan modes of communication.

The woman takes her problem to the head of her extended family, her *ebusuapanyin,* but he refuses to help. He asks, "Is she not a married woman? Is she not working with her husband at Tamale? Have they ever sent me a penny?" (1995, 4). Because the young couple did not remember the *ebusuapanyin* in times of financial security and good health, he will not assist them in their time of need. The *ebusuapanyin* tells the family, "I have no money. Solve your own problems." He says the family funds have run dry due to neglect, so he is unable to solve the girl's medical crisis. All the characters then contest the *ebusuapanyin*'s refusal. The girl's mother contends that the problem is not that her daughter failed to contribute money, but that she, the mother, has no direct close relatives among the male elders of her extended family. Her son challenges the *ebusuapanyin,* "You call yourself the head of the family. What happens when you ignore the responsibilities this position entails?" (1995, 7).

The sick girl soon dies. When the *ebusuapanyin* hears of her death, his attitude changes completely. He weeps and offers to pay all the funeral expenses, such as money for the coffin and drinks for the guests. The *ebusuapanyin*'s motive, which the other family members recognize immediately, is not altruistic. Rather, he wants to collect all the monetary donations people will bring to the funeral. Customarily, the one who pays for the funeral is the one who collects the proceeds.[36]

At the funeral, the *ebusuapanyin* sits at the donation table with his clerks. He transforms the audience into funeral guests as he calls out to them like an auctioneer petitioning for donations. The sister of the dead girl, unable to bear this abuse of the *abusua keseε,* intervenes by calling upon the moral authority of the audience. Her mode of addressing the audience is typical of the concert party. She speaks to them as brethren, thereby including them as part of the "family":

> Well, brothers and sisters, just imagine. My own sister was ill. The head of the family couldn't do anything to help, because he wanted her to die so that he could sell the corpse and enjoy the booty. With that idea in his head, he would not give us any money to treat our sister's illness, but he is now actively receiving donations after her death. What sort of family is this? (1961; 1995, 13)

The girl accuses the *ebusuapanyin* of wanting to trade on her sister's corpse. It is from this accusation the play gets its title, *Ebusua Dɔ Fun.* On one hand *ebusua dɔ fun* means "the family honors the dead," an expression which one might use to praise a well-performed funeral. If a family respects the deceased, they will honor him or her with a proper burial. But the phrase can also mean "the family loves the corpse," meaning they were not interested in the deceased when that person was alive.[37] It is an accusation one would level at family members who are only interested in the deceased for their own personal profit and enjoyment of the funeral celebration. This duplicity of meaning is typical of Akan proverbs, which communicate criticism through opacity. Akan indirection, or *akutia,* protects both the speaker and the target of the implied criticism (Yankah 1995, 51–52; 1997).

The Family Honors the Dead touched on delicate issues every spectator was likely to have experienced. Tensions and abuses within the extended family were at the very heart of Akan culture as it negotiated the economic and cultural strains of the colonial and postcolonial world. The play calls for ethical and moral accountability in contemporary life and a critical attitude toward tradition. Socioeconomic changes introduced during colonialism, such as wage and migrant labor, put new pressures on the family structure. Whereas tribute to an *ebusuapanyin* might once have been a much more fluid system of generosity and reciprocity among neighbors, in colonial Ghana, family members often migrated to distant cities where they performed work and sent wages back home. Their participation in the extended family system could thus become reduced to a quantifiable "bottom line." This is exactly what happened to the sick daughter in *The Family Honors the Dead.* She had moved with her husband far away to Tamale. The *ebusuapanyin* complains that when she and her husband migrated, they did not send money back home.

At the end of the play, all the characters sing a song that asks, "Has the family done the right thing? What the family has done isn't good. They trade on the dead." The *ebusuapanyin* then admits to the audience that "when my granddaughter was ill, I didn't go near her." He accepts the blame and then sings a song extolling the new nation of Ghana (at the time just four years old). He sings:

> The new Ghana is wonderful, beautiful,
> The new Ghana, and everybody.
> The new Ghana is fearful, wonderful, beautiful.
> The new Ghana and everybody.
> We thank God. (Ahanta Trio 1961; 1995, 14–15)

When he finishes singing, the *ebusuapanyin* tells the audience what he will do with the funeral donations he has collected. Like other characters, he addresses the audience as brethren, including them in the "family" conflict:

> Brothers and sisters gathered here, I have received 25 pounds in donation. I'm going to buy tobacco with it for my pipe. That's the news item I have for you. Whoever would do things the way I have done them will be disgraced one day. People will look on him with contempt. (*Audience laughs and makes comments.*)

And the play ends, just like that. While the plot seems to be heading toward a sober call for ethical accountability and an assurance that justice will be done, the final moments undermine such an interpretation. The *ebusuapanyin* appears to take responsibility for his wrongdoing and then praises the new Ghana with the empty adjectives "wonderful, beautiful." He deflects his culpability by using political rhetoric, and thereby moves the play's focus from the immediate sphere of the family to a more general public sphere of national pride. The *ebusuapanyin* then quips, in a lighthearted aside, that he plans to keep the funeral profits and squander them on a frivolous personal luxury item, tobacco. The audience that witnessed this play in 1961 merely laughed, the play ended, and everyone went home, presumably satisfied. In a few short minutes, *The Family Honors the Dead* moved from the domestic sphere of the Akan matrilineage to the new entity of the modern nation state, finally ending by dismissing the *ebusuapanyin*'s greed.

Concert parties are a highly didactic genre, so what "lesson" did this play teach? Its ambivalent conclusion and rather abrupt incorporation of nationalist rhetoric complicate any interpretation, though these elements are entirely consistent with what I identify as the concert party's paradoxical style, its thrilling rattle-trap roller-coaster ride. The *ebusuapanyin*'s allusions to Ghana suggest that the narrative is not only about individualistic greed in the extended family system but is also a parable about corruption in the larger arena of national politics.

In the play, the brother of the sick girl asks the family elder, "You call yourself the head of the family. What happens when you ignore the responsibilities this position entails?" According to Akan conventions of indirection, this question to the head of the family could also have been addressed to chiefs, parliamentarians, and even Ghana's head of state.[38] What happens when these leaders ignore the responsibilities their positions entail? Public perception of avarice and excess in Kwame Nkrumah's administration, which was in power at the time this play was staged, ultimately contributed to Nkrumah's downfall. The Ahanta Trio may have been implicitly criticizing the state by depicting such a morally reprehensible *ebusuapanyin*. As mentioned earlier, stories about the domestic sphere of the Akan matriclan imply the public sphere of the state, since the polity in Akan culture is often perceived as merely an extension of the extended family. Family and state are "not differentiated in kind but only in degree," according to A. N. Langley (1970, 35).[39]

The Family Honors the Dead is an example of how the concert party provided its audiences with a forum for reflecting critically on the uses and abuses of power and institutions in Ghanaian life in 1961. I want to turn now briefly, in the final section of this chapter, to look at a stock character from this period. I will focus on the character Felicia from the Akan Trio's 1961 play *Don't Covet Your Neighbors' Possessions* (*Mma W'enyi Mmber Obi N'adze*). In terms of the history of the concert party, Felicia represents a significant character because she is a continuity between prewar and postwar theatrical practices. Felicia is the 1960s version of the Anglicized Lady central to concert trios of the 1930s and 1940s.

Married to a wealthy man named Kwamena Left, Felicia is a frivolous woman whose penchant for speaking English is both loved and despised by her husband. "Behaving as if she were white!" he complains in an aside to the audience (Akan Trio 1961a; 1995a, 18). Kwamena married Felicia because he admires her Western ways. She is an appropriate wife for a man of his stature. However, the problem with Felicia is that she outclasses Kwamena. She speaks too much English, and he does not always understand what she is saying. He is also annoyed she cannot cook and do other chores that would be expected of any traditional Akan wife.

Felicia's behavior brilliantly captures the style and tone of classic concert party lady impersonation. All dialogue preceding Felicia's entrance is in Fante, but Felicia addresses her lover Kwamena exclusively in English. They take great pleasure in exchanging English greetings.

> *Felicia:* Hello there!
> *Kwamena:* Hello, hello, hello-oo, hello-ooo!
> *Felicia:* Good evening.
> *Kwamena:* Good evening my darling.
> *Felicia:* Where have you been for the past hour or two?! I haven't seen you for a long time.
> *Kwamena:* Oh, I've been lingering about. Lingering about.
> *Felicia:* Lingering about.
> *Kwamena:* Yeah. (*Addressing audience*) Now, before I say anything, I would like to make an informal introduction of my darling to you. (*Audience murmurs*)
> *Felicia:* Fine. (Akan Trio 1961a; 1995a, 9)

In her first scene, Felicia is completely at ease in English, but Kwamena's language abilities are more limited, and he soon falters and reverts to Fante. He asks Felicia to introduce herself to the audience, for they have never before "seen her kind."

Felicia speaks to the audience as if she were a guest on a television variety show. With a voice that sails erratically in the soprano registers, Felicia says she is "ex-TREME-ly happy to be given this GOLD-en oppor-TUN-ity" to say a few words. Having just returned from the United Kingdom, she is "HERE tonight to entertain you with a SPE-cial song entitled, 'I'm Just a Bubble.'" She begins singing an English-language song, "Reaching for Someone," at a slow, ambling pace, but the tempo soon lurches into a frenzied tap dance. Felicia finds the dance exhilarating, screeching, "I LOVE this!" Meanwhile Kwamena labors to keep up with her. In her next song, "In the Mood," the tempo again races out of control, and she and Kwamena are seized by a fit of rock 'n' roll dance hysteria, at the end of which Kwamena is left speechless and exhausted.

No explicit moral judgement or critique of Felicia is offered in the play. She remains throughout a sympathetic character, untroubled by an identity crisis and generally accepted by those around her. Many spectators came to concert parties expressly because they wanted to see and emulate characters such as Felicia, who could speak refined English, wear fashionable clothes from abroad, and dance the most up-to-date steps. Yet Felicia is a parody of an essential type; she is the prototype of an African woman who has "been to" England. Felicia's wildly exuberant performance of Western language and manners is a torrent of mimesis. All surface and no substance, this performance of European femininity by a Ghanaian man in drag deconstructs an ideal. No doubt English "ladyhood" held a powerful influence and legitimacy for many Ghanaians during colonialism. However, Felicia's mimetic excess divests English "ladyhood" of its power. Pushed to a disorienting extreme, the "lady" self-destructs, disintegrating into so many contrived gestures, fashion accessories, and falsetto squeals.

After dancing rock 'n' roll with Kwamena, Felicia cheerfully bids "bye-bye" and leaves a stunned and breathless Kwamena alone onstage. He slowly collects himself and tries to interpret the performance for the audience. He speaks English:

> Well, La . . . la . . . la . . . ladies . . . labi . . . (*He speaks gibberish.*) Ladies and gentlemen, this is actually a good inter-pre-ta-TION of modern civiliza-TION. I am not here to teach you what's happening behind the Iron Curtain. But I am here rather to DEMON-strate to you what is happening over THERE. Sure, everything will be nice, nothing but rock 'n' roll. (1961a; 1995a, 10)

This speech is what a number of people I interviewed call "concert nonsense," an absurd and delightfully free-ranging discourse.[40] While nothing about the show up to this point suggests anything beyond a local perspective on domestic life, Kwamena adds a note of global awareness, mentioning the Soviet Union, which in 1961 had extensive diplomatic relations with newly independent Ghana. He also alludes (presumably) to America, the birthplace of the rock 'n' roll craze that was then raging among Ghana's youth. Kwamena tells the audience "this is a actually good interpretation of modern civilization," a comment that may have referred to Felicia, the foreign pop ballads, the rock 'n' roll dancing, the careening tempo of the scene, or, indeed, the entire concert party play.

Kwamena Left's appraisal, "this is actually a good interpretation of modern civilization," can be extended to the entire history of the concert party genre. This popular, syncretic, improvised theatre form expresses a great deal about how some people in colonial and postcolonial Africa have creatively grappled with rapidly shifting identities, diverse cultural influences, and tumultuous social transformations of the twentieth century. The political significance of the concert party as it developed in the independence era was implicit in its careening and unpredictable style. Shows moved abruptly from local particularities to national and international generalities; from moral aphorisms to frivolous, amoral asides; from Akan proverbs to American rock 'n' roll. This topsy-turvy style expressed and helped constitute the concert party's public. As Ghanaians took possession of their country, concert parties became forums in which they envisioned themselves as part of larger communities, those defined not by face-to-face contact but by more abstract notions of ethnicity and nationalism. While concert parties of the earlier eras served a similarly integrative function, shows during the independence era blossomed, becoming far more aesthetically and thematically complex. By dramatizing social disruptions caused by inheritance disputes, migration, or a shifting economic base, concert parties addressed the concerns of its public— Ghanaian citizens busy assessing the legacy of colonialism and inventing a postcolonial future.

Epilogue

Though my study stops in the mid-1960s, the concert party continued through subsequent decades and was still active, if not thriving, in the mid-1990s when I did my research. The 1970s and 1980s saw an increase in the number of women in concert parties, and highlife music continued to dominate, for no troupe could be successful without a good band. The late 1970s were a particularly rough time for concert troupes. Political instability, drought, and famine took a toll on performers and audiences alike. But as the country got back on its feet in the 1980s, so too did concerts. In an effort to entice audiences away from television, the increasingly available rival entertainment form, concert parties grew in duration, stretching out further and further into the night. Troupes promised spectators a lot of entertainment for their money: A typical show of the early 1990s began at 9 P.M. with several hours of music as the band played covers of pop songs, then their own original compositions. Around 1 or 2 in the morning, a backdrop of cloth would be strung across the back of the stage and the dramatic portion of the program commenced. Typical plays—full of comic business, sub-plots, and musical interludes—lasted for several hours, concluding in the predawn morning. During these marathon events, which could be cold and long, spectators wandered in and out of the performance venue, often an open-air cinema hall or large family compound. Some spectators chewed cola nuts to keep awake, others gave in briefly to sleep, napping on benches or on a neighbor's shoulder as the actors declaimed into microphones, their voices crackling through loudspeakers and echoing in the surrounding neighborhood.

As the number of households in Ghana with access to television sets and video grew, the concert party began to experience a decline in popularity in the early 1990s. "Ghana films," narrative feature films often shot on consumer-grade VHS video, further eroded the concert party audience base. But when I arrived in Ghana in 1994 for a year's worth of research, the National Theatre in Accra was just beginning a concert party "revival" series. In an effort to fill its expansive and often empty auditorium, the National Theatre devised a regular concert party series that would appeal to middle-class audiences. Shows happened on weekend afternoons, so they provided entertainment for the whole family, adults and children. Afternoon shows also helped counter the stigma concert parties had acquired through association with alcohol and night-long frivolity. The National Theatre auditorium, with air conditioning and plush seats, was far more comfortable than open-air cinema halls, which usually had only hard wooden benches to sit on. But the real key to the success of the National Theatre revival series was that it was taped by the Ghana Broadcasting Corporation and televised throughout the country. This program became the most popular and talked-about show on Ghanaian television.

From the perspective of the performers, the success of the National Theatre concert party revival series was more qualified. Actors and bandleaders were dissatisfied by the low pay they were receiving for their National Theatre appearances in the mid-1990s. Artists were also apprehensive about their loss of producing autonomy, for their work at the National Theatre came under the artistic direction and financial control of a state-sponsored institution. Despite these reservations, concert performers generally agreed that the revival series was a good thing both for the concert party genre and for the careers of individual performers and troupes who appeared in this venue. Reportedly, there has been a recent wave of new, younger troupes forming who seem to be making a name for themselves. Whether the concert party will continue to withstand the growing competition from television and videos remains to be seen.

Kwame Anthony Appiah concludes in his epilogue to *In My Father's House* that "only something so particular as a single life—as my father's life, encapsulated in the complex pattern of social and personal relations around his coffin—could capture the multiplicity of our lives in a postcolonial world" (1992, 191). While concert parties do not represent single lives, they do represent the fullness and contradictions of life as lived by many average people in one formerly colonized nation. While shows may appear at first glance to be superficial melodramas, concert performances offer a far more complex perspective on the colonial and postcolonial situation than one sees in most mass media representations of Africa, or even in postcolonial literary theory. Though they have predictable plots and stereotypical characters, concert parties are as resistant to reductive binaries such as "tradition" and "modernity," "colonizer" and "colonized" as was the life of Appiah's father, "Paa Joe."

Since the concert party's inception at the turn of the century, it has constantly exploited the contradictions of its location in a cultural and geographic border zone. Early twentieth-century performances excited contentious interpublic relations in coastal society and addressed conflicts created by the introduction of new modes of social differentiation under colonial rule. Concert artists of the 1930s and 1940s appropriated ideas from Ananse, Charlie Chaplin, Kru laborers, Al Jolson, and Cab Calloway and transformed this material according to their own formulas of invention. What changed in the 1950s was not the eclecticism of the concert party's allusions, but the scope of its referents and the sheer velocity with which shows lurched between ostensibly disconnected, incongruous parts.

Even as concert parties of the 1960s satirized the affectations of the "been-to" colonial concert party Lady—the stereotype that dominated concert stages in the 1930s and 1940s—they also travestied the humble origins of their supposed heroes, rural agriculturalists. For instance, the Akan Trio's *Don't Covet Your Neighbor's Possessions* parodies farmer Koo Nimo's backwardness and lack of education. Koo Nimo is so simple-minded he becomes easily confused about basic issues such as who is in his family. He says all his brothers and sisters are dead, except for himself and his wife (an absurdity, of course, since his wife is not his sister) (1961a; 1995a, 3). When Koo Nimo tells about his courtship of Araba, the audience howls at his misuse of English: "I was making my *choose*" (6). Koo Nimo complains that when he met Araba's parents to ask for her hand in marriage, he was harassed by Araba's brothers' demands for *sekan,* or "knives." The audience roars at Koo Nimo for so hilariously misinterpreting requests for *akontansekan,* a customary donation a potential husband pays to his brothers-in-law. Koo Nimo appears as a comic "uncivilized bush man," subject to as much derision as the colonial "been-to" Lady Felicia.

At the end of *Don't Covet Your Neighbor's Possessions,* Koo Nimo's wife Araba advises married women to discourage the amorous overtures of men on the street. Meanwhile her husband appeals to the men in the audience to "leave other people's wives alone" (1961a; 1995a, 30). His advice concludes, "Praise God!," to which the spectators at the Swedru Sports Stadium in 1961 responded, "Hallelujah!" Finally Kwamena, the city-slicker who has been thoroughly disgraced for having tried to seduce Araba, steps forward. He offers another, less orthodox interpretation of the play, in English:

> Ladies and gentlemen, there is an epidemic which is even buried into the heart of the socialism of this country, and that sort of disease I term it socialmilation [*sic*]. You are all aware of this factor, and there is no need of saying anything about it. But rather, I am laying emphasis on what have been said: That he who ever does this kind of scandalous practice, we shall find you out, and deal with you according to our worship, because they are turning to degrade this dear Ghana of ours. Ladies and gentlemen, I am done.

Like the speech Kwamena gave earlier in the play in which he claimed "this is actually a good interpretation of modern civilization," this monologue is a delightfully free-ranging rumination. Kwamena temporarily shifts the play from domestic matters to the larger arena of national affairs. He uses abstract English language which would not have been understood by the majority of spectators. Kwamena's use of English is a power ploy, an attempt to regain the dignity and respect he lost in the course of the play. But his pseudo-political jargon is quickly dismissed by the other characters. Felicia rejects him by saying in Akan, "My husband has spoken English. Let him get away from this place!" And Koo Nimo complains, "Oh, Kwamena, you have spoken English again. You know I, Koo Nimo, don't understand English." Kwamena's attempt to appropriate the play's conclusion by speaking English is swiftly derailed. The Akan-speaking characters, unintimidated by the colonizer's language, easily dismiss Kwamena and proceed to "sum up" the show as they wish.

While the format of an epilogue invites a final summation, any single conclusion I could offer about the significance of the concert party feels as arbitrary as the end of concert party plays themselves. How can one "sum up" a theatre form so eclectic in derivation, so contradictory in style, so wide-ranging in audience appeal? I could underscore a theme pursued throughout this book—the concert party's re-invention of modernity—and explore the demands this African counter-discourse of modernity places on Eurocentric notions of the "modern." Or I could expand upon the performative dimensions of colonialism, the ways in which colonial ideologies were sedimented, made "real," and re-invented through embodied behavior. I might underscore the importance of deciphering Akan-based theories of communication implicit in concert party invention and production. How can a proverb like *"ohia ma adwennwen"* open up our understanding of this African performance genre? I could also return to my critique of postcolonial theory and argue for the need for more empirically detailed studies of postcolonial popular culture. Or I might end on a note not previously explored in this book: a discussion of the desire expressed by concert party practitioners with whom I worked for a coherent narrative history of their theatre form. How did I reconcile their desires with the current academic critique of narrative historiography? Like contending characters in a concert party play, each of these lines of argument clamors to have the last word. But with concert parties, one must look not to the end for meaning, but to the middle, and to the gaps, silences, and disjunctions as well as the implied messages suggested through Akan indirection, *akutia.*

Notes

1. Introduction

1. On *asafo* music, see Nketia (1974, 7, 24); on highlife, see Collins (1976b and 1994b).

2. See Bame (1985); Barber (1982, 1986, and 1995); Barber and Ògúndíjo (1994); Barber, Collins, and Ricard (1997); Clark (1979); Collins (1994a); Darkey (1991); Jeyifo (1984); and Ricard (1986).

3. Popular theatre forms are generally improvised and non-scripted. Only very recently have productions been recorded on videotape.

4. For more extensive treatment of the concert party from the mid-1960s through the 1990s, see also Bame (1985); Barber, Collins, and Ricard (1997); Collins (1994a); and Darkey (1991).

5. "Chop bars" are West African fast food stands.

6. See for instance Gates (1988); Mudimbe (1988); Drewal (1991); Appiah (1992); Taiwo (1995); Jeyifo (1996); Oyêwúmí (1997); and Adéèkò (1998).

7. While I considered trying to incorporate more of these archival sound recordings into this book because this material is so rich, I felt it was important to give a balanced treatment of each era of concert party history and not weight the study too heavily in the 1960s, the period when the archival recordings were made.

2. Reading Blackface in West Africa

1. For a similar critique of the status of history in Paul Gilroy's *The Black Atlantic,* see Dayan (1996).

2. See for instance an interview with Ghanaian playwright Mohammed ben Abdallah (1992, 33).

3. See for instance Scott (1998).

4. Whether or not there exists a direct relationship between American minstrelsy and performance traditions exported from Africa and retained by slaves in the New World is a notoriously vexed question in theatre historiography. See Ellison (1964, 45–59); Sacks and Sacks (1993); and Toll (1974, 40–51). Some scholars assume that there were no "genuine" elements of African and African American culture in minstrelsy; the genre was a white construction of blackness that had little to do with the "real" thing (Lyon 1980, 150–159). Although a number of early American minstrel performers claimed to have observed and copied the dances, dialects, and jokes of slaves, these claims may be interpreted as hyped-up fabrications created for advertisement. But this dismissal of the possibility that minstrelsy appropriated "genuine" African and African American performance traditions is premature. William Mahar's linguistic analysis of stage dialects used during the first forty years of blackface entertainment asserts that white Negro impersonators deployed three distinct varieties of black English: West African Pidgin English, Plantation Creole, and Black English vernacular (1985, 260–285). If "Negro" speech in minstrelsy was not based on observation of slaves, how could such distinct dialects have made their way into sheet music lyrics and sketch books? In addition, Howard L. Sacks and Judith Rose Sacks's groundbreaking study *Way Up North in Dixie* persuasively demonstrates that minstrel entertainers had ample opportunity to observe and indeed collaborate with black musicians in the north, not simply on southern plantations as white performers often claimed (1993).

5. While minstrelsy scholarship is vast, no single study has yet considered the genre's international dimensions. On Jamaica, see Hill (1992); on Nigeria, see Owomoyela (1991, 199–201); on South Africa, see Coplan (1985, 37–42) and Erlmann (1991, 27–37); on Australia, see Waterhouse (1990).

6. My analysis of minstrel dramaturgy is informed by extensive examination of the Harvard Theatre Collection's (HTC) holdings of minstrel playbills, posters, sheet music, jokebooks, and dialogue pamphlets, as well as the University of Chicago Library's Atkinson Collection of Ethiopian Drama (ACED). On the dramaturgy of minstrel shows, see Toll (1974, 51–57).

7. The written history of the concert party credits solo comedian Teacher Yalley as having created the concert party form (Bame 1985, 8–9; Collins 1976a, 50–57; Darkey 1991, 30–31; Sutherland 1970, 6–7). However, my interviews of older residents in Sekondi and Tarkwa, oral histories of veteran performers, and archival research in colonial newspapers and the files of the Optimism Club of Sekondi indicates that the perceived importance of Yalley may be the result of an over-reliance on Sutherland's biography of Bob Johnson as a sole source of primary documentation. Colonial newspapers give evidence that African amateur comedians performed at elite social gatherings, quite possibly in blackface makeup, as early as 1903 (*Gold Coast Leader* 1903). While numerous secondary sources on the concert party credit Yalley with having begun his performing career at the Optimism Club in 1918, there does not seem to be any documentary evidence to support this. The Optimists did not have their own building with a stage and facilities for social gatherings until the mid-1920s. In addition to Yalley, there were a number of amateur comedians performing in Sekondi in the 1920s (Ruhle 1925).

8. For a description of the structure of a typical concert party show, see Collins (1994b, 19–23).

9. On the sociology of concert party performers, see Chapter 4.

10. Kwame Mbia Hammond says the word "trant" came from a substance that was used in the colonial days to color school chalkboards. Actors would rub this black paste on their faces to create blackface (#93.6).

11. A $5 million lawsuit over a blackface skit staged at a conference attended by African Americans at Club Med in Senegal suggests how disastrous such a performance could have been at Ghana's Panafest (*Chicago Tribune* 1996).

12. While rituals and festivals in Ghana often have a serious premise, they can also include humor and more light-hearted activity. For instance, the Akwambo festival in Swedru is a carnivalesque event in which men comically dress as women and paint their faces garish colors.

13. Thomas to Sir Philip Cunliffe-Lister, January 3, 1934, ADM 12/5/103, NAG, quoted in Shaloff (1972, 243).

14. On literature deemed subversive by the Gold Coast government, see the *Negro Worker* (September 1935); Spitzer and Denzer (1973, 428); Shaloff (1972, 250–251f); and Cunard ([1933] 1970).

15. See *The Negro Worker* (September 1934) and Shaloff (1972, 250).

16. Many veteran concert performers whom I interviewed believed Al Jolson was of African descent.

17. For recent theories on the performativity of identity see Butler (1990, 1993); see also Parker and Sedgwick (1995).

3. "THE ROWDY LOT CREATED THE USUAL DISTURBANCE"

1. According to colonial newspapers, the name "concert party" does not appear at all in the historical record until 1933, when it was used by a short-lived Accra troupe called the Co-Optimists Concert Party (*Gold Coast Independent* 1933). Therefore, in this chapter, I adopt the more historically accurate term "concert" to describe the early forms of this emergent theatre form.

2. On storytelling, see Yeboa-Dankwa (1988). On "traditional" music, see Cole and Ross (1977, 170–179) and Nketia (1963a, 15–26).

3. This group may well have fashioned themselves after a British troupe by the same name. See Sterne and de Bear (1926). On a visit to the Gold Coast by the British Royal Air Force Concert Party, see the *Gold Coast Independent* (1943a).

4. "Fante" is a term that indicates both language and ethnicity. The Fante language is a dialect of the Akan language, Asante Twi being the other prominent dialect. The Fante people, who live along Ghana's coast, are a segment of the Akan ethnic group.

5. On counterpublics, see Fraser (1992).

6. A Standard VII certificate indicated that a student had completed at least ten years of formal schooling (Foster 1965, 118).

7. On Gold Coast newspapers, see Jones-Quartey (1965, 1968).

8. On "radical bilingualism," see Mehrez (1991).

9. Although Kemp lived in the Gold Coast for nine years, he never learned to speak any local language. See Kemp (1898, 66)

10. Singing-band music was popular in Christian circles, for it helped win new converts (Kemp 1898, 81, 181). This music also helped pioneer African-language education, for singing bands taught members how to read and write Fante and other Ghanaian languages (*Gold Coast Spectator* 1929). On the development of new music styles in turn-of-the-century Gold Coast, see Mensah (1966, 20). On *adenkum* songs, see Nketia (1963a, 67–74).

11. See *Gold Coast Nation* (1914d, 1914c) and Kemp (1898, 169–170).

12. Kobina Sekyi's *The Blinkards* translates "scholar" as *aburoba,* literally "child of overseas."

13. This play was performed at the Kumasi Oddfellows dance with the Accra Orchestra in 1934 (*Gold Coast Spectator* 1934c).

14. The identity of this couple remains obscure: Bob Vans believes they were Jamaican, John Collins and Kwabena Bame think this team was of African American descent, and John Darkey gives evidence that they were Liberians (Bame 1985, 9; Collins 1976a, 52; Darkey 1991, 25–28; Vans #95.30). Based upon the language Glass and Grant spoke

in private and the style of dancing they occasionally performed, August Williams suspects Glass and Grant were Kru people from Liberia (Williams #95.52). A review printed in the *Gold Coast Spectator* in 1932 corroborates: It compares Williams to J. C. Glass "the Liberian comedian" with whom he had studied (*Gold Coast Spectator* 1932h).

15. "Blues" in Ghanaian parlance denotes a style of highlife music with somber lyrics.

16. The neighboring city of Takoradi soon became a rival for commercial preeminence. In 1920, the colonial government chose Takoradi as the site for a new deepwater harbor, the construction of which was completed in 1928 (Busia [1950] 1951, 2). Sekondi's economy further declined when the Railway Headquarters moved from Sekondi to Takoradi in 1934 (Cudjoe 1995, 1).

17. The Sekondi Palladium was distinct from the Accra theatre of the same name discussed earlier.

18. While the Sekondi Optimism Club has many affinities with an American-based organization known as Optimist International, there does not appear to have been any formal affiliation between these two organizations (Thompson 1966).

19. On Bob Johnson, see Sutherland (1970, 25). "Bobs" continued to be a standard feature of the National Theatre of Ghana's concert party series in the 1990s.

20. See *Gold Coast Times,* 4 June 1938, quoted in Darkey 1991, 30–31; see also Yalley (1927a, 1927b, 1927c, 1927d).

21. See Bame (1968, 31); Collins (1976a, 50); Darkey (1991, 30); Kerr (1995, 74–78); and NCC (1985).

4. *"Ohia Ma Adwennwen,"* or *"Use Your Gumption!"*

1. Previous histories of the concert party identify a "Charles Hutton" as its pioneer. However, his name was in fact spelled "Horton," according to his family in Sekondi and Esikado. On Empire Day, see the *Gold Coast Nation* (1912). See also the description of an Empire Day concert at the Bishop's School in Accra in 1930 recounted in Chapter 2 of this book.

2. Among the many scholars who have tackled this question are Wole Soyinka (1976); Onwuchekwa Jemie Chinweizu and Ihechukwu Madubuike (1980); Ngũgĩ wa Thiong'o (1986); V. Y. Mudimbe (1988); Christopher Miller (1990); Margaret Thompson Drewal (1991, 27–33); Kwame Anthony Appiah (1992, 47–72); Kwasi Wiredu (1996); Oyèrónké Oyêwùmí (1997); and Adéléké Adéèkó (1998).

3. Concert actors in Ghana are drawn from the same "intermediate sector" of the economy as the popular theatre practitioners Karin Barber studied in Nigeria (1995, 8).

4. Although Christaller's dictionary first appeared over one hundred years ago, it continues to be the authoritative reference on Akan, according to linguist Dr. Gilbert Ansre and K. Keelson and O. Adu-Gyamfi, Akan language instructors at the University of Ghana Language Center.

5. Kakaiku's use of the tortoise is, as far as I can tell, very unusual. While Ghanaian *anansesɛm* feature many different animals, I never encountered any other story with a turtle. However, the tortoise is the primary trickster of Yorùbá folklore from Nigeria (Sekoni 1994).

6. In Ghana, as in many parts of Africa, funerals are important occasions, marking the transition of a person from life into the land of the ancestors. Funerals are rituals that relatives and friends often feel more compelled to attend than other ceremonies of passage such as weddings, cyclical festivals, or blessings of new babies.

7. *Ohia ma adwennwen* is analogous to de Certeau's theory of the "tactic." De Certeau distinguishes strategies—calculated actions based on a powerful agent's distanced observation and appraisal of a situation—from tactics, the myriad small tricks and improvisational sleights of hand through which the weak "put one over" on the strong ([1984] 1988, xix, 37–38).

8. This is the explanation given by Kakaiku's son, Moses K. Oppong II (Kakaiku's Band #95.37).

9. The following are brief biographical sketches of older performers I interviewed: Augustus Williams staged with J. T. Marbel at the Accra Palladium in the early 1920s; Bob S. Ansah founded the Gold Coast Two Bobs, a group that often entertained the British West African Frontier Force during World War II; Joseph Benjamin Amoah, Emmanuel Baidoe and Jimmie Narkwa gained their reputations with the West End Trio and the Dix Covian Jokers during the 1940s. Emmanuel Baidoe later went on to become a celebrated female impersonator with the Akan Trio; Bob Vans started his acting career in Burma, where he was stationed during World War II and was appointed to entertain the troupes. After the war, Vans and I. K. Ntama founded the Burma Jokers, which later became the Ghana Trio; Kwame Mbia Hammond and Y. B. Bampoe got their start in show business as school boys when they imitated the Dix Covian Jokers and the West End Trio. In 1946, Bampoe and Hammond formed the Yankey Trio, a short-lived troupe. Kwame Mbia Hammond continued his career with Bob Cole's Ghana Trio in the 1950s. Y. B. Bampoe briefly joined the City Trio, and then he founded the Jaguar Jokers with Hammond's brother, K. Acquaah Hammond, in 1954. The Jaguar Jokers are still intermittently active today.

10. Mercantile trade was important in the family lives of the oldest concert party practitioners about whom I was able to gather information, those who began performing in the 1930s: E. K. Dadson of the Axim Trio (born 1915), Bob Johnson of the Axim Trio (born 1904), and Bob S. Ansah of the Gold Coast Two Bobs (born 1918). However, actors who began their performance careers in the 1940s came from families employed in mining, railways, and cocoa farming and trade.

11. On the history and sociology of railway workers in Ghana, see Jeffries (1978).

12. The rise of a genuine mercantile class in the Gold Coast happened in the nineteenth century, but its impact on social change continued to be felt in the early twentieth century (Akyeampong 1996c, 47–69; Arhin 1983, 15–19).

13. The *Gold Coast Census of Population 1948* revealed a striking relationship between education and urbanization. The percentage of the population with six years of education or more was considerably higher in the cities: between 10 and 25 percent in the cities as compared with 4 percent in the country at large (discussed and interpreted by Foster 1965, 128–133).

14. According to the *Gold Coast Census of Population 1948,* in 1948 only 1.6 percent of the colony had this much education (in Foster 1963, 118–119).

15. By professional, I am referring here to the economics of performance as defined by concert actors themselves. To be "professional," one had to pursue concert parties as a primary source of income. Concert performers from the 1920s such as Augustus Williams and Teacher Yalley were essentially amateurs who continued to hold other full-time jobs. The earliest evidence of concert performers pursuing their art professionally can be found in a letter from J. B. Ansah of the Two Bobs and Their Carolina Girl to the Optimism Club in 1934, in which he stated, "Staging movements have been our sole profession with which we are gradually confronting the World's Depression" (Ansah 1934).

16. Jimmy Narkwa recalls that "for a whole year we could not come back home. We just moved from village to village, and from town to town. We could not make any money. People who showed interest in us often gave us *gari* [dried cassava], or beans and other things. When we went to Ho during mango season, it was mango in the morning, mango in the afternoon, mango all the time. We went to the mango growing areas and picked the mangoes lying on the ground and ate them" (CPMR #95.27).

17. Parents of concert performers were most distressed by the extremely itinerant nature of the acting profession. While migrant labor was common in the Gold Coast, it usually entailed workers moving from one part of the country to one other location, where they would establish a new semi-permanent household. Concert acting, by way of contrast, required performers to be in a new town almost every night of the week.

18. *Dipo* rituals are puberty rites held in the Eastern Region every March (Cole and Ross 1977, 209; Opoku 1970, 79).

19. On the Deer-Catching Festival of the Effutu of Winneba, see Opoku (1970, 33–39).

20. Both the Kwawu region and the city of Akropong had a long Christian missionary presence, which may account for the importance of Easter and Christmas in these areas (Debrunner 1967; Miescher 1997).

21. Outgoing Correspondence (London Office to Obuasi Office) of the Ashanti Gold-fields Corporation, Guildhall Library, London, quoted in Crisp (1984, 73).

22. Mine workers often came from the Northern, Volta, and French territories, as well as from Nigeria (Crisp 1984, 46–53, 62).

23. In the 1930s, manual laborers in the mines earned between 1 and 3 shillings per day (Crisp 1984, 62).

24. In addition to Bob Vans, Bob Cole and I. K. Ntama were other important concert party artists who served in Burma (Ntama #95.41; Saidu #94.19).

25. On Bartholomew and Co., see MacMillan ([1920] 1968, 175–176).

26. The files of the Optimism Club provide evidence of regular performances by the Two Bobs and Their Carolina Girl and the Axim Trio during the 1930s.

27. The Co-Optimists Concert Party held a performance at the Rodger Club in honor of the King's birthday on June 3, 1933 (*Gold Coast Independent* 1933). The Axim Trio performed at the Domarch Club in Nsawam in 1934 (*Gold Coast Spectator* 1934h). On elite clubs in the Gold Coast, see Agovi (1990, 8–9) and K. Hagan (1968).

28. For example, the Axim Trio performed at the Sekondi Palladium in 1932 (*Gold Coast Nation* 1932), the Co-Optimists Concert party performed at the Merry Villas in 1933 (*Gold Coast Spectator* 1933), and the Two Bobs and Their Carolina Girl performed at the Accra Palladium in 1933 (*Gold Coast Spectator* 1934a).

29. For instance, the Two Bobs and Their Carolina Girl performed at the Etsiapa Memorial School in Elmina in 1938 (*Gold Coast Spectator* 1938). The Axim Trio performed in the Methodist Chapel in Winneba in 1936 (*Gold Coast Spectator* 1936). On open yards, see Ansah (#93.10). On compounds, see CPMR (#95.27). For illustrations of various performance spaces, see Bame (1981, 50).

30. For insight into the regional web of trade surrounding Kumasi and how transportation systems can impact local markets, see Clark (1994, 34–72).

31. On this Nigerian tour, see also Horton (1935) and *Gold Coast Spectator* (1935).

32. See Chapter 5 for how Bob S. Ansah used his wits to borrow musical instruments from the schoolmaster free of charge.

5. IMPROVISING POPULAR TRAVELING THEATRE

1. See Chapter 4.

2. For an overall introduction to the field of performance studies, see Carlson (1996). For recent collections of scholarship, see Diamond (1996); Parker and Sedgwick (1995); and Phelan and Lane (1998).

3. On performativity, see Butler (1990, 1993, and 1997) and Parker and Sedgwick (1995).

4. While the Akan have maintained the corpus of *anansesɛm* orally for centuries, the earliest and most extensive written collection of *anansesɛm* to date is Capt. R. S. Rattray's *Akan-Asante Folklore* (1930). Rattray's book is extremely useful to this study inasmuch as the tales were collected in the late 1920s, the same historical period when the concert party became a recognized performance genre among the Akan. While Rattray's study is textually rich, providing both Twi transcriptions and English translations, it is contextually poor. Rattray gives no information about who told particular stories, when each story was told, how music and dance were incorporated into the performance, who was in the

audience, or what the occasion was that prompted the telling. Akan Ananse stories, like proverbs, are a means of indirect communication and social criticism, so the context and tone of performance and reception are crucial to their interpretation (Yankah 1989b). Considering the centrality of *anansesɛm* to Akan oral arts, the absence of a performance-based, contextual study is indeed unfortunate. Published sources on *anansesɛm* tend to be either collections of tale texts (Addo 1968; Appiah 1966) or articles outlining the general parameters of the genre as performance (Dseagu 1976; Sutherland 1960, 1987, 3–5; Yankah 1983, 1989a; Yeboa-Dankwa 1988).

5. For instance, see "How It Came About That Many Diseases Came among the Tribe," "How Kwaku Ananse Got Aso in Marriage," and "How Elephants Came to Go Off to the Long Grass Country" in Rattray's collection of folktales (1930, 76–81, 132–137, 146–151).

6. When people talked about "picking" and "polishing" in the context of our interviews, they always used English rather than Twi words, even if their sentences were otherwise in Twi or Fante. The Akan language has many verbs for "picking," depending on the type of item being picked. For instance, one verb (*to*) is used for uprooting tubers, another verb (*ti*) is used for plucking peppers, and still another (*paw*) is used for selecting fowls. *Tew*, one of the several words for polishing, has at least twenty-six different connotations (Christaller [1881] 1933, 507–508). Actors may have chosen to use English because in this language "pick" and "polish" have a more generic meaning than Akan alternatives.

7. On a similar process of domesticating cultural difference in Nigeria, see Barber and Waterman (1995).

8. *Kenkey*, or *dɔkono*, is a ball of fermented cornmeal that is wrapped in corn husks and boiled.

9. On *akutia*, see Yankah (1995, 51–52).

10. Videographer of this interview.

11. I am grateful to Stephan Miescher for bringing this citation to my attention.

12. This comment comes at the end of a scene depicting the arbitrary and devastating impact of a school inspector's visit (Awoonor 1972, 33–37).

13. Occasionally a fourth part, the Cloth Woman, would be added.

14. For instance, when the Gold Coast Two Bobs performed for the RWAFF, the army limited their shows to forty-five minutes. But if they did a show for the general public in the town hall at Obuasi, the performance might last between two and two-and-a-half hours.

15. See Adams and Amoah (#93.8); Amegatcher (1968, 35–36); Ansah (#93.10); Bampoe and Hammond (#95.55); CPMR (#95.27); Dadson and Dadson (#93.3); Hammond (#93.6); and Narkwa (#94.26).

16. This landmark phrase "I dey for top" is well remembered by practitioners and spectators alike, as it invariably came up when I asked about the dramaturgy of early trio shows. As Pidgin English, this expression would be associated with the Krus, and accordingly seems to have migrated from concert parties into popular slang usage in the early 1960s, when "I dey for top" became the term by which people referred to night soil (sewage) removal vans (Awoonor 1972, 80). Prior to the introduction of vans, night soil collectors were stereotypically Krus, who made their rounds with their canisters balanced atop their heads.

17. This story was narrated by Bob Vans (#95.33).

18. This story resembles an Ananse tale in which the spider impresses everyone at a funeral because he can mourn in three voices (Rattray 1930, 249).

19. In 1958, "School Girl" was recorded by E. T. Mensah and His Tempos Band, Decca West Africa WA 857, KWA 5854 (see BAPMAF Collection). The song was re-released in the United States in the 1990s on the Original Music compact disc *Giants of Dance Band Highlife*, catalogue number OMCD011.

20. On the Kru influence on Ghanaian music see Collins (1976b) and Coplan (1978,

101–102). Emmanuel Akyeampong (1993, 129) cites a 1924 newspaper report complaining about a group of fifty to sixty Krus in an Accra neighborhood disturbing their neighbors by playing "tambourines, accordions, mouth-organs and a medley of other musical instruments." Kwame Mbia Hammond says the Krus from Liberia were notorious for cracking jokes, playing guitar, and being very good dancers. "They brought typical high life to the Gold Coast" (#93.6).

21. Johnson's biography indicates that he was a great admirer of Chaplin; he particularly liked the way Chaplin wore his shoes (Sutherland 1970, 7).

22. The one exception to this was a woman named Christina Wilmot, who performed with the Axim Trio when that group was just getting started. According to Bob S. Ansah (#93.10) and Bob Vans (#95.30), Christina Wilmot left the group when they began to tour regularly.

23. According to one Christian missionary: "In many instances (the Gentleman) has . . . adopted European dress: this touches what to some is a sore spot. . . . There is great tendency to carry the fashion to absurd lengths: the tall silk hat, high collar, patent leather shoes, must be as uncomfortable to the aristocrat, as the gorgeous Christy-minstrel attire of the humbler classes is grotesque" (Kemp 1898, 59). This description conflated the social type of the Fante gentleman with a minstrel show dandy, making him into a sort of West African "Zip Coon." Zip Coon is a stock character from the American minstrel tradition. He was supposed to represent the ostentatious behavior of former slaves who had migrated to northern cities (Toll 1974, 34, 123).

24. On concert party blackface, see Chapter 2.

6. "This Is Actually a Good Interpretation of Modern Civilization"

1. On the demographics of the Royal West African Frontier Force, see Manns (1984).

2. See in particular the *Gold Coast Independent* and the *Gold Coast Times*.

3. "Fanti," "Akan," and "Ahanta" are terms that simultaneously indicate ethnicity, language, and region. "Abuakwa" is a region of Ghana, otherwise referred to as Akyem Abuakwa.

4. "Ghana" is the name of an ancient empire of the western Sudan, from which the Akan are said to have migrated (Apter 1963, 22; Mauny 1954; Ward [1948] 1969, 45–50). As independence became an increasingly viable prospect in the 1950s, Ghana became popular as the new name for the Gold Coast. The name Ethiopian Jokers reflected the tremendous symbolic importance of Ethiopia among nationalists in West Africa for, as Elizabeth Isichei says, it was an "island of freedom in a colonised continent" ([1977] 1985, 270). Burma was where the majority of Gold Coast soldiers fought during World War II (Haywood and Clarke 1964).

5. For a lists of concert party troupes from the years 1955, 1960, and 1978, see Collins (1976a, 52) and Bame (1985, 24, 26).

6. See also Bame (1985, 57–62).

7. See Cole and Ross (1977, 44–46) and Yankah (1989a, 1989b, 1995, and 1997).

8. The Gold Coast was the target of so much wartime British propaganda because this colony was the primary training site for the West African Frontier Force. It also supplied a disproportionate number of soldiers for the Allied armies and served as the assembly stage for fighter planes and bombers, which were then flown to Egypt and the Middle East war theatres.

9. According to Clarke, a number of plays about Hitler were also staged in villages in Nigeria (1986, 89). Bob S. Ansah talked extensively about the role of concert parties in Gold Coast war propaganda (#95.34a; #95.57).

10. On this period of Ghanaian history, see Allman (1993); Apter (1963); Austin (1964); Bourret (1949, 150–203); Clarke (1986); Fortes (1945); Holbrook (1978, 1982); Killingray (1982, 94–95); Manns (1984); and Rathbone (1973; 1993).

11. As John Collins's research demonstrates, the roots of highlife extend into many cultures outside of Ghana, including Liberia, Sierra Leone, Nigeria, Cuba, Jamaica, and America. However, there is a strong perception in Ghana that highlife is 'Ghana's most important modern homegrown dance-music' (1994b, preface). Concert party artist Kwaw Prempeh identifies highlife music not just with Ghana, but with black people in general. He says "highlife is our black people's greatest music" (#95.39).

12. For an Africanist critique of Gilroy's book, see the special edition of *Research in African Literatures* on the "Black Atlantic" edited by Simon Gikandi (1996).

13. In the early 1960s, the Nkrumah administration launched a seven-year agricultural development plan. Its aims, according to J. A. Dadson, were "(1) to raise agricultural output and efficiency by introducing technology into agriculture, and by expanding the area under cultivation; (2) to alter the structure of commodity production in favor of industrial and export crops and livestock; 3) to supply the urban populations with low-cost foodstuffs; 4) to attract the rural educated youth into agriculture, and thus to reduce unemployment and improve the quality of human resources in agriculture" (1993, 309–310).

14. M. Cameron Duodu's short story "Tough Guy in Town" describes a dance from the Takoradi pubs that appears to be the same one danced in the Fanti Trio play: "He jived and shook his waist, went back body bent as if about to fall down, leapt up suddenly, and held on to his partner's hands and it began all over again. It was hot, and it seemed as if Tennessee Ernie had specially composed 'Rock City Boogie' for Tough Guy" (1958, 138).

15. See Chapter 4.

16. See also *Sunday Mirror* (1960b).

17. Van's meditation eventually bore fruit. He came up with the idea of amplifying the concert party, an innovation that significantly impacted staging practices. With microphones, concert parties could perform in large auditoriums; actors without innately strong voices no longer had to worry about vocal projection; and amplification also flattened actors' blocking, as they grouped around microphones placed downstage in a line.

18. A description of an Akan Trio performance from 1960 in the *Sunday Mirror* indicates the extent to which their shows were still closely aligned with the trio format of the 1930s and 1940s: "The Trio trod the stage constantly and its tipsy jocularities in which were featured two 'gents' with blackened faces and whitened lip-lines and an impersonated 'lady' were popular everywhere" (*Sunday Mirror* 1960b).

19. The song is about the perils of migration, for it says, "If I were to be in my home town, this would not have been my lot" (Koomson #95.42; Owusu 1963).

20. On Kakaiku plays, see Grant (#95.46); Kakaiku's Band (#95.37); Koomson (#95.42); and Oppong and Oppong (#95.40). For a synopsis of the social role of the *egyankaba,* see the play entitled *Treat Somebody's Child As Your Own* in Bame (1985, 84–87).

21. For descriptions of this story, see Bame (1985, 84–87); Kakaiku's Band (#95.37); and Oppong and Oppong (#95.40).

22. On Akan matrilineage, see Appiah (1992, 181–192); Danquah (1928, 201–212); McCaskie (1995, 77); Miescher (1997); and Rattray ([1929] 1969, 1–32).

23. For instance, four out of the eight plays Kwabena Bame synopsized in *Come to Laugh* are about orphans and housegirls (1985, 83–96). The theme of orphans is also prominent in Ghanaian highlife lyrics (Yankah 1984, 572–577).

24. On the problems of Akan inheritance, see Appiah (1992); Danquah (1928, 201–218); Miescher (1997); and Nzegwu (1996).

25. The current government of Jerry Rawlings has even issued a decree expanding widow's property rights (Appiah 1992, 192).

26. See for example Kusum Agoromba (1997).

27. Appiah, a professor at Harvard University, has a complicated family background. His mother is British and his father was a member of the Asante royalty. Appiah's situation is further complicated by the fact that his mother's country, Britain, tends to follow

patrilineal inheritance customs, whereas among Asantes, one's inheritance and ethnic identity are determined solely through maternal lines.

28. Undergraduate students to whom I taught the Jaguar Jokers' play *Onipa Hia Moa* (1995a), or *Mankind Needs Help* (1995b), were very confused by reading the text. Only when they saw a videotape of this performance did they understand the tone of the piece, the function of repetition, and the nature of the show's stock characters, presentational style, and satire on contemporary life.

29. Veteran performers who listened to the tapes with me were also able to identify dances based upon the rhythm of footsteps in the recordings.

30. For an analysis of the "Bob" houseboy character, see Chapter 5.

31. Among concert party practitioners, the word "drama" connotes written plays in English (Ghana Concert Parties Union 1995, #95.54).

32. These song lyrics are from the plays *Life Is Like a Mirror* (Akan Trio 1961b; 1995b, 5) and *Beautiful Nonsense* (Fanti Trio 1961a; 1995a, 18, 5).

33. *Ebusuapanyin* literally translates as "family elder."

34. R. S. Rattray wrote in 1929 that the extended family structure "is one reason why, up to the present, we have not had any paupers and workhouses in West Africa" ([1929] 1969, 18). In subsequent years, the family social welfare system has undergone enormous strains as it has adjusted to new political regimes, inflation, droughts, military dictatorships, and neocolonial structural adjustment programs. However, this system still appears to be effective. One almost never sees in urban Ghana paupers living in the inhumane conditions typically found among homeless people in American cities. Considering that Ghana's per capita income is roughly USD 400 per year, the absence of public human misery is an impressive testimony to the strength and power of the extended family. This structure has continued to serve as a far more comprehensive safety net than anything most so-called developed nations have managed to devise.

35. An Akan proverb says, *"Abusua te sɛ kwaeɛ, wowɔ akyiri a ɛyɛ kusuu, wopini ho a, na wohunu sɛ dua koro biara wɔ ne siberɛ"* ("The matriclan is like the forest; if you are outside it is dense, if you are inside you see that each tree has its own position") (Appiah 1992, 192). The woman in the play laments because her position in the "forest" of the matrilineage is so unfavorable.

36. For further background on the cultural customs, history, and economic aspects of Akan funerals, see Appiah (1992, 181–192); Arhin (1994); and Nketia (1955).

37. This is the same accusation Anthony Appiah levels at his father's matriclan in his book *In My Father's House*: "This wrangling over my father's corpse (as it struck me) by people who had ignored his suffering when he was living, apparently without any concern for those of us who had loved and cared for him, was more than I could bear" (1992, 186). The socio-economic disparity between Appiah and the woman in this play gives some indication of the ubiquity of such problems among all social classes in Akan society.

38. In Akan culture, superiors tend to be confronted only through opaque references and indirect allusions (Yankah 1989a; 1989b).

39. On the connection between narratives of domestic conflict and the larger arena of national politics, see also Priebe (1978).

40. "Concert nonsense" frequently came up in my translation work with K. Keelson, especially when I asked questions about why some particular aspect of a play provoked laughter among the audience. I talked extensively about "concert nonsense" with actor K. A. Hammond on May 30, 1995. See also Bame (1968, 34).

Bibliography

ABBREVIATIONS

ACED. Atkinson Collection of Ethiopian Drama, Department of Special Collections, University of Chicago
BAPMAF. Bokoor African Popular Music Archives Foundation
CPMR. Concert Party *Mpaninfoɔ* Reunion
GBC. Ghana Broadcasting Corporation
GCPU. Ghana Concert Parties Union
GNEA. Ghana National Entertainment Association
HTC. Harvard Theatre Collection, The Houghton Library
MUSIGA. Musicians Union of Ghana
NAG. National Archives of Ghana
NCC. National Commission on Culture, Ghana
RWAFF. Royal West African Frontier Force
UGAA. Audio Archives, Institute for African Studies, University of Ghana, Legon
USIS. United States Information Service

ARCHIVES CONSULTED

Atkinson Collection of Ethiopian Drama (ACED)
Housed in the Department of Special Collections at the University of Chicago Library, the Atkinson Collection includes over three hundred minstrel show scripts, including afterpieces, jokebooks, and practical handbooks. These scripts provided me with a basis for dramaturgical comparisons between minstrel sketches and concert party plays.

Bokoor African Popular Music Archives Foundation (BAPMAF)
Established in 1990 by Dr. John Collins, BAPMAF has a wide-ranging collection of ma-
    terials on African popular culture, including over 400 hours of recorded music. Most
    relevant to this present study were BAPMAF recordings of early highlife music and
    photographs documenting key personalities and innovators of the concert party the-
    atre.

Harvard Theatre Collection (HTC)
The Harvard Theatre Collection has an extensive collection of material on American min-
    strelsy. Under the guidance of the HTC staff, I conducted a systematic survey of this
    material, including posters, playbills, and photograph.

National Archives of Ghana (NAG)
An introductory survey of the holdings of NAG can be found in Henige (1973). I prima-
    rily consulted the newspaper collections of the Accra and Cape Coast branches. The
    regional administrative files at the Sekondi branch were also particularly useful for
    gathering information on the history of social clubs in the Western Region.

Optimism Club
During a research trip to Sekondi, I discovered a privately held collection of papers docu-
    menting the history of the Optimism Club from the early 1920s, and the club rector,
    Lawrence Cudjoe, generously gave me access to these materials. Among the files, I
    found letters from some of the earliest concert party troupes, such as the Two Bobs
    and Their Carolina Girl, Teacher Yalley (the "Laughter-Maker of Tarkwa"), the Co-
    Optimists Concert Party, and the Axim Trio. These files also contained letters from
    Gold Coast luminaries such as J. B. Danquah, copies of lectures delivered at the
    Club, and evidence of how economic fluctuations, changes in the railway system,
    and the building of Takoradi Harbor affected the people of Sekondi. I brought these
    files to the attention of Joseph Justice Turton Mensah, the regional archivist of the
    National Archives of Ghana, Western Region. The records have since been moved to
    the Sekondi branch of NAG.

University of Ghana
I used several different collections at the University of Ghana. The Balme Library and the
    Institute of African Studies Library were particularly important in terms of providing
    access to colonial newspapers. (For an overview of the Ghanaian depositories of
    colonial newspapers and their holdings, see Jones-Quartey 1975, 102–113.) The In-
    stitute of African Studies Audio Archives played a central role in my research, for
    they have concert party recordings from the early 1960s. These tapes provided an
    unprecedented opportunity for me to do close analysis of plays from the era of Gha-
    na's independence.

WORKS CITED

Abdallah, Mohammed ben. 1992. "Interview." Conducted by Jane Wilkinson. In *Talking
    with African Writers: Interviews with African Poets, Playwrights, and Novelists,* ed-
    ited by Jane Wilkinson, 32–45. Portsmouth, N.H.: Heinemann.
Acquah, Ioné. [1958] 1972. *Accra Survey: A Social Survey of the Capital of Ghana.* Accra:
    Ghana Universities Press.
Adams, Frank Emmanuel, and J. B. Amoah. #93.8. Interview with author. Video record-
    ing, filmed by Nathan Kwame Braun. Sekondi, 17 August 1993.

Addo, Peter Eric Adotey. 1968. *Ghana Folk Tales: Ananse Stories from Africa.* New York: Exposition Press.

Adéẹ̀kọ́, Adélékè. 1998. *Proverbs, Textuality, and Nativism in African Literature.* Gainesville: University Press of Florida.

Agawu, Kofi. 1992. "Representing African Music." *Critical Inquiry* 18 (2): 245–266.

Agovi, Kofi E. 1990. "The Origin of Literary Theatre in Colonial Ghana, 1920–1957." *Research Review* 6 (1): 1–23.

Ahanta Trio. 1961. *Ebusua Dɔ Fun* (*The Family Honors the Dead*). Performed 4 March. Audiotaped and preserved by UGAA.

———. 1995. *The Family Honors the Dead* (*Ebusua Dɔ Fun*). Translated by K. Keelson. Unpublished manuscript, based on UGAA audio recording of 1961 performance.

Ahmad, Aijaz. 1996. "The Politics of Literary Postcoloniality." In *Contemporary Postcolonial Theory: A Reader,* edited by Padmini Mongia, 276–293. London: Arnold.

Akan Trio. 1961a. *Mma W'enyi Mmber Obi N'adze* (*Don't Covet Your Neighbor's Possessions*). Performed in Swedru, 1 March. Audiotaped and preserved by UGAA.

———. 1961b. *Ɔbra Tse Dɛ Ahwehwɛ* (*Life Is Like a Mirror*). Performed in Cape Coast, 5 August. Audiotaped and preserved by UGAA.

———. 1995a. *Don't Covet Your Neighbor's Possessions* (*Mma W'enyi Mmber Obi N'adze*), Translated by K. Keelson. Unpublished manuscript based on UGAA audio recording of 1961 performance.

———. 1995b. *Life Is Like a Mirror* (*Ɔbra Tse Dɛ Ahwehwɛ*). Translated by Catherine M. Cole and K. Keelson. Unpublished manuscript based on UGAA audio recording of 1961 performance.

Akyeampong, Emmanuel Kwaku. 1993. "Alcohol, Social Conflict and the Struggle for Power in Ghana, 1919 to Recent Times." Ph.D. diss., University of Virginia.

———. 1996a. Letter to author, 20 January.

———. 1996b. "What's a Drink? Class Struggle, Popular Culture and the Politics of Akpateshie (Local Gin) in Ghana, 1930–67." *Journal of African History* 37: 215-236.

———. 1996c. *Drink, Power, and Cultural Change: A Social History of Alcohol in Ghana, c. 1800 to Recent Times.* Portsmouth, N.H.: Heinemann.

Allman, Jean Marie. 1993. *The Quills of the Porcupine: Asante Nationalism in an Emergent Ghana.* Madison: University of Wisconsin Press.

Amartey, Robert Jamieson, and Augustus Williams. #95.51. Interview with author. Video recording, filmed by Nathan Kwame Braun. Accra, 19 May 1995.

Amegatcher, Adelaide. 1968. "The Concert Parties: A Manifestation of Popular Drama in Ghana." Master's thesis, University of North Carolina, Chapel Hill.

Anderson, Benedict. [1983] 1991. *Imagined Communities: Reflections on the Origin and Spread of Nationalism.* Rev. ed. London: Verso.

Ansah, Bob S. #93.10. Interview with author. Video recording, filmed by Nathan Kwame Braun. Accra, 22 August 1993.

———. #94.14. Interview with author and Nathan Kwame Braun. Audio recording. Accra, 23 October 1994.

———. #95.34a. Interview with author and Nathan Kwame Braun. Audio recording. Accra, 12 February 1995.

———. #95.34c. Interview with author. Video recording, filmed by Nathan Kwame Braun. Bekwai, 2 March 1995.

———. #95.57. Interview with author. Video recording, filmed by Nathan Kwame Braun. Accra, 26 July 1995.

Ansah, J. B. 1934. Letter to Optimism Club. Optimism Club Files, 17 September.

Appiah, Kwame Anthony. 1992. *In My Father's House.* New York: Oxford University Press.

Appiah, Peggy. 1966. *Ananse the Spider: Tales from an Ashanti Village.* New York: Pantheon Books.

Apter, David E. 1963. *Ghana in Transition*. Rev. ed. New York: Atheneum.

Arhin, Kwame. 1983. "Rank and Class among the Asante and Fante in the Nineteenth Century." *Africa* 53 (1): 2–22.

———. 1994. "The Economic Implications of Transformations in Akan Funeral Rites." *Africa* 64 (3): 307–322.

Arhin, Kwame, ed. 1993. *The Life and Work of Kwame Nkrumah*. Trenton, N.J.: Africa World Press.

Arkhurst, Sandy. #95.58. Interview with author. Video recording, filmed by Nathan Kwame Braun. Legon, 27 July 1995.

Ashcroft, Bill, Gareth Griffiths, and Helen Tiffin, eds. 1995. *The Post-Colonial Studies Reader*. London: Routledge.

Austin, Dennis. 1964. *Politics in Ghana, 1946–1960*. London: Oxford University Press.

Awoonor, Kofi. 1972. *This Earth, My Brother*. London: Heinemann.

Bame, Kwabena N. 1968. "Comic Play in Ghana." *African Arts* 1 (4): 30–34, 101.

———. 1981. *Come to Laugh: A Study of African Traditional Theatre in Ghana*. Accra: Baafour Educational Enterprises.

———. 1985. *Come to Laugh: African Traditional Theatre in Ghana*. New York: Lilian Barber Press.

Bampoe, Y. B. 1995. Letter to author, 19 October.

Bampoe, Y. B., and K. Acquaah Hammond. #93.11. Interview with author. Video recording, filmed by Nathan Kwame Braun. Adoagyiri, 25 August 1993.

———. #95.55. Interview with author. Video recording, filmed by Nathan Kwame Braun. Nsawam, 7 July 1995.

Barber, Karin. 1982. "Popular Reactions to the Petro-Naira." *Journal of Modern African Studies* 20 (3): 431–450.

———. 1986. "Radical Conservatism in Yoruba Popular Plays." In *Drama and Theatre in Africa*, Bayreuth African Studies Series no. 7, 75–82.

———. 1987. "Popular Arts in Africa." *African Studies Review* 30 (3): 1–78.

———. 1995. "Literacy, Improvisation and the Public in Yorùbá Popular Theatre." In *The Pressures of the Text: Orality, Texts and the Telling of Tales*, edited by Stewart Brown, 6–27. Birmingham: Centre of West African Studies.

Barber, Karin, ed. 1997. *Readings in African Popular Culture*. Bloomington: Indiana University Press.

Barber, Karin, and Báyọ̀ Ògúndíjọ, eds. 1994. *Yorùbá Popular Theatre: Three Plays by the Oyin Adéjọbí Company*. African Studies Association Press.

Barber, Karin, John Collins, and Alain Ricard. 1997. *West African Popular Theatre*. Bloomington: Indiana University Press.

Barber, Karin, and Christopher Waterman. 1995. "Traversing the Global and the Local: Fújì Music and Praise Poetry in the Production of Contemporary Yorùbá Popular Culture." In *Worlds Apart: Modernity through the Prism of the Local*, edited by Daniel Miller, 240–262. London: Routledge.

Berliner, Paul F. 1994. *Thinking in Jazz: The Infinite Art of Improvisation*. Chicago: University of Chicago Press.

Bhabha, Homi K. 1986. "Signs Taken for Wonders: Questions of Ambivalence and Authority under a Tree outside Delhi, May 1817." In *Race, Writing, and Difference*, edited by Henry Louis Gates Jr., 163–184. Chicago: University of Chicago Press.

———. 1994. *The Location of Culture*. London: Routledge.

Blankson, D. K. #95.44. Interview with author and K. Acquaah Hammond. Video recording, filmed by Nathan Kwame Braun. Aboso, 23 April 1995. Translated by Moses Narh.

Bourret, F. M. 1949. *The Gold Coast: A Survey of the Gold Coast and British Togoland, 1919–1946*. Stanford: Stanford University Press.

Braun, Nathan Kwame. 1997. *passing girl; riverside—An Essay on Camera Work.* Video recording made in collaboration with Catherine M. Cole. Boston: Documentary Educational Resources.

Brempong, Owusu. 1986. "Akan Highlife in Ghana: Songs of Cultural Transition." Ph.D. diss., Indiana University.

British Empire Exhibition. 1925. *Gold Coast Railway.* Wembly: British Empire Exhibition, Gold Coast Section.

Brooks, George E. Jr. 1972. *The Kru Mariner in the Nineteenth Century: An Historical Compendium.* Newark, Delaware: Liberian Studies Association in America.

Busia, K. A. [1950] 1951. *Report on a Social Survey of Sekondi-Takoradi.* London: Crown Agents for the Colonies.

Butler, Judith. 1990. *Gender Trouble: Feminism and the Subversion of Identity.* London: Routledge.

———. 1993. *Bodies that Matter: On the Discursive Limits of "Sex."* London: Routledge.

———. 1997. *Excitable Speech: A Politics of the Performative.* New York: Routledge.

Cardinall, A. W. 1931. *The Gold Coast, 1931: A Review of the Conditions in the Gold Coast in 1931 as Compared with Those of 1921.* Accra: Government Printer.

Carlson, Marvin. 1996. *Performance: A Critical Introduction.* New York: Routledge.

Carr, Edward Hallett. 1961. *What Is History?* New York: Random House.

Casely-Hayford, Augustus. 1991. "Prosopographical Approaches to Fante History." *History in Africa* 18: 49–66.

Casely-Hayford, Augustus, and Richard Rathbone. 1992. "Politics, Families and Freemasonry in the Colonial Gold Coast." In *People and Empires in African History: Essays in Memory of Michael Crowder,* edited by J. F. Ade Ajayi and J. D. Y. Peel, 143–160. New York: Longman.

Chicago Tribune. 1996. "Blackface Skit Sparks Lawsuit for Club Med." 9 May. sec. 1, p. 22, col. 6.

Chinweizu, Onwuchekwa Jemie, and Ihechukwu Madubuike. 1980. *Toward the Decolonization of African Literature.* Enugu, Nigeria: Fourth Dimension Publishers.

Christaller, J. G. [1879] 1990. *Three Thousand Six Hundred Ghanian Proverbs (From the Asante and Fante Language),* translated by Kofi Ron Lange. Lewiston: Edwin Mellen Press.

———. [1881] 1933. *Dictionary of the Asante and Fante Language Called Tshi (Twi).* 2nd. ed. Basel: Basel Evangelical Missionary Society.

Clark, Ebun. 1979. *Hubert Ogunde: The Making of the Nigerian Theatre.* Oxford: Oxford University Press.

Clark, Gracia. 1994. *Onions Are My Husband: Survival and Accumulation by West African Market Women.* Chicago: University of Chicago Press.

Clarke, Peter B. 1986. *West Africans at War 1914–18, 1939–45: Colonial Propaganda and Its Cultural Aftermath.* London: Ethnographica.

Cole, Herbert M. 1975. "The Art of Festival in Ghana." *African Arts* 8 (3): 12–23, 60–62, 90.

Cole, Herbert M., and Doran H. Ross. 1977. *The Arts of Ghana.* Los Angeles: Museum of Cultural History, University of California.

Collins, John E. 1976a. "Comic Opera in Ghana." *African Arts* 9 (2): 50–57.

———. 1976b. "Ghanaian Highlife." *African Arts* 10 (1): 62–68, 100.

———. 1987. "Jazz Feedback to Africa." *American Music* 5 (2): 176–193.

———. 1992. *West African Pop Roots.* Philadelphia: Temple University Press.

———. 1994a. "The Ghanaian Concert Party: African Popular Entertainment at the Cross Roads." Ph.D. diss., State University of New York at Buffalo.

———. 1994b. *Highlife Time.* Accra: Anansesem Publications.

Concert Party Mpaninfoɔ Reunion (CPMR). #95.27. Reunion of concert party elders: Bob S. Ansah, Joseph Emmanuel Baidoe, Y. B. Bampoe, K. Acquaah Hammond, and

James Kwaku Narkwa. Convened by author and Nathan Kwame Braun. Video recording, filmed by Nathan Kwame Braun. Sekondi, 21 January 1995. Translated by
K. Keelson.

———. #95.28. Reunion of concert party elders: Bob S. Ansah, Joseph Emmanuel Baidoe, Y. B. Bampoe, K. Acquaah Hammond, and James Kwaku Narkwa. Convened
by author and Nathan Kwame Braun. Video recording, filmed by Nathan Kwame
Braun. Takoradi, 22 January 1995. Translated by K. Keelson.

———. #95.29. Reunion of concert party elders: Bob S. Ansah, Joseph Emmanuel Baidoe, Y. B. Bampoe, K. Acquaah Hammond, and James Kwaku Narkwa. Convened
by author and Nathan Kwame Braun. Video recording, filmed by Nathan Kwame
Braun. Sekondi, 23 January 1995. Translated by K. Keelson.

Conquergood, Dwight. 1991. "Rethinking Ethnography: Towards a Critical Cultural Politics." *Communication Monographs* 58: 179–194.

———. 1992. "Ethnography, Rhetoric, and Performance." *Quarterly Journal of Speech*
78: 80–97.

Cooper, Frederick. 1994. "Conflict and Connection: Rethinking Colonial African History." *American Historical Review* 99 (5): 1516–1545.

Coplan, David. 1978. "Come to My Town, Cape Coast!: The Social History of Ghanaian
Highlife." In *Eight Urban Musical Cultures*, edited by Bruno Nettl, 96–114. Urbana:
University of Illinois Press.

———. 1985. *In Township Tonight!: South Africa's Black City Music and Theatre.* Johan-
nesburg: Ravan Press.

———. 1994. *In the Time of Cannibals: The Word Music of South Africa's Basotho Migrants.* Chicago: University of Chicago Press.

Crenshaw, Kimberlé. 1992. "Whose Story Is It, Anyway? Feminist and Antiracist Appro-
priations of Anita Hill." In *Race-ing Justice, En-Gendering Power: Essays on Anita
Hill, Clarence Thomas, and the Construction of Social Reality,* edited by Toni Mor-
rison, 402–440. New York: Pantheon.

Crisp, Jeff. 1984. *The Story of an African Working Class: Ghanaian Miners' Struggles,
1870–1980.* London: Zed Books.

Cudjoe, Lawrence. 1995. "On Sekondi." Unpublished manuscript in author's possession.

———. #94.25. Interview with author and Nathan Kwame Braun. Audio recording. Sekondi, 29 December 1994.

Cunard, Nancy, ed. [1933] 1970. *Negro.* New York: Ungar Press.

Dadson, Beatrice, and Kojo Dadson. #93.3. Interview with author and Nathan Kwame
Braun. Accra, 26 July 1993.

Danquah, J. B. 1928. *Cases in Akan Law: Akim Abuakwa.* London: Routledge.

———. 1943. *The Third Woman: A Play in Five Acts.* London: United Society for Christian Literature.

Darkey, John C. A. 1991. "Popular Theatre in Ghana: Its Social Concerns, Artistic Form and
Traditions." Master's thesis, Institute of African Studies, University of Ghana, Legon.

Davy, Kate. 1994. "Fe/male Impersonation: The Discourse of Camp." In *The Politics and
Poetics of Camp,* edited by Moe Meyer, 130–148. New York: Routledge.

Dayan, Joan. 1996. "Paul Gilroy's Slaves, Ships and Routes: The Middle Passage as Metaphor." *Research in African Literatures* 27 (4): 7–14.

de Certeau, Michel. [1975] 1988. *The Writing of History.* Translated by Tom Conley. New
York: Columbia University Press.

———. [1984] 1988. *The Practice of Everyday Life.* Translated by Steven Rendall. Berkeley: University of California Press.

de Graft, J. C. 1976. "Roots in African Drama and Theatre." In *Drama in Africa. African
Literature Today* no. 8, 1–25. London: Heinemann.

de Graft Johnson, J. C. 1932. "The Fanti Asafu." *Africa* 5 (3): 307–322.

Debrunner, Hans W. 1967. *A History of Christianity in Ghana.* Accra: Waterville Publishing House.

Diamond, Elin, ed. 1996. *Performance and Cultural Politics.* New York: Routledge.

Drewal, Margaret Thompson. 1991. "The State of Research on Performance in Africa." *African Studies Review* 34 (3): 1–64.

Dseagu, S. A. 1976. "Proverbs and Folktales of Ghana: Their Form and Uses." In *Traditional Life, Culture and Literature in Ghana,* edited by J. M. Assimeng, 80–92. New York: Conch Magazine.

Duodo, M. Cameron. 1958. "Tough Guy in Town." In *Voices of Ghana: Literary Contributors to the Ghana Broadcasting System 1955–57.* Accra: Ministry of Information and Broadcasting.

Ebron, Paulla A. 1996. "Narratives of Difference: Ideas of Music in a Global Imaginary." Paper presented at the Institute for Advanced Study and Research in the African Humanities, Northwestern University, 3 April.

Ellison, Ralph. 1964. *Shadow and Act.* New York: Random House.

Ephirim-Donkor, Anthony. 1997. *African Spirituality: On Becoming Ancestors.* Trenton, N.J.: Africa World Press, Inc.

Erlmann, Veit. 1991. *African Stars: Studies in Black South African Performance.* Chicago: University of Chicago Press.

———. 1996a. *Nightsong: Performance, Power, and Practice in South Africa.* Chicago: University of Chicago Press.

———. 1996b. *Nightsong: Performance, Power, and Practice in South Africa.* Videotape. Chicago: Chicago University Press.

Fanti Trio. 1961a. *Beautiful Nonsense.* Performed in Swedru. Audiotaped and preserved by UGAA. 4 March.

———. 1961b. *Onyimpa Yɛ Edwuma Ana Oedzidzi (Man Must Work Before He Eats).* Performed in Cape Coast. Audiotaped and preserved by UGAA. 4 August.

———. 1995a. *Beautiful Nonsense.* Translated by K. Keelson. Unpublished manuscript, based on UGAA audio recording of 1961 performance.

———. 1995b. *Man Must Work Before He Eats (Onyimpa Yɛ Edwuma Ana Oedzidzi).* Translated by Catherine M. Cole and K. Keelson. Unpublished manuscript, based on UGAA audio recording of 1961 performance.

Fiawoo, F. K. 1943. *The Fifth Landing Stage: A Play in Five Acts.* London: United Society for Christian Literature.

Fortes, M. 1945. "The Impact of the War on British West Africa." *International Affairs* 21 (2): 206–219.

Foster, Philip. 1965. *Education and Social Change in Ghana.* Chicago: University of Chicago Press.

Fraser, Nancy. 1992. "Rethinking the Public Sphere: A Contribution to the Critique of Actually Existing Democracy." In *Habermas and the Public Sphere,* edited by Craig Calhoun, 109–142. Boston: MIT Press.

Garber, Marjorie. 1992. *Vested Interests: Cross-Dressing and Cultural Anxiety.* New York: HarperCollins Publishers.

Gates, Henry Louis, Jr. 1988. *The Signifying Monkey: A Theory of Afro-American Literary Criticism.* New York: Oxford University Press.

Ghana Concert Parties Union (GCPU). 1993. Author's notes from Union meeting, 26 August.

———. 1995. Author's notes from Union meeting, 23 March.

———. #95.54. Interview with author. Video recording, filmed by Nathan Kwame Braun. Accra, 6 June 1995. Translated by O. N. Adu-Gyamfi.

Ghana National Entertainment Association (GNEA). 1961. Correspondence to J. H. Nketia, February 20. Private collection of J. H. Nketia.

Gikandi, Simon, ed. 1996. Special Issue on the "Black Atlantic." *Research in African Literatures* 27 (4).

Gilbert, Michele. 2000. *Hollywood Icons, Local Demons: Ghanaian Popular Paintings by Mark Anthony.* Hartford, Conn.: Trinity College.

Gilroy, Paul. 1993. *The Black Atlantic: Modernity and Double Consciousness.* Cambridge: Harvard University Press.

————. 1995. "'. . . To be real': The Dissident Forms of Black Expressive Culture." In *Let's Get It On: The Politics of Black Performance,* edited by Catherine Ugwu, 12–33. London: Institute of Contemporary Arts.

Goffman, Erving. 1959. *The Presentation of Self in Everyday Life.* New York: Doubleday.

Gold Coast Independent. 1921. "Entertainment." 27 August.

————. 1924a. "The Palladium." 2 August, p. 609.

————. 1924b. "Advertisement for the Palladium." 2 August, p. 611.

————. 1924c. "Advertisement for the Merry Villas." 2 August, p. 611.

————. 1933. "The 'Co-Optimists' Concert Party." 1 April.

————. 1943a. "RAF Concert Party." 27 March, p.74.

————. 1943b. "Editorial: Colonial Reconstruction." 29 May, p. 128.

Gold Coast Leader. 1903. "Amagic Costume Ball and Concert." 21 February.

Gold Coast Nation. 1912. "The Moral Lessons of Empire Day." 30 May, p. 55.

————. 1914a. "Seccondee." 11 June.

————. 1914b. "The Wesleyan School Concert: A Critique by a Young Student." 27 August.

————. 1914c. "The Ladies' Club Concert." 12 November.

————. 1914d. "The Singing Band Fanti [*sic*] Sacred Concert." 3–10 December, p. 773.

————. 1914e. "Boy Scouts Association." 17–24 December.

————. 1932. "Sekondi—Concert." 5 March.

Gold Coast Spectator. 1929. "Editorial." 23 November, p. 522.

————. 1932a. "Musical Dragons." 23 January, p. 109.

————. 1932b. "West African National Club." 30 January, p. 141.

————. 1932c. "West Virginia Business Men Brutally Lynch Two Negro Workers." 6 February, p. 171.

————. 1932d. "World Situation and the Negro." 16 February, p. 194.

————. 1932e. "Seen the Ghost." 12 March, p. 339.

————. 1932f. "Al Jolson's *Big Boy* at the Palladium. His Excellency Attends Empire Day School Concerts." 28 May, pp. 715 and 719.

————. 1932g. "What Would You Do If You Were a Teacher?" 18 June, p. 832.

————. 1932h. "Short Sketches of Musicians and Actors: Mr. Augustus Williams." 25 June, p. 853.

————. 1932i. "The First Show He Attended." 2 July, p. 887.

————. 1932j. "Suggestions for Fancy Dress and Make-up for Xmas." 24 December. p. 8019.

————. 1933. "The Co-Optimists—Merry Villas." 10 June, p. 745.

————. 1934a. "Drama." 13 January, p. 51.

————. 1934b. "Musician Hit in Two-fold Manner." 10 March, p. 371.

————. 1934c. "The Two Bobs in Akropong." 29 March, p. 491.

————. 1934d. "'Blackman, blackman, take him away . . .': What the Negro Suffers in England, by One Who Has Suffered." 16 June, p. 926.

————. 1934e. "Accra Orchestra at Kumasi." 1 September, p. 2228.

————. 1934f. "Axim Trio at Suhum." 15 September, p. 2299.

————. 1934g. "Entertainment at Abosso." 29 September, p. 2371.

————. 1934h. "Axim Trio at Nsawam." 27 October, p. 2521.

————. 1934i. "'Paul Small' Scores in Variety Performance." 1 December, p. 2720.

————. 1935. "Two Bobs and Girl Propose Nigerian Tour." 13 April, p. 571.

———. 1936. "Axim 3 Entertain." 2 May, p. 772.

———. 1938. "Two Bobs Charm in Entertainment." 7 May, p. 597.

Gold Coast Times. 1930. "A Grand Night at the Bishops School." 7 June, p. 11.

———. 1932a. "West African Comedians and Entertainers." 30 January, p. 10.

———. 1932b. "Empire Day." 14–21 May.

Grant, George Benjamin. #95.46. Interview with author and K. Acquaah Hammond. Video recording, filmed by Nathan Kwame Braun. Sekondi, 25 April. Translated by Lydia Addi.

Gyegye, Kwame. [1987] 1995. *An Essay on African Philosophical Thought: The Akan Conceptual Scheme.* Rev. ed. Philadelphia: Temple University Press.

Hagan, George. 1993. "Nkrumah's Cultural Policy." In *The Life and Work of Kwame Nkrumah,* edited by Kwame Arhin. Trenton, N.J.: Africa World Press.

Hagan, Kwa O. 1968. "The Literary and Social Clubs of the Past: Their Role in National Awakening in Ghana." *Ɔkyeame* 4 (2): 81–86.

Hammond, Kwame Mbia. #93.6. Interview with author. Video recording, filmed by Nathan Kwame Braun. Adoagyiri, 9 August 1993.

Haywood, Col. A., and Brigadier F. A. S. Clarke. 1964. *The History of the Royal West African Frontier Force.* Aldershot, England: Gale and Polden.

Henige, David P. 1973. "The National Archives of Ghana: A Synopsis of Holdings." *International Journal of African Historical Studies* 6 (3): 475–485.

Hill, Errol. 1992. *The Jamaican Stage, 1655–1900: Profile of a Colonial Theatre.* Amherst: University of Massachusetts Press.

Hill, Polly. 1963. *The Migrant Cocoa-Farmers of Southern Ghana: A Study in Rural Capitalism.* Cambridge: Cambridge University Press.

Hinderink J., and J. Sterkenburg. 1975. *Anatomy of an African Town: A Socio-Economic Study of Cape Coast, Ghana.* Utrecht, The Netherlands: Geographical Institute, State University of Utrecht.

Holbrook, Wendell Patrick. 1978. "The Impact of the Second World War on the Gold Coast: 1939–1945." Ph.D. diss., Princeton University.

hooks, bell. 1992. *Black Looks: Race and Representation.* Boston: South End Press.

Horton, Charles B. 1935. Letter to Optimism Club. Optimism Club Files, 31 March.

Hughes, Langston. 1932. "The Same." *Negro Worker,* June, 31–32.

Isichei, Elizabeth. [1977] 1985. *History of West Africa since 1800.* London: Macmillan.

Jaguar Jokers. 1995a. *Onipa Hia Moa (Mankind Needs Help).* Performed in Teacher Mante, 15 July. Videotaped by Catherine Cole and Nathan Kwame Braun.

———. 1995b. *Mankind Needs Help (Onipa Hia Moa).* Translated by O. N. Adu-Gyamfi. Unpublished manuscript based on performance in Teacher Mante, 15 July.

Jeffries, Richard. 1978. *Class, Power and Ideology in Ghana: The Railwaymen of Sekondi.* Cambridge: Cambridge University Press.

Jeyifo, Biodun. 1984. *The Yoruba Popular Travelling Theatre of Nigeria.* Lagos: Nigeria Magazine.

———. 1996. "The Nature of Things: Arrested Decolonization and Critical Theory." In *Contemporary Postcolonial Theory: A Reader,* edited by Padmini Mongia, 158–171. London: Arnold.

Johnson Family. 1985. *Program of the Burial Services and Requiem Mass for the Late Ishmael Bob Johnson.* 19–20 July.

Jones-Quartey, K. A. B. 1965. "A Note on Press-Archives Research as an Approach to West African History." *Research Review* 2 (1): 48–57.

———. 1967. "Kobina Sekyi: A Fragment of Biography." *Research Review* 4 (1): 74–78.

———. 1968. "The Gold Coast Press: 1822–c. 1930, and the Anglo-African Press: 1825–c. 1930—The Chronologies." *Research Review* 4 (2): 30–46.

———. 1975. *History, Politics and Early Press in Ghana: The Fictions and the Facts.* Accra: Afram Publications.

Kakaiku's Band. n.d. Band Record Book, c. 1954–1957. Private collection of Samuel Kwame Koomson, Tarkwa.

——. #95.37. Interview with author and band members, including: Moses K. Oppong II, Idrisu Abduallahi, David Kwame Blankson, Nathaniel Ekɔw Browne, Romeo Ampofo Dadah, Grace Adom Oppong, Moses K. Oppong Jr., and Kwaw Prempeh. Video recording, filmed by Nathan Kwame Braun. Aboso, 20 April 1995. Translated by K. Keelson.

Kedjanyi, John. 1966. "Observations on Spectator-Performer Arrangements of Some Traditional Ghanaian Performances." *Research Review* 2 (3): 61–66.

Kemp, Rev. Dennis. 1898. *Nine Years at the Gold Coast.* New York: Macmillan.

Kerr, David. 1995. *African Popular Theatre: From Pre-Colonial Times to the Present Day.* London: James Currey.

Killingray, David. 1982. "Military and Labour Recruitment in the Gold Coast During the Second World War." *Journal of African History* 23 (1): 83–95.

Kimble, David. 1963. *Political History of Ghana: The Rise of Gold Coast Nationalism, 1850–1928.* Oxford: Clarendon Press.

Koomson, Samuel Kwame. #95.42. Interview with author and K. Acquaah Hammond. Video recording, filmed by Nathan Kwame Braun. Tarkwa, 23 April 1995. Translated by Charlotte Akyeampong.

Krakue, Frank. 1926. Letter to Optimism Club. Optimism Club Files, 27 December.

Kusum, Agoromba. 1997. *Heni Bedi M'ade? (Who Will Be My Heir?).* Videorecording by Nathan Kwame Braun.

Langley, J. Ayo. 1970. "Modernization and Its Malcontents: Kobina Sekyi of Ghana and the Re-statement of African Political Theory (1892–1956)." *Research Review* (Ghana) 6 (3): 1–61.

Livingston, Jennie. 1992. *Paris Is Burning.* Video recording. Chatsworth, Calif.: Academy Entertainment. Distributed by Image Entertainment.

Lokko, Sophia D. 1980. "Theatre Space: A Historical Overview of the Theatre Movement in Ghana." *Modern Drama* 23 (3): 309–319.

Lott, Eric 1993. *Love and Theft: Blackface Minstrelsy and the American Working Class.* New York: Oxford University Press.

Lyon, David. 1980. "The Minstrel Show as Ritual: Surrogate Black Culture." In *Rituals and Ceremonies in Popular Culture,* edited by Ray B. Browne, 150–159. Bowling Green, Ohio: Bowling Green Popular Press.

MacKenzie, John M. 1994. "Edward Said and the Historians." *Nineteenth-Century Contexts* 18 (1): 9–25.

MacMillan, Allister [1920] 1968. *The Red Book of West Africa.* London: Frank Cass and Co.

Mahar, William J. 1985. "Black English in Early Blackface Minstrelsy: A New Interpretation of the Sources of Minstrel Show Dialect." *American Quarterly* 37 (2): 260–285.

Manns, Adrienne. 1984. "The Role of Ex-Servicemen in Ghana's Independence Movement." Ph.D. diss., Johns Hopkins University.

Manuh, Takyiwah. 1993. "Women and Their Organizations during the Convention People's Party Period." In *The Life and Work of Kwame Nkrumah,* edited by Kwame Arhin. Trenton, N.J.: Africa World Press.

——. 1996. Interview with author. Chicago, March 11.

Mauny, R. A. 1954. "The Question of Ghana." *Africa* 24 (3): 200–213.

McCaskie, T. C. 1995. *State and Society in Pre-Colonial Asante.* Cambridge: Cambridge University Press.

McClintock, Anne. 1992. "The Angel of Progress: Pitfalls of the Term 'Post-Colonialism.'" *Social Text* 31/32: 84–98.

McKillican, E. H. 1934. "Some Experiments in Dramatic Work at the Presbyterian Girls' School, Aburi." *Gold Coast Teachers Journal* 6 (3): 218–220.

Mehrez, Samia. 1991. "The Subversive Poetics of Radical Bilingualism: Postcolonial Francophone North African Literature." In *The Bounds of Race: Perspectives on Hegemony and Resistance,* edited by Dominick LaCapra, 255–277. Ithaca: Cornell University Press.

Mensah, Atta Annan. 1966. "The Impact of Western Music on the Musical Traditions of Ghana." *Composer* 19: 19–22.

Meyer, Moe, ed. 1994. *The Politics and Poetics of Camp.* New York: Routledge.

Miescher, Stephan F. 1997. "Of Documents and Litigants: Disputes on Inheritance in Abetifi—A Town of Colonial Ghana." *Journal of Legal Pluralism and Unofficial Law* (39): 81–119.

Miller, Christopher. 1990. *Theories of Africans: Francophone Literature and Anthropology in Africa.* Chicago: University of Chicago Press.

Mudimbe, V. Y. 1988. *The Invention of Africa: Gnosis, Philosophy, and the Order of Knowledge.* Bloomington: Indiana University Press.

Musing Light. 1932a. "Vaudeville by Ladies Musical League." *Gold Coast Spectator.* 23 January, p. 109.

———. 1932b. "Advanced Musical and Dramatic Culture: The Future Gold Coast Music and Drama, Ideal Audience." *Gold Coast Spectator.* 23 July, p. 991.

Narkwa, James Kwaku. #94.21. Interview with author. Video recording, filmed by Nathan Kwame Braun. Shama, 16 November 1994.

———. #94.26. Interview with author. Video recording, filmed by Nathan Kwame Braun. Shama, 29 December 1994.

National Commission on Culture (NCC). 1993. *Funeral Program for Lord Bob Cole.* 30 July to 1 August.

Negro Worker. 1931. "Contents." January, p. 1.

———. 1933. "Our Aims." April/May, p. 33.

———. 1934a. "Freedom under British Rule." May, p. 31.

———. 1934b. "This 'Foul and Obnoxious' Tract." September, p. 1.

———. 1935. "Sedition Craze." September, p. 20.

Newton, Esther. 1972. *Mother Camp: Female Impersonators in America.* Chicago: University of Chicago Press.

Ngũgĩ wa, Thiong'o. 1986. *Decolonising the Mind: The Politics of Language in African Literature.* Portsmouth, N.H.: Heinemann.

———. 1993. *Moving the Centre: The Struggle for Cultural Freedoms.* Portsmouth, N.H.: Heinemann.

Nketia, J. H. Kwabena. 1955. *Funeral Dirges of the Akan People.* New York: Negro Universities Press.

———. 1963a. *African Music in Ghana.* Evanston: Northwestern University Press.

———. 1963b. *Folk Songs of Ghana.* Legon: University of Ghana.

———. 1965. *Ghana—Music, Dance and Drama: A Review of the Performing Arts of Ghana.* Legon: Institute of African Studies, University of Ghana.

———. 1974. *The Music of Africa.* New York: W.W. Norton.

Ntama, Issac Kweku. #95.41. Interview with author. Video recording, filmed by Nathan Kwame Braun. Tarkwa, 22 April 1995.

Nzegwu, Nkiru. 1996. "Questions of Identity and Inheritance: A Critical Review of Kwame Anthony Appiah's *In My Father's House.*" *Hypatia* 11 (1): 175–201.

Okome, Onookome, and Jonathan Haynes. 1995. *Cinema and Social Change in West Africa.* Plateau State, Nigeria: Nigerian Film Corporation.

Opoku, A. A. 1970. *Festivals of Ghana.* Accra: Ghana Publishing Corporation.

Oppong Family. 1986. *Funeral Program of Moses Kweku Nyamekye Oppong, alias Kakaiku.* 3–5 October.

Oppong, Grace Adom, and Moses K. Oppong II. #95.40. Interview with author. Video recording, filmed by Nathan Kwame Braun. Aboso, 21 April 1995.

Optimism Club. 1915. *Constitution and Laws of "Optimism Club" Sekondi.* Sekondi: Church Press.

Otoo, E. C. 1927. Letter to Optimism Club. Optimism Club Files, 29 January.

Owomoyela, Oyekan. 1991. "Yoruba Folk Opera: A Cross-cultural Flowering." In *Visions and Revisions: Essays on African Literatures and Criticisms,* 199–217. New York: Peter Lang.

Owusu, G. B. K. 1963. "Kakaiku—The Musician and Comedian." *Ghana Radio Review and TV Times,* 11 October.

Oyêwùmí, Oyèrónké. 1997. *The Invention of Women: Making an African Sense of Western Gender Discourses.* Minneapolis: University of Minnesota Press.

Padmore, George. 1932. "What Is Empire Day?" *Negro Worker* (June): 1–3.

Parker, Andrew, and Eve Kosofsky Sedgwick, eds. 1995. *Performativity and Performance.* New York: Routledge.

Phelan, Peggy. 1993. *Unmarked: The Politics of Performance.* New York: Routledge.

Phelan, Peggy, and Jill Lane, eds. 1998. *The Ends of Performance.* New York: New York University Press.

Pilton, Patrick. 1976. *Every Night at the London Palladium.* London: Robson.

Prakash, Gyan. 1994. "Subaltern Studies as Postcolonial Criticism." *American Historical Review* 99 (5): 1475–1490.

Prempeh, Kwaw. #95.39. Interview with author and K. Acquaah Hammond. Video recording, filmed by Nathan Kwame Braun. Aboso, 21 April 1995. Translated by Moses Narh.

Priebe, R. 1978. "Popular Writing in Ghana: A Sociology and Rhetoric." *Research in African Literatures* 9 (3): 395–342.

Rathbone, Richard. 1973. "Businessmen in Politics: Party Struggle in Ghana, 1949–57." *Journal of Development Studies* 9 (3): 391–401.

———. 1993. *Murder and Politics in Colonial Ghana.* New Haven: Yale University Press.

Rattray, Capt. R. S. [1929] 1969. *Ashanti Law and Constitution.* Negro Universities Press.

———. 1930. *Akan-Ashanti Folk-Tales.* Oxford: Clarendon Press.

Rehin, George F. 1975. "Harlequin Jim Crow: Continuity and Convergence in Blackface Clowning." *Journal of Popular Culture* 9: 682–701.

Ricard, Alain. 1974. "The Concert Party as a Genre: The Happy Stars of Lomé," *Research in African Literatures* 5 (2): 165–179.

———. 1986. *L'Invention du Théâtre: Le Théâtre et les comédiens en Afrique noire.* Lausanne: Editions l'Age d'Homme.

Riggs, Marlon T. 1986. *Ethnic Notions.* Video distributed by California Newsreel, San Francisco.

———. 1991. *Color Adjustment.* Video distributed by California Newsreel, San Francisco.

Roach, Joseph R. 1996. *Cities of the Dead: Circum-Atlantic Performance.* New York: Columbia University Press.

Roediger, David R. 1991. *The Wages of Whiteness: Race and the Making of the American Working Class.* New York: Verso.

Rogin, Michael. 1996. *Blackface, White Noise: Jewish Immigrants in the Hollywood Melting Pot.* Berkeley: University of California Press.

Ruhle, C. H. B. 1925. "Report on the Orchestra for the Period 1923–1924." Optimism Club Files, 15 January.

———. 1927. Letter to Optimism Club. Optimism Club Files, 3 April.

Sacks, Howard L., and Judith Rose Sacks. 1993. *Way Up North in Dixie: A Black Family's Claim to the Confederate Anthem.* Washington: Smithsonian Press.

Saidu, Nelson. #94.19. Interview with author and Nathan Kwame Braun. 14 November 1994.

Sarbah, John Mensah. [1906] 1968. *Fanti National Constitution.* 2nd ed. London: Frank Cass.

Schechner, Richard. 1985. *Between Theater and Anthropology.* Philadelphia: University of Pennsylvania Press.

Scott, Anna. 1998. "It's All in the Timing: The Latest Moves, James Brown's Grooves, and the Seventies Race-Consciousness Movement in Salvador, Bahia-Brazil." In *Soul: Black Power, Politics, and Pleasure,* edited by Monique Guillory and Richard C. Green, 9–22. New York: New York University Press.

Sekoni, Ropo. 1994. *Folk Poetics: A Sociosemiotic Study of Yoruba Trickster Tales.* Westport, Conn.: Greenwood.

Sekyi, Kobina. 1917. "The Future of Subject Peoples." *African Times and Orient Review,* October-December, 78, 94, 109–110.

———. 1974. *The Blinkards.* London: Heinemann.

Shaloff, Stanley. 1972. "Press Controls and Sedition Legislation Proceedings in the Gold Coast, 1933–39." *African Affairs* 71 (284): 241–263.

Slemon, Stephen. 1994 . "The Scramble for Post-colonialism." In *De-scribing Empire: Post-colonialism and Textuality,* edited by Chris Tiffin and Alan Lawson, 15–32. New York: Routledge.

Smith, Edwin W. [1929] 1932. *Aggrey of Africa: A Study in Black and White.* 8th ed. London: Student Christian Movement Press.

Soyinka, Wole. 1976. *Myth, Literature and the African World.* Cambridge: Cambridge University Press.

Spitzer, Leo, and LaRay Denzer. 1973. "I. T. A. Wallace-Johnson and the West African Youth League." *International Journal of African Historical Studies* 6 (3): 413–452.

Spivak, Gayatri Chakravorty. [1987] 1988. *In Other Worlds: Essays in Cultural Politics.* New York: Methuen.

Stanley, Liz, and Sue Wise. 1991. "Feminist Research, Feminist Consciousness, and Experiences of Sexism." In *Beyond Methodology: Feminist Scholarship as Lived Research,* edited by Mary Margaret Farnow and Judith Cook, 265–283. Bloomington: Indiana University Press.

Sterne, Ashley, and Archibald de Bear. 1926. *The Comic History of the Co-Optimists.* London: Herbert Jenkins.

Sunday Mirror. 1960a. "A Profile of Ghana's Very Own Pop Idol." 1 May.

———. 1960b. "He's Successful, But Not Yet Rich." 8 May.

———. 1960c. "40 Years a Comedian." 29 May.

Sutherland, Efua. 1960. "Venture into Theatre." *Ɔkyeame* 1: 47–48.

———. 1969. "Theatre in Ghana." In *Ghana Welcomes You,* edited by Janice Nesbitt, 83–87. Accra: Orientation to Ghana Committee.

———. 1970. *The Original Bob: The Story of Bob Johnson, Ghana's Ace Comedian.* Accra: Anowuo Educational Publications.

———. 1987. *Two Plays: The Marriage of Anansewa and Edufa.* Essex: Longman.

Taiwo, Olufemi. 1995. "Appropriating Africa: An Essay on New Africanist Schools." *Issue: A Journal of Opinion* 23 (1): 39–45.

Taussig, Michael. 1993. *Mimesis and Alterity: A Particular History of the Senses.* New York: Routledge.

Taylor, Diana. 1997. *Disappearing Acts: Spectacles of Gender and Nationalism in Argentina's "Dirty War."* Durham: Duke University Press.

Thompson, Gordon S. 1966. *Of Dreams and Deeds: The Story of Optimist International.* St. Louis, Mo.: Optimist International.

Toll, Robert C. 1974. *Blacking Up: The Minstrel Show in Nineteenth-Century America.* New York: Oxford University Press.

Vans, Bob. #95.30. Interview with author and Nathan Kwame Braun. Audio recording. Accra, 6 February 1995.

———. #95.31. Interview with author and Nathan Kwame Braun. Audio recording. Accra, 8 February 1995.

————. #95.33. Interview with author and Nathan Kwame Braun. Audio recording. Accra, 10 February 1995.

————. #95.49. Interview with author and Nathan Kwame Braun. Audio recording. Accra, 10 May 1995.

Vansina, Jan. 1985. *Oral Tradition as History.* Madison: University of Wisconsin Press.

Versatile Eight. 1929a. Letter to the Optimism Club. Optimism Club Files, 12 June.

————. 1929b. Letter to the Optimism Club. Optimism Club Files, 17 July.

————. 1930. Letter to the Optimism Club. Optimism Club Files, 27 January.

Wallerstein, Immanuel Maurice. 1962. "The Emergence of Two West African Nations: Ghana and the Ivory Coast." Ph.D. diss., Columbia University.

Ward, W. E. F. [1948] 1969. *A History of Ghana.* Rev. 4th ed. London: George Allen and Unwin.

Warner Brothers. 1985. *The Greatest Legal Fake Book of All Time.* Secaucus, N.J.: Warner Brothers.

Waterhouse, Richard. 1990. *From Minstrel Show to Vaudeville: The Australian Popular Stage, 1788–1914.* Kensington, New South Wales: New South Wales University Press.

Waterman, Christopher Alan. 1990. *Jùjú: A Social History and Ethnography of an African Popular Music.* Chicago: Chicago University Press.

Wilks, Ivor. [1975] 1989. *Asante in the Nineteenth Century: The Structure and Evolution of a Political Order.* London: Cambridge University Press.

Williams, Augustus A. S. 1995. "Entertainment in Ghana." Unpublished manuscript in author's possession.

————. #95.52. Interview with author. Video recording, filmed by Nathan Kwame Braun. Accra, 29 May 1995.

Wiredu, Kwasi. 1996. *Cultural Universals and Particulars: An African Perspective.* Bloomington: Indiana University Press.

Yalley, J. D. 1927a. Letter to the Optimism Club. Optimism Club Files, 6 April.

————. 1927b. Letter to the Optimism Club. Optimism Club Files, 12 April.

————. 1927c. Letter to the Optimism Club. Optimism Club Files, n.d. June.

————. 1927d. Letter to the Optimism Club. Optimism Club Files, 8 August.

Yankah, Kwesi. 1983. *The Akan Trickster Cycle: Myth or Folktale?* Bloomington: African Studies Program, Indiana University.

————. 1984. "The Akan Highlife Song: A Medium of Cultural Reflection or Deflection?" *Research in African Literatures* 15 (4): 568–582.

————. 1989a. "From Africa to the New World: The Dynamics of the Anansi Cycle." In *Literature of Africa and the African Continuum,* edited by Jonathan A. Peters, Mildred P. Mortimer, and Russell V. Linnemann, 115–128. Washington, D.C.: Three Continents Press and the African Literature Association.

————. 1989b. *The Proverb in the Context of Akan Rhetoric: A Theory of Proverb Praxis.* New York: Peter Lang.

————. 1995. *Speaking for the Chief: Okyeame and the Politics of Akan Royal Oratory.* Bloomington: Indiana University Press.

————. 1997. "The Sung Tale as a Political Charter in Contemporary Ghana." Paper presented at the international conference Words and Voices: Critical Practices of Orality in Africa and in African Studies, Bellagio Study and Conference Center, Bellagio, Italy, 24–28 February.

Yeboa-Dankwa, Jonas. 1988. "Storytelling of the Akan and Guan in Ghana." In *Ghanaian Literatures,* edited by Richard K. Priebe, 29–42. New York: Greenwood Press.

Zynenwartel, Abe B. O. n.d. "Emmanuel Kwamina Dadson: A Biographical Tribute." Unpublished paper in author's possession.

Index

CATHERINE M. COLE is Assistant Professor in the Department of Dramatic Art at the University of California, Santa Barbara. She is author of numerous articles on African theater and has collaborated with filmmaker Nathan Kwame Braun on *"passing girl; riverside,"* a video essay on ethical dilemmas in visual anthropology.